Introduction to Early Childhood Education and Care

Introduction to Early Childhood Education and Care

An Intercultural Perspective

CAROLE MASSING

MARY LYNNE MATHESON

www.brusheducation.ca

Brush Education Inc.
www.brusheducation.ca
contact@brusheducation.ca

Cover and interior design: Carol Dragich, Dragich Design
Cover artwork by children, families, and educators of the 1000 Women Child Care Centre (Edmonton, Alberta). Photograph by Tracey Findlay.
Editing: Kay Rollans

Library and Archives Canada Cataloguing in Publication

Title: Introduction to early childhood education and care : an intercultural perspective / Carole Massing, Mary Lynne Matheson.

Names: Massing, Carole, 1946- author. | Matheson, Mary Lynne, 1953- author.

Description: Includes bibliographical references.

Identifiers: Canadiana (print) 20210144912 | Canadiana (ebook) 20210145072 | ISBN 9781550598841 (softcover) | ISBN 9781550598858 (PDF) | ISBN 9781550598872 (EPUB)

Subjects: LCSH: Early childhood education—Canada. | LCSH: Multicultural education—Canada. | LCSH: Culturally relevant pedagogy—Canada. | LCSH: Child care—Canada.

Classification: LCC LB1139.3.C3 M37 2021 | DDC 372.210971—dc23

We acknowledge the support of the Government of Canada
Nous reconnaissons l'appui du gouvernement du Canada | Canadä

Table of Contents

List of Tables

Acknowledgments

We are deeply grateful to the educators, brokers, students, friends, and family members from many different cultures who have shared their experiences and insights with us over the years. The Multicultural Health Brokers Cooperative (MCHB) showed us the challenges that immigrant and refugee families face in Canada. The thoughtful women in the Bridging Program for Immigrant Child Care Educators alerted us to the cultural discontinuities that newcomer educators experience in the Canadian system. We appreciate the talented educators at the Intercultural Child and Family Centre and 1000 Women Child Care Centre for their dedication to providing culturally responsive care and thank them for allowing us to build this book around their experiences. Echo Roth, Chelsea White, Sadia Ibrahim, Nirmali Warnakula, Rita Rudometkina, Tiffany Tse, and Francine Moosomin have agreed to let us use their real names in the stories we tell. Others have preferred to remain anonymous. In both instances, we treasure their willingness to share their practices. Jasvinder Heran, the executive director of both child care centres, is a committed partner in developing and modelling wise intercultural practice.

Thank you, as well, to our New Zealand colleagues, Wendy Lee and Chrissy Lepper, for showing us what is possible when a government is committed to an intercultural model, and for reinforcing our belief in the power of story.

Christine Massing's thoughtful critique, as well as suggestions from Bonnie Anderson and Becky Kelly, have added value to the book. Elena Massing helped to shape our process by reminding us tactfully that, as White settlers of a certain age, we are writing about interculturalism from a position of privilege.

Awareness of our privilege prompted us to form two advisory groups to help guide our process. Jasvinder Heran, Afshan Amjad, Bejuna Joshi, Echo Roth, and Francine Moosomin told us about their own teaching and learning experiences, while Yvonne Chiu and the group of multicultural health brokers she brought together—Mulki Ali, Tsedale Aragawi, Helen Ling Ling Zhao, Sabah Tahir, and Irene Dormitorio—offered insights on the experiences and needs of newcomer children and families.

Thank you to editor Kay Rollans for cheerfully polishing our work and to Brush Education for seeing its potential.

Each of us has special people in our lives who have supported and inspired us through our work and writing. Our children, grandchildren, and spouses have each contributed in their own way, from allowing us to use their stories, to critiquing and suggesting, to providing chocolate at just the right time. We are especially grateful to our husbands, Geoff Matheson and Duane Massing, for their support and companionship over the years and, most recently, for their patience and contributions during our many online collaborations as we were writing this book.

Preface

In the course of our careers, we have been privileged to work with early childhood students and educators from many different cultures. As long-time instructors, consultants, and researchers, we were entrusted with conveying the norms, expectations, and methods of mainstream early childhood practice. In conveying these norms, however, we quickly discovered that educators and families from diverse cultures have their own knowledge to share. That knowledge can help us understand and respond more sensitively to children, families, and colleagues from diverse cultures. More importantly, it can open the way to new possibilities for being and thinking—allowing us to get beyond the taken-for-granted and find common ground with difference. We can enrich our practice and our profession by challenging accepted norms with diverse cultural insights.

For some time now, we have been committed to building a truly inclusive practice in which every child and family—regardless of race, ethnicity, language, gender orientation, abilities, or socioeconomic status—feels genuinely valued. We certainly don't think we've found all the answers. We hope, though, that the experiences and thoughts we share will encourage an approach to practice that is characterized by thoughtfulness, discussion, and discovery.

When we decided to write this book, we formed two advisory groups: one with cultural brokers from the Multicultural Health Brokers Coop (MCHB) and the other with educators from Intercultural Child and Family Centre (ICFC), 1000 Women Child Care Centre, and some early learning and child care instructors from NorQuest College. We met with each of these groups to gather their experiences and discuss our ideas. When, eventually, the first draft of the book was completed, we sent it to each participant for their suggestions and approval. Having said that, responsibility for the content of final text is entirely our own.

One of the questions we asked educators and instructors was "In your early childhood studies or teaching, what could you relate to in terms of your culture?" Jasvinder Heran, the Executive Director at ICFC, answered as follows:

> I really cannot recall any moment in my schooling that we talked about culture. That's only happened recently…It seems that we hold a dominant image of children and, at times, taken-for-granted assumptions. I know for myself I needed to dig deeper and widen the understanding that situates children within historical, sociocultural, and economic contexts.

"How," Jasvinder asks, "can we go beyond the single, dominant view in order to truly honour differences?" More specifically, she asks the following questions:

- How do we establish professional relationships with families who have different values, customs, and identities than the educators?
- How do we truly honour differences with colleagues and other professionals?
- How do we teach educators that caring for children is rooted in a cultural community, that children are not separate from family, and that family includes extended family members such as grandparents, aunts, and uncles?
- How do we apply current regulations to our practice? For example, when children are required [in an educational or care setting] to eat at a table with no sharing, how do we still honour the communal practices of families? How do we advocate for families when our practice can't adapt in meaningful and relevant ways?

Yvonne Chiu of MCHB captured the sentiments of the group of cultural brokers by reminding us that "children of cultural minority backgrounds will encounter an immediate sense of not being part of the dominant culture and question their identity and sense of belonging." What, then, is necessary in an education and care context to nurture a sense of identity and belonging in these children? The brokers reflected on the important elements of an intercultural setting, and highlighted the following:

- Having early childhood educators that reflect the cultural diversities and identities of the children with whom they work
- Hearing multiple languages spoken, including the children's first languages, to affirm their sense of belonging and their interest in multilingual development

- Having parents actively engaged, whenever possible, in the sharing of culturally affirming experiences, routines, and resources for play
- Actively and creatively mediating between the cultural ways of raising children
- Adopting strategies for "guiding" and disciplining children that are rooted in hearing their voices and helping them understand the impact of their behaviours on others

Later, Yvonne emphasized that, in all aspects of early childhood education and care, we must be committed to the following:

- Identifying and addressing the cultural biases inherent in the "dominant" cultural perspectives on early childhood education and care
- Revealing and discerning the benefits of incorporating cultural ways of knowing and being into early childhood education and care beyond those of the "dominant" culture
- Recognizing that early childhood education and care can be antioppressive and antiracist in the efforts to address systemic, institutional, and interpersonal racism that impact children and their families

In our discussions, a highly educated college instructor spoke movingly about the difficulties she has experienced when working with students who dismissed what she had to offer because of her accent. Her experience left us determined to find ways to help students appreciate the immense value of diverse perspectives and ways of being.

All of the participants in our advisory groups offered stories and examples to be used in this book. We have incorporated this information, along with our own experiences, in two ways. First, we have used it to provide examples of key elements of early childhood education and care (ECEC) in practice. Second, we have used it to tell longer stories, both inside and outside of child care centres, that reflect on early childhood experiences from the perspectives of ECEs, children, and their families.

We hope this book feels like it belongs to those who have contributed their stories, and to the many other individuals who have helped us over the years to discover and develop good intercultural practice.

Notes on Terminology

We have used the term *early childhood education and care* (ECEC) throughout this text. Other terms that are used elsewhere to describe the same field include *early childhood development, early learning and child care*, and *early learning and care*.

We refer to people who work in ECEC as *early childhood educators* (ECEs), early childhood professionals, or simply *educators*.

The term *culture* can be defined in many different ways. For the purpose of our work, we are defining it broadly as the lifeways (beliefs, values, behaviours, etc.) that are distinctive of a group of people. This broad definition can include many aspects of diversity, such as religion, language, ethnicity, abilities, sexual orientation, socioeconomic status, and gender identity.

Introduction

I know there is strength in the differences between us. I know there is comfort where we overlap.
—ANI DIFRANCO

A textbook on intercultural early learning and child care seems particularly well-suited to our Canadian context and to this time in our history. It reflects both the aspirations that are foundational to the Canadian identity and current issues in navigating that identity.

The Canadian Multicultural Act builds upon the Canadian Charter of Rights and Freedoms, which forms the first part of the Constitution Act (1982). Enacted in 1988, the Canadian Multicultural Act begins by stating that "multiculturalism reflects the cultural and racial diversity of Canadian society and acknowledges the freedom of all members of Canadian society to preserve, enhance and share their cultural heritage" (§3.1.a). It ensures that every person has equal rights under the law and "has the freedom of conscience, religion, thought, belief, opinion, expression, peaceful assembly and association and guarantees those rights and freedoms equally to male and female persons" (preamble). Although not without problems and challenges, Canada's commitment to multiculturalism can be seen as unique, largely successful, and a defining part of Canada's national identity.

While multiculturalism is often interpreted as referring to distinct ethnic cultures, this statement makes clear that the Canadian Multicultural Act ensures equal rights to all persons regardless of race, ethnicity, sex, gender orientation, ability, religion, language, or socioeconomic status. However, at this time in our history there is growing awareness that, in fact, not everyone is treated equally. Various conditions within our society highlight the inequities that exist. Some prominent issues include the following:

- The growing and overdue awareness about historical and contemporary injustices dealt to Indigenous Peoples
- The systemic racism experienced by many in Canadian society
- Inequities based on gender and on sexual and gender identities
- The need to create inclusive environments and experiences for persons with challenges and exceptionalities
- The changing demographics of our population as a result of immigration and the opportunities these changes offer to draw upon the strengths of diversity
- The importance of being able to recognize and reject efforts by some groups to encourage distrust and divisiveness for political or other reasons
- National climate, health, and economic crises—including the COVID-19 pandemic, which we are living through at the time of writing—that disproportionately affect those already struggling with systemic inequities and that demonstrate the importance of caring for and about one another

This is a time for us to talk with one another across cultures—to bring divergent views into the open and to resolve conflicts in an honest and respectful manner so we can work together to resolve them. *Interculturalism* gives a name to this process. For Schreifer (2016), the term *intercultural*

> describes communities in which there is a deep understanding and respect for all cultures. Intercultural communication focuses on the mutual exchange of ideas and cultural norms and the development of deep relationships. In an intercultural society, no one is left unchanged because everyone learns from one another and grows together. (para. 4)

But what does that mean for us as early childhood educators (ECEs)? We believe that ECEs are in a unique position to contribute to building a fair and equitable society by

- Recognizing the inequities that exist in society and committing to addressing them
- Collaborating with and learning from colleagues and families from diverse cultures
- Creating environments where all children and families feel comfortable and valued
- Responding to and planning for children in ways that are respectful of who they are and what they bring to our program

- Modelling openness and interest in learning about difference
- Affirming that difference is positive—that we are all the same in some ways and different in others, and that is okay
- Helping to build strong communities by bringing people together and encouraging dialogue across cultures

Through the years, we (the authors) have been privileged to explore with educators from diverse backgrounds. We have seen areas where Canada's mainstream early childhood theory and practice fits or complements their cultural knowledge. We have seen other places where the two differ quite drastically. These areas of difference can be confusing and even painful for educators, children, and families. Consider Amelia's experience, for example:

> Amelia, an early childhood education student who has been placed in a kindergarten classroom, is distressed because she has been told by her supervisor that she is not to help the children get dressed to go outside because they need to learn to be independent. She believes that helping them get dressed is a way to show her caring and to teach them to be caring people.

Or take a look at Mathew and Mark, children at an early childhood education centre:

> Two brothers, Mathew (4 years old) and Mark (2 ½ years old), are new to the centre. Because of their ages, they are placed in separate rooms. The educators in both rooms are finding that the boys are adjusting well but find it difficult to settle down at nap time. When the educators talk with Matthew and Mark's parents, they learn that the boys are used to sharing a bed at home.

As these kinds of differences surfaced, we began to work to find ways to combine the best of cultural practices with the best of early childhood practices. We call this *wise practice*, a term first used by Joy Goodfellow (2001). We have come to believe that there is no end point to this exploration—no definitive model of "best cultural care." Instead, this work is a process that is best exemplified in the definition of *interculturalism*: it involves a respectful exchange of ideas that serves to develop mutual trust and deeper relationships.

Interculturalism and wise practice frame our approach to this book. We believe that they allow us to address multiple dimensions of diversity, including language, culture, gender identity, sexual orientation, abilities, religion, and socioeconomic status. Our intention is to provoke dialogue by presenting mainstream early childhood theory and practice alongside cultural perspectives that offer an alternative or additional view. Sometimes the two conflict; other times they complement each other.

Some approaches may resonate with you more than others. Inevitably they will alert you to the possibility that others may not think the same way you do. In the course of this reflection and discussion, individuals and programs may come to different resolutions depending on their particular situations, and that is fine.

We invite you to join us in considering how we can bring diverse perspectives into the work we do in early childhood education in order to create environments in which all children and families feel they belong, are respected, and are valued.

What to Expect from This Book

In this book, we will explore central themes, concepts, approaches, and strategies that every intercultural ECE should know. We illustrate this information with examples drawn and adapted from our own experiences, and the experiences of our colleagues, the advisory groups that guided us in writing this book, and the children with whom we have worked. We will also hear some longer stories that reflect on aspects of work and play from the perspectives of ECEs, children, and their families.

Each chapter begins with some questions about target learning outcomes to orient you to the content along with a brief introduction. We have included many real-life stories, photos, and questions in the chapters to bring you into the life of an early childhood setting. *What Do You Think?* and *Who Am I?* sections encourage you to apply concepts in each chapter to practical situations and to your own life. Each chapter ends with a *Takeaways* section that gives an overview of the main points as well as a short *Reflection and Discussion* section to support your discussions with colleagues and encourage you to reflect on the skills, attitudes, experiences, and beliefs that you bring to your work with children. Some chapters contain sidebars that highlight extra materials, points of interest, and related theory. Some will also touch on a few of the figures of historical influence on North American early childhood education and care (ECEC) theory and practices, including Montessori, Piaget, Vygotsky, and Erikson. These are names that you will meet, if you haven't already, in the course of your early childhood studies.

While we both have experience in other kinds of early education programs, the examples of intercultural practice in this book come mainly from our work in early childhood centres. We believe that the practices we propose will be applicable in most early childhood settings.

What does it mean to be an ECE in Canada? Whatever the answer to this question, we believe interculturalism lies at its heart. The chapters in this book attempt to flesh out this question, and to offer frameworks with which ECEs can begin to answer it for themselves.

Part I introduces the theoretical bases of this book. In Chapter 1 you will learn about the kinds of work that ECEs do and the settings in which they are employed. The chapter provides information on ethics, professionalism, and reflective practice. You will be invited to consider the benefits of a culturally diverse workforce. Chapter 2 applies a socio-cultural perspective to explore implications for early childhood practice and to introduce the chapters that follow. Chapter 3 focusses on celebrating difference. This is a topic that is particularly relevant to this time in our history when there is heightened awareness about issues of social justice and concern for redressing past wrongs. Then, in Chapter 4, we discuss how ECE professionals can develop an intercultural lens. This chapter describes the evolution of wise practice and shows how an intercultural dialogue supports wise practice. It also considers the impact of ethnocentrism and the importance of self-reflection.

Part II explores children's physical, cognitive, and emotional development and wellbeing. Chapter 5 looks at aspects of diversity beyond ethnicity, citing brain and body research as a foundation for evidence-based practice. It explores the effects of negative childhood events and suggests ways that we can support children in developing resiliency. In Chapter 6, we consider ways of encouraging relationship building in order to support the social and emotional wellness of children.

Part III addresses how to create environments that contribute to children's wellbeing and affirm their identity. Rituals, routines, and transitions are important components of the child care day, as we discuss in Chapter 7. Play, too, has a key role in children's development and learning. Chapter 8 introduces theories about the nature and value of play and discusses the role of the adult in children's play. Chapter 9 addresses ways to create environments that support children's play and learning and details how one playroom was transformed to respond to the cultural diversity of its children, families, and educators. Finally, recognizing the benefits of time spent in nature, Chapter 10 looks at how ECEs can bring children to nature and nature to children, both inside and outside of the playroom.

Part IV looks at how we support children's creativity, literacy, and inquiry skills, identifying intercultural considerations. In Chapter 11, we explore ways to support these skills through visual arts, music and movement, and dramatic play. Chapter 12 contains information about language development and tips for supporting language learning. It details various emerging literacy skills to help you recognize and support literacy development and contains important information about the value of maintaining children's home language and of preserving Indigenous languages. Finally, of course, learning begins with asking questions. Chapter 13 discusses ways to support inquiry generally, then focuses on the importance of numeracy skills, the nature of math skills as one aspect of numeracy, and ways that we can support children's emerging math skills.

The final chapters in this book—Part V—look at the skills, responsibilities, and challenges of the ECE professional working in an intercultural context. ECEs are guided by regulations, policies, and broad curriculum frameworks, but decisions about the kinds of day-to-day experiences they will offer children are left to the professionals themselves. Chapter 14 describes planning that is based on the interests and abilities of children. Chapter 15 addresses observation, documentation, and assessment, with a focus on learning stories. Building close relationships with families is key to offering care that is truly responsive to culture. Chapter 16 explores the attitudes and strategies needed to build strong intercultural relationships and resolve differences that might arise. Finally, Chapter 17 describes challenges and opportunities that exist in the field of early childhood education and care and offers some tips to help you survive and thrive as a ECE professional.

PART I

Theoretical Beginnings

1

What Does It Mean to Be an ECE Professional?

History will judge us by the difference we make in the everyday lives of children.
—*NELSON MANDELA*

||||||||||||||||||||||||||||||||||||||||||||||||||||||||||||||||||||||||||||||||||||||||||||||||||||||||||||||||||||||||||||||||||||||||||||||||||||||||||||||

LEARNING OUTCOMES

When you have read this chapter, you will be able to answer these questions:

- What are the roles and responsibilities of an ECE?
- Why is it important to maintain a professional attitude and professional behaviours at all times?
- What is the purpose and significance of a professional code of ethics?
- What are some characteristics of an effective ECE?
- Why is reflective practice considered a tool for ongoing personal and professional development?
- What value does diversity bring to ECEC practice?
- What skills, attitudes, and knowledge could you personally bring to the profession?

Introduction

This chapter introduces you to the roles and responsibilities of an early childhood professional. If you are already working in the field, much of the information will be familiar to you. If you are just beginning your career, however, it will give you an idea as to the nature of the profession and will help you evaluate whether or not it is for you.

We begin with a description of events in the life of an ECE, Sadia, and invite you to reflect on the attitudes, skills, and characteristics that she brings to her work with children. We then list settings where you might be employed and the kinds of work you might do as part of your job. Sadia's stories may inspire you to think about the characteristics of an effective ECE and consider the attitudes and skills that you would bring (or hope to bring) to your work with children.

The ability to be self-reflective and to be willing to consider experiences and perspectives that are different from your own allows you to grow as a person and as a professional. A diverse ECEC staffing component gives you this opportunity and enriches the experiences of children and families.

Snapshots from an Educator's Day

What is it like to work as a child care educator? If you are in a child care centre, you might be working any one of several different shifts. Sadia, for instance, begins work at 6:30 and finishes at 3:30. She has a half-hour lunch break and a 15-minute coffee break in that time.

Sadia is expected to attend staff meetings, to be involved in professional development activities, and to participate in planning meetings. She is responsible for observing and documenting children's activities on an ongoing basis and writes learning stories to make children's learning visible.

We could describe the work Sadia does as a practice of relationships. She forms vitally important relationships with the children, as you will see in the snapshots below. She also works closely with the other two educators in her playroom, with the families of the children, and with colleagues in her centre and in her profession.

In the course of a day, Sadia will use her observations and interactions with the children to provide materials and experiences that support their interests. She will involve them in meaningful ways in the tasks of the playroom. She will spend time with them both indoors and out. Routines—taking children to the bathroom, ensuring they wash their hands well, serving and clearing up from lunch, helping children settle for a nap, providing snacks, greeting children, and saying goodbye—provide structure for her day.

Let's take a closer look at Sadia's playroom and see how she navigates some of the routines and other activities of her day:

Sadia sits at a small table with two 4-year-olds, Jai-jin and Marcus, as they explore the sand dough and implements. Sadia describes what Jai-jin is doing—"You cut the ball, Jai-jin!"—as she makes a cutting motion with her fingers. Jai-jin smiles at her and repeats, "Cut." Sadia knows that Jai-jin's home language is Korean and that he is just beginning to learn English, so she uses simple sentences and adds gestures to help him understand what she is saying.

When Sadia notices the first sign of frustration from Marcus, she scoots down the bench to be closer to him and offers assistance if he needs it. "Oh no, it's crumbling, breaking into bits, isn't it?" she says. With her gentle acknowledgment and her close presence, Marcus is able to figure out how to roll the sand dough on his own without it crumbling into many pieces.

Later that morning, knowing it will soon be time to get ready to play outside, Sadia visits each group of children playing to let them know what will be happening next: "We will be going outside soon. If there is something you really need to do before we clean up, now is the time." When it is time to clean up, Sadia invites Sabina's help by asking if Sabina would like to pick up the red or the yellow pieces. When Sabina hesitates, Sadia playfully picks up a yellow block, saying, "Oh look, I have a yellow block. I'm going to put it in the basket." She pauses and then says, "Hmmm, what should I put away next? Another yellow block or a red one?" Before she can pick one up, Sabina grabs a red block exclaiming, "The red ones are mine! I'm putting the red ones away!" The relaxed and playful manner in which Sadia approaches cleanup engages Sabina's cooperation—this time, anyway!

At lunchtime, Sadia heads to the sink with the children to wash her hands. "I'm going to wash my hands, too. They are pretty dirty from playing outside, aren't they?" She wants to be a good role model, and she wants children to notice what she is doing, so she intentionally calls attention to her actions. At the table, she eats some pasta and fruit with the children while asking what fruit they like the best. Conversation is encouraged; no one is rushed to finish as she knows that children (and adults, too) eat at different paces.

Eva, the youngest and newest child in the playroom, has finished eating, and Sadia invites her to scrape her plate into the scrap bowl. Eva seems a little reluctant, so Sadia shows her what to do by scraping her own plate. She then says, "Your turn, Eva." Sadia models where to stack drinking cups and where to place used cutlery on the trolley. Since everything on the trolley is at the children's level, it is easy for Eva and the other children to participate in this self-help task. Sadia supports Arwin by scraping his plate hand-over-hand when he has some difficulty with the maneuver; she recognizes that individual children's needs differ.

Sadia is a responsive and skilled ECE. She is compassionate and knows how important it is to acknowledge children's frustration. Her focus is on engaging children's cooperation rather than getting caught up in power struggles when children are reluctant to help out, a trap that many educators fall into when they engage in teacher-centred and authoritarian ways of interacting with children. Sadia is also aware of her role in supporting children's English language acquisition; since she does not speak Korean herself, she uses other intentional strategies to communicate with Jai-jin. She has also picked up a few words in his home language from another educator that she can use to make a connection with this child. Sadia models what is expected of the children in her playroom; modelling is an indirect strategy that can be powerful in guiding children's positive behaviours.

Sadia is employed in a child care centre, but as you will see in the next section, this is only one of the settings in which an ECE might work.

Who Is an ECE?

We are using the term *early childhood educator* (ECE) to refer to a professional who works with children aged birth to 12 years in a variety of settings, including the following:

- Child care centres
- Preschool programs
- Family day homes
- School-aged care

WHAT DO YOU THINK?

Now that you've read about Sadia's typical day with children, think about these questions and discuss them with your classmates:

- What words would you use to describe Sadia's interactions with the children?
- What do you notice about the attitudes, skills, and knowledge she brings to her work?
- How do you think Sadia sees the work she is doing? Does she believe it is important work? How does she see herself in relation to her work?
- Sadia is employed at a centre where families come from many different cultures and have many different child-rearing beliefs and aspirations for their children. How might she respond to these?
- Can you see yourself doing the work Sadia is doing? What parts would be satisfying for you? What parts would be challenging at this point in your career?

- Recreational programs
- Family resource centres
- Schools (as educational assistants)
- Government (e.g., as a licensing officer)
- Inclusive care settings with children who have exceptionalities

The role of the ECE will vary according to the setting but usually includes the following components:

- Planning and providing play-based learning and care program experiences that promote the wellbeing and holistic development of children
- Documenting children's development and learning
- Communicating with parents or guardians about their children's activities at home and in the program
- Ensuring that every child is included in the activities of the centre regardless of race, ethnicity, abilities, religion, language, or socioeconomic status
- Forming collaborative, respectful, relationships with children and families
- Using community resources to enhance program resources
- Working cooperatively and productively as a member of a team
- Demonstrating professional behaviour at work and in the community, including maintaining confidentiality while keeping appropriate records and documentation
- Possibly advocating for support from government agencies and associations
- Maintaining ongoing professional development

WHAT DO YOU THINK?

Which of the components of an ECE's role did you see in the description of Sadia's day? Which weren't mentioned?

The Effective ECE

Several key characteristics help ECEs be effective in their complex roles:

- **Physical and emotional stamina**: ECEs are on the move and on demand for most of the day. A high energy level is an asset and good wellness practices are very important.
- **Interpersonal skills**: Early learning and care is sometimes referred to as a relationship-based practice because ECEs interact with children, families, and colleagues all throughout the day. Effective communication and relationship skills are critical.

- **Self-awareness**: Effective ECEs are aware of their personal beliefs, values, feelings, biases, assumptions, and behaviours to ensure that their responses to situations are in the best interests of children, families, colleagues, and others. Self-awareness is a critical component of reflective practice, enabling ECEs to effectively explore puzzling situations and find explanations and solutions.
- **Curiosity**: Curiosity drives learning. Effective ECEs encourage children's curiosity through their own interest in the world around them.
- **Creativity and playfulness**: Children learn through their play, and the effective ECE can appreciate the value of play and enter into the spirit of imagination and innovation that are a part of play.
- **Cultural humility**: Effective ECEs understand that there are many ways of looking at, and being in, the world. They are interested in learning how other people live and experience the world.

Other characteristics that are often mentioned include commitment, patience, and caring. Can you think of still more?

Ethical Standards

One of the characteristics of a *community of practice* (Wenger, 1998) is a shared sense of what good professionals should be like and how they should behave. These shared ethical standards are particularly important in ECEC because we are in a position of power in working with young, vulnerable children.

A code of ethics helps to define and unite a profession. It gives its members common goals to work toward and provides a basis for ethical decision-making. Some provincial child care organizations have developed their own codes of ethics. At the national level, the Canadian Child Care Federation, the CCCF, (2020) has developed a code of ethics for early childhood professionals that consists of eight principles:

1. Child care practitioners promote the health and well-being of all children.
2. Child care practitioners enable children to participate to their full potential in environments carefully planned to serve individual needs and to facilitate the child's progress in the social, emotional, physical, and cognitive areas of development.
3. Child care practitioners demonstrate caring for all children in all aspects of their practice.
4. Child care practitioners work in partnership with parents, recognize that parents have primary responsibility for the care

of their children, value parents' commitment to the children, and support parents in meeting their responsibilities to their children.

5. Child care practitioners work in partnership with colleagues and other service providers in the community to support the well-being of children and their families.

6. Child care practitioners work in ways that enhance human dignity in trusting, caring and cooperative relationships that respect the worth and uniqueness of the individual.

7. Child care practitioners pursue, on an ongoing basis, the knowledge, skills, and self-awareness needed to be professionally competent.

8. Child care practitioners demonstrate integrity in all of their professional relationships.

The CCCF Code of Ethics describes what each of these principles looks like in practice. The complete CCCF ethics document is included in Appendix A.

Whether or not the professional organization in your area has developed a code of ethics, it is critically important that you always demonstrate professional behaviour. This allows parents and colleagues to have confidence in you and it helps to confirm that ECEC is a credible and important profession with a defined body of skills, knowledge, and beliefs.

Professionalism

The ECEC field has worked hard to establish itself as a profession and to demonstrate that it is far more than "just babysitting." However, salaries still tend not to fully recognize the training and skills that educators bring to their work, nor the critical importance of the field to children, families, and the economy. You can help to raise the profile of the profession by always representing it in a professional manner.

Professionalism in ECEC includes usual workplace expectations such as being reliable and punctual, and being respectful, considerate, and kind in your dealings with others. However, the nature of the work is such that some behaviours are particularly important. Consider a few examples of professional and unprofessional responses to typical situations (Table 1.1).

Each of the examples in Table 1.1 addresses a different aspect of professionalism in an ECEC setting. Let's take a moment to look at each of them a little more closely.

Table 1.1. Examples of Professional and Unprofessional Responses

	THE SITUATION	PROFESSIONAL RESPONSE	UNPROFESSIONAL RESPONSE
A	You feel that your teammate, Jane, is being unduly harsh with a child who is new to the centre.	You express your concerns to Jane privately and tactfully.	During coffee break in the staff room, you complain to other staff members about Jane's behaviour.
B	You are often a few minutes late coming back from lunch.	You realize that your lateness is upsetting the schedule of the room and decide to be on time in the future.	You tell yourself that a few minutes can't make that much difference and continue to be a bit late.
C	A parent who is a personal friend of yours asks you questions about one of the other families in your room.	You tell the parent that you're sorry but that you can't discuss the other family because of privacy concerns.	You give her information and express your impressions of the family.
D	You are working with the children on a project when a colleague comes into the room and asks how it's going.	You ask the children to tell your colleague how they feel it's going.	Within the children's hearing, you say, "Alicia is so smart she knows exactly what to do, but Mikey is all over the place."
E	At a community gathering, an acquaintance says to you, "I hear things aren't going that well with your new director, Nasima."	You say, "I can't really talk about that."	You say, "She's new, of course, but some of the things she's doing have people pretty upset."
F	Your teammate says, "Look at this picture that Elena did! I'm going to post it on my Facebook."	You say, "Don't forget to get permission from Elena and her parents before you post it."	You say, "Sure—go for it."

Example A: Resolving conflict. The web of relationships in a child care environment can give it the intimacy of a family. This can help to create a warm work environment, but also one where it's difficult to maintain boundaries. It's very important for the wellbeing of the workplace to avoid gossip and to settle disagreements in a professional manner. If you have an issue with a colleague, you should always discuss it with them first. If you are unable to arrive at a resolution, you can take the matter to your supervisor or director.

Example B: Being on time. This is an easy one. In child care centres, shifts are usually tightly scheduled. If one person is late arriving or coming back from break, the other educators in the room are impacted. Being on time is the considerate and responsible thing to do.

Example C: Privacy. As an ECE, you are in a position to know a great deal about many children and families and you have a responsibility to keep that information safe and private. You should only reveal private information about children when it's in their best interests and you have their family's permission. Privacy information in various provinces will dictate the handling of sensitive documentation. Check your program's policies and, if you are in doubt, consult your director or supervisor.

Example D: Respect. Talking about children as if they aren't there suggests they don't matter. When someone speaks about a child in their presence, a good strategy is to redirect the conversation in a way that includes the child.

Example E: Representing your organization. You represent your organization in the community and have a responsibility to ensure its positive reputation. Gossiping about internal affairs can create a negative perception in the community and doesn't reflect well on you as a professional.

Example F: Responsible use of social media. Using children's work requires permission. Beyond that, however, are issues of social media usage. Your organization may well have policies about social media use and about the use of cell phones while you are at work. Be aware that anything you post on social media remains there forever. Know that your online presence reflects upon you as an individual and upon the profession.

Reflective Practice

Effective educators are self-reflective; that is, they are committed to understanding and examining their own thoughts, feelings, and actions. This is a practice that allows for ongoing professional and personal growth.

You can develop a habit for self-reflection by taking time to think through puzzling or new situations and being open to the perspectives of others. Let's see how ECE Clara uses self-reflection to understand a new situation in her playroom:

It just snowed for the first time this season and is cold enough outside that the children need to wear warm winter clothes. When it's time to go out to play, Cara's class of 5-year-olds proceeds to the coat area where they get dressed. Some need a bit of help with zippers and there are some whose hats are askew, but basically they are making good progress. At the end of the row of children, however, Cara comes upon Carlos, who is sitting by his locker making no effort to get ready. Cara encourages him to get dressed and, when he makes little progress, proceeds to dress him herself.

Later, in reflecting on the incident, she realizes that she felt impatient with Carlos, that she felt he should have been able to help himself, and that her actions with him may have revealed her impatience. Cara is upset with herself for behaving in this way and decides that she needs to draw on her colleagues for insights into the situation.

Fortunately, a colleague from the same cultural background as Carlos's family is able to clarify the situation. "In my culture," she points out, "adults dress children as a way of showing they care and teaching the children to be caring people. Carlos has probably never had to dress himself." This understanding helps Cara to be patient with Carlos and to gently encourage him to take pride in his increasing ability to dress himself.

Reflection also happens at the group level, among colleagues, and within organizations. Let's look at ECE Jody's experience, in which reflection enables not only her but a group of her colleagues to become better able to meet the needs of a particular child and of other children with nontraditional gender expressions.

Keagan, who is 5 years old, is a child in Jody's playroom. Keagan identifies as a boy-girl. Their parents accept Keagan's identity. Jody feels it's important that she and her colleagues explore their feelings about Keagan's fluid gender identity. Today in the staff meeting, she asks for their opinions. Her colleagues come from many different ethnic and religious backgrounds, and their answers are varied. Here are a few of their responses:

Back home where I am from, this is completely unacceptable. We were not allowed to show any kind of support and parents had to disown their children. Also, this is against our religion. Personally, I don't mind as long as it's not my own children.

—NATASHA

As a member of the queer community, I see a lot of similarities between this child and me when I was younger in terms of the experiences they are going through. In their gender exploration, I would see this child guiding us in how to talk to them and address them.

—ALEX

> This was a first for me. Back home, I never heard stories about this. I might feel uncomfortable because it would be unfamiliar. However, this is a child and so I would treat them no different than any other child.
>
> —*FATIMA*

This discussion was part of a larger process of learning and reflection. The centre had already brought in a presenter to speak on gender, sexuality, and identity. This prompted educators to think deeply about their own responses to Keagan's gender expression. The next step for the organization is to reflect on whether the mission, values, policies, and practices of the organization ensure that children with nontraditional gender identities have the best possible experience in the centre.

As you can see, self-reflection is a tool for your development as an educator. Reflection is also an invaluable tool for an organization's growth.

Valuing Diversity in ECE Practice

Just as it is important to value diversity among the children in an ECEC program, it is important to value diversity among our ECE colleagues. Indeed, the two go hand in hand. An ECEC program with a diverse population of child care educators is a gift to children and families:

- It can help children and families "see" themselves in playrooms and feel they belong.
- It provides opportunities to demonstrate and teach respect for diversity.

? WHAT DO YOU THINK?

If Keagan were a child in your care, how would you feel and think about their fluid gender identity? How might you respond to the child and their family?

? WHO AM I?

Knowing ourselves is the first step in becoming culturally competent. How would you describe yourself with respect to these various dimensions of diversity?

- Ancestry
- Ethnicity
- Race
- Religion
- Language
- Culture
- Gender identity
- Family composition
- Abilities (physical, intellectual, social, etc.)
- Socioeconomics

How might the person you are affect your relationships with, or expectations of, persons who are different from yourself?

- It can support families in preserving their home languages.
- It is a source of cultural knowledge that can inform programming by recognizing and building upon cultural play in meaningful and authentic ways.
- It can help other educators understand the life circumstances and experiences of families.
- It allows us to enrich and expand theory and practice in ECEC in order to reflect the diversity of families in our population.

To truly benefit from diversity among child care educators, however, it is important that we, ourselves, are willing to be self-reflective and are open to exploring the possibilities of perspectives and experiences that are different from our own.

TAKEAWAYS

Early childhood education and care is a critically important, but often under-valued, profession. As you saw in the brief sketch of Sadia's day, the work is intense and challenging, but also satisfying. It involves critical relationships with children, families, and the community. Commitment, energy, caring, and self-awareness are valuable characteristics for ECEs. Openness to diverse perspectives and lifestyles enables you to build effective relationships with children, families, and colleagues. It is critically important that you act with professionalism at all times. Ethical and professional standards can guide you in making difficult decisions and also demonstrate the integrity of the profession. Self-reflection is a tool for your ongoing professional growth.

If you are an ECE student, we hope that this chapter has helped you to visualize yourself in an educator role and consider what you bring to the profession.

REFLECTION AND DISCUSSION

- When you read about Sadia's day at the beginning of this chapter, did you notice aspects of her work that you would find particularly satisfying? That you might find challenging?

- What skills, knowledge, values, and characteristics do you see as important for an effective ECE?

- What skills, knowledge, values, and characteristics do you bring to your work with children? What are areas that you would like to develop?

- What steps would you take to ensure that your interactions with children and families are professional in nature?

2

Framing Our Practice

There is not likely to be One Best Way...
(which does not mean all ways are fine).
—*BARBARA ROGOFF*, THE CULTURAL NATURE
OF HUMAN DEVELOPMENT *(2003, P. 6)*

||||||||||||||||||||||||||||||||||||||||||||||||||||||||||||||||||||||||||||||||||||||||||||||||||||||||||||||||||||||||||||||||||||||||||||||||||||||||||||||||||||||

LEARNING OUTCOMES

When you have read this chapter, you will be able to answer these questions:
- What is a sociocultural perspective?
- What implications does a sociocultural perspective
  have for our practice as ECEs?
- Why is it important to think about our own image of the child?
- How might an image of the child be reflected
  in curriculum documents?

Introduction

When we get to know the children and families in our care, we see that there is a great deal of diversity among them. This may include differences in such areas as lifestyle, history, religion, and language. Children grow up in the context of their families, their community, and the larger society, so all of these characteristics help to define the people they become. This chapter introduces you to a sociocultural framework for looking at child development and explains why it is important to take into account the diverse experiences of children and families.

The ways in which we conceptualize childhood and children in general—our "image of the child" (Malaguzzi, 1994)—play a large role in determining how we interact and work with children. Our child-hood experiences and our observations of children are reflected in our image of the child, but cultural and societal expectations also play a large part. This chapter will encourage you to spend some time reflecting on your own image of the child and the implications it has for you as an educator.

Our Diverse Families

In 2010, filmmaker Thomas Balmès, in his film *Babies,* introduced us to four newborn babies: Ponijao from rural Namibia; Bayar from rural Mongolia; Mari from Tokyo, Japan; and Hattie from San Francisco, United States. His delightful film follows the babies through the first year of their lives as they reach typical milestones: nursing, eating, crawl-ing, walking. It highlights similarities and differences in the children's experiences during this year. We see a goat come to drink from Bayar's bathwater as he's taking a bath; Hattie being bored during an organized play session; Mari's tantrum when she is frustrated with a toy; and Ponijao fighting with her brother or, in another scene, casually wielding a machete.

The environments in which these children live are diverse and their experiences very different. However, even within a Canadian preschool group, we can see that children come from diverse families and have very different family experiences. Let's meet a few of the children in one preschool playroom:

- Dakota, who is of Indigenous heritage and spends his summers on the land with his family. Dakota's family is anxious to reconnect with their traditional culture and hope that Dakota will learn to speak their Cree language.
- Jack, who, with his three siblings, was recently apprehended by Children's Services and placed in foster care. Jack's foster parents were able to take Jack and his younger sister, but unfortunately could not accommodate his two older brothers, who went to different homes. He is protective of his younger sister and misses his brothers.
- Joey, whose father is profoundly disabled as a result of an industrial accident. His mother is the sole earner in the family and looks after his dad as well. Prior to the accident, Joey and his family had travelled extensively and had many adventures together.
- Cassidy, whose single parent mother is a student who goes to evening classes three days a week and works at a convenience

store during the day. Cassidy has a large extended family with grandparents and aunts who spend a lot of time with her.

- Matija, who came to Canada recently with his Serbian parents after living in a refugee camp from the time he was born. He has just started in the program and is learning English. Matija's family, which includes his parents, a sister, and three brothers, has the support of a community group that is helping them settle in Canada.
- Emily, whose father works while her mom stays at home with a newborn baby. Her mother attends a parenting support group at the centre.

As you can see, even though it might not be immediately obvious, there will probably be tremendous diversity in the family structures that children bring to your program. Some children may have same-sex parents, some may have parents whose work schedules don't allow a great deal of time with their children, some may have close ties with their religious or cultural community. These are just a very few of the diversities that you might encounter.

Sociocultural Views of Development

Urie Bronfenbrenner (1917–2005) was a Russian-born American developmental psychologist whose ecological theory of development (Figure 2.1) is consistent with a sociocultural view of development.

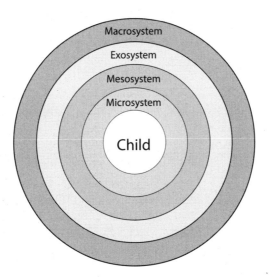

Figure 2.1. Bronfenbrenner's (1979) ecological system

Bronfenbrenner believed that a child develops through interactions with the environment and depicted these interactions as a series of systems, each of which affects the others. For example, the child is influenced by their family but certainly shapes the family as well. At a broader level, the child is impacted by policies affecting them and their family, but in a more general sense, is considered in those policies.

Bronfenbrenner called the environment closest to the child the *microsystem*. Let's look at another child, Zoe, to understand Bronfenbrenner's ecological system. Zoe's microsystem normally consists of her parents, the grandparents who she sees regularly, her child care centre, and her friends. The ways these individuals or groups interact with Zoe will affect how she develops. In return, Zoe's particular characteristics—her temperament, her abilities—will influence the people around her. Interestingly, Zoe's brother may have quite a different experience within his microsystem, even if it is largely the same as Zoe's, because *he* is not Zoe: he has a different personality and skills. His development might proceed quite differently from hers.

The next layer, the *mesosystem*, represents the connections between different microsystems. In Zoe's case, these would include the connections between her home and her child care centre, between her parents and grandparents, and between her parents and her friends. For this reason, warm relationships between Zoe's parents and her educators at the child care centre contribute to her sense of harmony and belonging.

Further out in the model, the *exosystem* refers to settings in which Zoe isn't directly involved but which may indirectly affect her life. These could include her family's places of work, the neighbourhood in which she lives, and perhaps more distant family members. The influence of Zoe's exosystem on her life was starkly apparent during the COVID-19 lockdown, for example: Zoe's parents had recently opened a restaurant and, though they tried to hide it from Zoe, were very stressed about their finances. Her child care centre was closed, and she missed the daily contact with her friends and the educators there.

The *macrosystem* is the most distant layer of influences and is composed of cultural patterns and values as well as political and economic systems. Again, the COVID-19 pandemic shows how this system can impact a child's life: political policies around providing financial assistance to people and businesses temporarily alleviated some of the stress that Zoe's parents were feeling, which helped her to feel more secure.

Bronfenbrenner (1979) later added the dimension of time to his ecological system; he called this dimension the *chronosystem*. The chronosystem shows the influence of change and consistency in the child's environments. Certainly the pandemic caused significant change for Zoe. She has gone from spending her days with friends in child care and in the neighbourhood to staying at home and being warned not to get close to people. Her more distant grandparents are unable to visit. Her parents are worried about whether their restaurant will survive; they also try to keep her away from distressing news, but she knows that many people are sick and dying. Who knows what long-term effect this massive upheaval will have on her development?

Bronfenbrenner's chronosystem would be a particularly important aspect of Indigenous child development, given the intergenerational effects of residential schools and other colonial practices that disrupted traditional lifeways. (Truth and Reconciliation Commission [TRC], 2015) It would also play a significant role in the lives of children whose families have experienced deprivation or violence prior to coming to Canada. Even those families who come to Canada under less traumatic conditions typically experience significant culture shock, and this influences their children's development.

Bronfenbrenner's (1979) ecological system is one way of showing the interrelated influences on children's development. As you can see, each child's experience will be different. Family structures, resources, and experiences will be different, as will the broader influences such as culture, politics, and religious beliefs.

There are many different ways to conceive of the influences on children's lives; Bronfenbrenner's theory provides just one. Indigenous Elders, in a project in Southern Alberta, developed an alternative model of child development that is also represented as a series of concentric circles that represent different influences on a child's development (Lindstrom et al., 2016). In this case, the circles were labelled, beginning at the centre, as "child," "family," "community," "knowledge keepers," "culture," and "Creator."

These representations tell us that we can't consider child development without looking at the broader

WHAT DO YOU THINK?

Sociocultural theory tells us that family and community experiences have a profound influence on the way children learn and grow (Rogoff, 2003; Vygotsky, 1978). How do you think the family experiences that Dakota, Jack, Joey, Cassidy, Matija, and Emily are having might influence their growth and development? How could their experiences in child care add to the mix?

context in which the child grows. Different families and communities have different hopes and expectations for children. Some may place more emphasis on developing literacy skills, while others are more concerned with social competence. Religious adherence and traditions are more important to some families than to others. We also have to consider the family's experiences over time. These might include residential school or refugee experiences or other significant events in the family's history, such as addiction or family violence.

Until recently, early childhood practice was determined by a one-size-fits-all approach to assessing and judging children's abilities. We see this in developmental checklists and developmentally appropriate practice (DAP) publications. Our early childhood practice and the DAP documents were based on the work of developmental psychologists such as Piaget and Erikson. It is important, therefore, to approach these theories with a sociocultural lens. While these psychologists' work has value to us, it must be viewed with the awareness that it was based on a limited sample of White, middle-class children and reflects the individualistic values of European and Euro-American society (Katz, 1996).

Because these measures of what is "normal" were based on this limited sample, children from any other background may not score as well. These children are then judged to be inadequate and in need of remediation. By extension, their parents are considered to be deficient and in need of "fixing." This kind of thinking has led to the development of Head Start and other remedial programs. However, it is important to ask: Are these measures able to account for the influence of diverse backgrounds on a child's development? In many cases, the answer is no, and families and their children end up being judged by cultural standards that are not their own (Cannella, 2008).

Different cultures have differing expectations regarding the age at which children can or should be able to perform certain tasks. In some cultures, children are expected to look after younger children by the age of 4; in Canada, while there is no legal age requirement, 12 is typically considered to be the minimum age at which a young person can babysit. There are cultures in which toddlers are allowed to handle sharp knives and be near fires—something that many Euro-Canadian parents would consider to be unsafe (Rogoff, 2003).

On the other hand, some Canadian child care practices are distressing to newcomers. Christine Massing (2015) reports that her immigrant ECEC students were appalled that their practicum supervisors wouldn't allow them to help children eat or dress themselves. She quotes a student, Asmaa, who talked about her experience with a child in an infant room:

> She can't eat. I ask if I could help her and they [the educators] say "no." I go to the washroom after and cry and cry. I feel very bad. She's crying, she's hungry, and she needs to eat. The others know how [to feed themselves] but some kids can't eat and they [the educators] don't care. (p. 170)

These were conflicting cultural perspectives: the supervisors were trying to encourage independence and self-help skills, while the ECEC student valued caring. If this group of immigrant ECEC students was creating a developmental checklist, it would probably look quite different from the one their supervisors would put forward.

The point is that expectations for children's development are influenced by their social and cultural context, so it would be very inappropriate, and quite possibly harmful, to assess children exclusively according to Eurocentric, middle-class standards. Families have very different priorities, lifestyles, histories, and hopes for their children; these are a part of the children's everyday experiences and influence their development.

INTRODUCING...BARBARA ROGOFF

Psychologist Barbara Rogoff (2003) compared the learning processes of children in remote Mayan communities with the learning experiences of children in middle-class American families. She was curious about why Mayan children participated willingly and without prompting in the tasks of the household and community, well past the stage where middle-class North American children have to be prompted (or bribed) to perform chores.

Rogoff concluded that this difference stems from the fact that the Mayan children are made a part of the community and learn from pitching in and paying attention. Their involvement in meaningful tasks is a source of dignity and value. In contrast, North American children are segregated from community life and placed in settings (e.g., school, child care) made only for children but controlled by adults.

Rogoff makes the point that the Mayan children are learning to collaborate: to align themselves with one another, to be alert to what is going on, to help without being asked, and to be considerate of others. She explores differences in the roles and interactions of adults and children in the two cultural contexts.

How does Rogoff's analysis reflect the sociocultural context described in this chapter?

What opportunities do children in early childhood settings have to do meaningful work? What opportunities could they have?

 Learn more about Rogoff's research by watching her presentation *Learning Through Pitching In* (UC Davis School of Education, 2013), part of the UC Davis's Distinguished Educational Thinker Series.[1]

---

1 UC Davis School of Education. (2013, April 18). *Professor Barbara Rogoff – Learning through pitching in* [Video]. YouTube. https://www.youtube.com/watch?v=jdh_GjBsphg&ab_channel=UCDavisSchoolofEducation

Implications for Practice

Sociocultural theory has implications for our work in child care: with the children themselves, with families, as a community, and as representatives of the profession in the larger society. We'll be addressing all of these areas in more detail in future chapters, but let's look briefly now at what a sociocultural approach to ECEC means for each of these four levels.

1. **The child.** The children are, of course, the primary focus for all of our days as ECEs. Sociocultural theory tells us that if we are to support them well, we need to take into account the whole context of their lives. This means the following:
   - Getting to know them very well as individuals so we can see and support their strengths and interests
   - Building close, trusting relationships with them so they feel safe and valued
   - Collaborating with them wherever possible so they can contribute to the child care community

2. **The families.** The fact that children develop within the context of their families and the communities to which they belong makes it very important that we find ways to learn about the aspirations and expectations that the family has for a child to know how the child is developing and how we can support that growth. Relationships with families build bridges between the home and the program that can support home languages, culturally affirming experiences, and access to cultural resources.

3. **The community.** The child care program is one of the communities in a child's life, one that plays an important role.

This means that the culture we establish and model should be one where children feel they belong, can pursue their interests, and feel respected and valued.

4. **The profession.** Chapter 1 introduced you to the role of the ECEC educator. As an early childhood professional, you belong to a community of practice that is defined by certain skills and knowledge. You have a responsibility to represent yourself in the community beyond your ECEC colleagues in a manner that sheds a positive light on the profession. You may also advocate for the profession—in order, for example, to gain more recognition, better funding, or higher standards for the profession.

The Broader Society

We should consider that the norms that societies adopt for child-rearing and education reflect the priorities of that society. As a child care community, our practice will also be guided by the kind of society we want in the future—one that is strengthened and enriched by the participation of every individual regardless of culture, ethnicity, ability, gender, socioeconomic status, religion, and language.

Your views of children and childhood will be influenced by your own experiences within your family, community, and the larger society. The image of the child that you have built is an important factor in your practice as an ECE.

Image of the Child

Each one of you has inside yourself an image of the child that directs you as you begin to relate to a child. This theory within you pushes you to behave in certain ways; it orients you as you talk to the child, listen to the child, observe the child. It is very difficult for you to act contrary to this internal image. For example, if your image is that boys and girls are very different from one another, you will behave differently in your interactions with each of them. (Malaguzzi, 1994, p. 1)

It is important for educators to self-reflect, as well, on their own expectations of the children they work with. Loris Malaguzzi, the father of Reggio Emilia, tells us that our image of the child is where teaching begins. It determines how we relate to and observe children, as well as the kinds of environments we create for them.

There are many possible images of the child: the child as an "empty vessel" to be filled with knowledge, the child as innocent, the child as a miniature adult, and so on. Malaguzzi (1994) suggests that educators adopt an image of the child as agentic; that is, the child as a competent, active person who makes sense of their world through their active involvement with it. In this view, adults and children are co-learners and equal partners in educational decision-making. The adult uses observations, documentation, and discussion as a basis for planning, then sensitively guides, challenges, and discovers with children.

The image of the agentic child has been highly influential in the theory and practice of European and North American early education and care, but it is not the only image of the child that we see among educators. In one program designed to prepare immigrant and refugee ECEs to pursue postsecondary studies in ECEC in Canada (discussed in Chapter 4, p. 45), we asked a group of immigrant and refugee educators what words they would use to describe children. Some of the words they suggested were *innocent, our heart, precious, special, unique, a treasure, a flower, our roots,* and *our future.* These responses are consistent with an ethic of caring and a belief that children would learn to care for others by being cared for themselves. However, ECE students whose actions reflected this image were sometimes rebuked in their practicum settings. They reported being criticized for feeding children rather than letting them eat by themselves and for helping them to dress rather than encouraging them to learn to dress independently. They described the expectation that children would do these things for themselves as cold or even abusive (Christine Massing, 2015, 2018; Massing & Shortreed, 2014).

These experiences show two contrasting images of the child: one as vulnerable and needing protection and nurturing, the other as competent

❓ WHO AM I?

Here are some questions to help you think about your own image of the child:

- What words would you use to describe children?
- What is childhood?
- What is the role of the adult in children's lives?
- How do children learn?
- What is the role of the educator in children's learning?
- How does your image of the child fit with the image of the child as competent, capable, and able to direct their actions and learning? Is this an image that you agree with? Why or why not?
- What are the implications of your image of the child for your role as an educator?

and independent. Each of these perspectives has value. We can draw from the strengths of each, but in order to do so we need first of all to be aware of our own image of the child. This image is built from several influences: our own childhood experiences, our observations and experiences with children, our own values and beliefs, and the values and beliefs that our culture and society holds for children.

We need to be open to exploring the roots of behaviours that are different from our own. Discrepancies in our images of children open exciting possibilities for exploration. As Peter Moss has said, the early childhood program becomes "a place of encounter, interaction, connections among citizens in a community, with many possibilities—social, cultural...and others new and surprising" (cited in Inuit Tagataga Inc., 2008).

||||||||||||||||||||||||||||||||||||||||||||||||||||||||||||||||||||||||||||||||||||||||||||||||||||||||||||||||||||||||||||

TAKEAWAYS

Sociocultural theory provides a solid foundation for working with children in a way that is respectful and inclusive. It makes sense, from a sociocultural perspective, that our image of the child is strongly influenced by the expectations of our culture and society. Seeing children in relation to their families, communities, and the broader society helps us understand each child better, gives us access to a broader base of ideas and resources, and makes our daily practice both more interesting and maybe a little more challenging.

In the chapters that follow, we'll discuss ways to build these connections with families and communities and bring them into the work we do with children. In Chapter 3, however, we'll look at issues that threaten harmony within our society and the wellbeing of individuals living in it. As ECEs, we have an opportunity to help children learn to celebrate the differences that add interest and build strength in our society.

||||||||||||||||||||||||||||||||||||||||||||||||||||||||||||||||||||||||||||||||||||||||||||||||||||||||||||||||||||||||||||

REFLECTION AND DISCUSSION

- If you were to depict your own development using Bronfenbrenner's model, what would it look like?

- What do you think our society might be like in 25 years? What skills, knowledge, and characteristics will individuals need to succeed? How can we promote these in a child care setting?

3

Celebrating Difference

It is not our differences that divide us.
It is our inability to recognize, accept,
and celebrate those differences.
—AUDRE LORDE

IIIIIIIIIIIIIIIIIIIIIIIIIIIIIIIIIIIIIIIIIIIIIIIIIIIIIIIIIIIIIIIIIIIIIIIIIIIIIIIIIIIIIIIIIIIIIIIIIIIIIIIIIIIIIIIIIIIIIIIIIIIIIIIIIIIIIIIIIIIIIIIIIIIIIIIII

LEARNING OUTCOMES

When you have read this chapter, you will be able to answer these questions:
- How do children learn their attitudes toward race, ethnicity, gender, ability, and appearance?
- What is cultural humility?
- How can we help children value diversity and social justice?
- What are some specific ways to combat stereotyping, prejudice, discrimination, and racism?

Introduction

As ECEs, we have a responsibility to help children learn to be comfortable with, and appreciate, people who are different from themselves. Differences in appearance, ability, family composition, language, ethnicity, religion, gender, socioeconomic status, and other characteristics offer rich possibilities for sharing and learning. By working with children in ways that support this learning, we contribute to a just and equal society, one that is free from discrimination and racism.

In this chapter, we'll explore how children acquire attitudes about difference and what we, as educators, can do to help them learn to value fairness and justice.

Children, Bias, and the Social Environment

Josh is an ECE in an intercultural playroom. The children in Josh's play-room are fortunate to live day-by-day with classmates who are richly diverse in appearance. Let's take a look at one of their interactions:

> Emily and her playmate Amita are working at the craft table when Emily suddenly lays her hand flat on the table and says to Amita, "Put your hand here." Amita lays her hand flat beside Emily's. Then Emily calls to Romy, "Put your hand here." Romy comes from around the table and does as she is told. "Look, teacher," Emily calls out, "Three colours." Educator Josh replies by putting his hand beside theirs. "Four colours!" the girls cry.
>
> The three girls do indeed have three different skin colours. Emily's family has Scandinavian origins, Amita's family is from Ethiopia, and Romy has Asian and Caribbean roots. To add to the diversity, Josh's family is from the Philippines. Josh knows that the children's discovery calls out for an exploration of skin colours, hair, and facial features. He gathers together mirrors and crayons with various skin shades, and encourages the children to continue their exploration of physical differences by making self-portraits. Throughout the week, as he reads storybooks with characters who have varying skin colours, he draws this to the children's attention. Soon many of the children in the room are noticing and pointing out differences and similarities in their physical features. As their interest grows, Josh suggests that they could make a mural of their face drawings, and Romy says they should call it, "Our Beautiful Faces."

By building on the children's interest in these differences and emphasizing that all are equally beautiful, Josh is working toward a society where diversity is valued and everyone is respected.

Early childhood educators are with children for a substantial portion of their day during a developmentally significant part of their lives. Along with children's families, they can have a very strong influence on children's attitudes and behaviour toward others. However, as we saw in Chapter 2, there are other, broader influences as well, and they don't just influence children.

Take Harriet, an ECE administrator, for example. Harriet is open and honest with herself about her biases as an adult, and how they could have been shaped by her social environment growing up:

> I grew up seeing myself as a fat person, although, looking back at photos, I was more solid than fat. People would look at me when I was young and say, "My, she's big for her age, isn't she!" My mom was slim and attractive, and you could tell from the stories she told that she had been very popular when she was young. She was careful with her eating and exercised to stay in shape. She wasn't critical of my weight, but I picked up a clear, though indirect, message that it was important

to be popular and that you needed to be slim for that to happen. At the same time, I was watching TV and reading teen magazines where all of the main characters were slim and beautiful. I dieted off and on from the time I hit my teens and had an eating disorder that I was thankfully able to overcome after a couple of years.

As an adult, I am an average weight, and my mind tells me that people are beautiful at all sizes. However, I still have a nagging bias about people who are obese. I sometimes catch myself looking at them and thinking, "Surely they can do something about that! I'm responsible for hiring at my child care centre, and I have to be careful not to let that bias influence my decisions."

Harriet is aware of her bias about obesity and is working to get past it. Her story gives some clues as to the influences that led her to this way of thinking: comparisons with her mother, the comments of neighbours and friends, and the images she saw on TV and in magazines. Some things she doesn't mention but may also influence her are the comments of classmates and peers and, at a broader level, the influence of a multibillion-dollar diet industry that thrives on people's insecurities about their weight.

Harriet's story helps us to see how bias—the unreasoned tendency to prefer one characteristic over another—and prejudice—preconceived opinions not based in evidence—can limit opportunities for herself and for others. If she stereotypes people who are obese as "not making an effort," she might engage in discriminatory practices in her work, giving preferential treatment to those whose body type she finds acceptable.

As we can see, our opinions about ourselves and others are influenced by messages from many levels of society. However, research suggests that we learn many of these attitudes early in life and that they reflect the modelling we receive from those around us. This means that the work we do as ECEs is vitally important in building a fair and just society.

Understanding attitudes that stand in the way of valuing diversity can help us to recognize these in ourselves and others and to take steps to combat them.

 WHO AM I?

DIVERSITY INFLUENCES

This exercise will help you understand how biases develop.

In Chapter 2 (p. 15), we talked about the social context of children's development. Indigenous Elders depicted the influences on development as concentric circles labelled "child," "family," "community," "knowledge keepers," "culture," and "Creator" (Lindstrom et al., 2016). Bronfenbrenner's (1979) ecological model is similar, with influences ranging from immediate contacts, such as family and child care at the centre; to the connections between different microsystems; to the larger community; and finally to cultural patterns, political and economic systems, and beliefs and values.

Consider the Bronfenbrenner ecological model and the Indigenous model of children's sociocultural development discussed. How might the levels of influence in these models affect the ideas that children develop about the following:

- Diverse physical characteristics and abilities
- Ethnicity, culture, and religion
- Gender and gender identification
- Socioeconomic status
- Family composition

Now, think about the influences at various levels in your own life. Here are some questions to get you started:

- As a child, what messages did you receive from your family and other close influences about treating people fairly? What messages did you receive about people whose cultures and religions were different from yours?
- What messages did your friends and classmates send about how you should look, act, and think in order to be accepted?
- What did the media tell you about various groups of people in society?
- Did religion play a role in your early life? What messages did you receive there about fairness and justice?
- What was the structure of your family? Was this the same or different from that of your friends and classmates?
- What exposure did you have to diversity and what did you learn from this? (Your experience might have been affected by policies about education, housing, basic income, and so on. For example, changes in policies around the provision of services to children with exceptionalities might influence your exposure to children with diverse abilities.)

Understanding Stereotypes

A *stereotype* is a generalization about an individual or a group. Have you ever heard statements like these?

- Asian Canadian students are academic achievers.
- Women do the best job of looking after children.
- Teenagers are difficult.
- Boys are better at math than girls.

Psychologists call stereotyping a "cognitive shortcut" because it helps us to quickly make sense of the world by reducing complexities into more manageable (because more simplistic) generalities. Unfortunately, it leads us to make judgments without having actual knowledge of a particular person or situation.

Overall, stereotyping creates and reinforces cultural barriers. It is harmful to the people who are stereotyped because people make assumptions about them, and these assumptions may limit their opportunities. For example, if a teacher assumes that a group of students is less likely to achieve, the teacher will be less likely to recognize their strengths. Consequently, it will be more difficult for those students to demonstrate success.

Even positive stereotypes can be harmful. For example, looking at the examples above, we can see that the Asian Canadian student who struggles in school can be further damaged by their failure to live up to the stereotype. As well, the child who is described by their family as "the smart one," "the pretty one," or "the athletic one"—or the person who is assumed to be "good at math"—may find it hard to break out of that label to achieve in other areas.

Stereotyping is also detrimental to the person who stereotypes because it narrows their view of the world: they miss out on the opportunity to get to know individual members of a group they stereotype and to learn from them.

Combating Stereotyping

Many families and early childhood programs are guilty of stereotyping with respect to gender. The idea that boys and girls require different toys and clothing greatly limits children's options (not to mention that there is no acknowledgment of children who do not identity in either category). Not only do children not get to experience certain forms of play, but they also absorb messages about how they should be as adults: girls should be pretty and boys should be active or even violent.

WHAT DO YOU THINK?

The next time you are in a toy store, compare the toys in the "boys'" aisles with those in the "girls'" aisles. What do you see? What messages are these gender divisions sending to children?

One way that we can combat stereotyping by gender is to pay attention to the way we talk to children about their appearance and their play. Do we comment on girls' pretty clothes or fancy hairstyles? Do we comment on boys' physical prowess? Do we tend to steer boys and girls to different kinds of play? Ideas about gender are so ingrained in our society that it's difficult to change some of these patterns. It's important that we do so, however, in order to give children a full range of opportunities.

Understanding Discrimination

> Discrimination refers to treating individuals badly because of characteristics such as gender identification, age, gender expression, weight, religion, disability, sexual orientation, language or immigration status. Many people have experienced some sort of discrimination but racial and ethnic minorities are most likely to experience day-to-day discrimination. (APA, 2016)

Discrimination hurts families and children in a number of ways. Discriminatory hiring practices limit employment opportunities; this impacts the family's ability to provide the necessities of life for their children. Discrimination makes victims feel unworthy; it can undermine their self-confidence so they are less likely to achieve. It is often associated with bullying and exploitation.

Discrimination can lead to chronic stress, which can have physical consequences, including increasing inflammation in the body. Discrimination has been linked to physical and mental problems including anxiety, depression, obesity, high blood pressure, and substance abuse (APA, 2016). The experiences with discrimination that mothers have during pregnancy can even have physical and hormonal effects on children before they are born (McCarthy, 2019).

Combating Discrimination

Celebrating diversity, as Josh does in the example above, is an important way to combat discrimination. As an educator, you can express delight in the range of physical characteristics, abilities, experiences, and interests among the children in your care, and you can encourage children to see this diversity as an opportunity for learning.

Adults may hesitate to talk with children about discrimination and bias, but talking openly about these topics can be important. It can prepare children for dealing with instances of discrimination and let them know that it's okay to share their frustration, hurt, and disappointment with an adult. Such discussions can open the way for children's questions and provide opportunities to challenge stereotypes. Discussing differences, as Josh did in the example above, helps children both appreciate diversity and recognize discrimination when they encounter it.

Here are some things you can do to address diversity and discrimination with children:

- Pay attention to your own comments and behaviour; children are learning from you.
- Include discussions of discrimination on an ongoing basis as situations arise.
- Don't give too much information at once and use age-appropriate language.
- Help children understand that diversity means opportunity: the greater the range of experiences there are to draw from, the greater the opportunities for learning.
- Read age-appropriate books that address diversity issues.
- Help children plan responses to discriminatory comments: for example, "That's not a kind thing to say," or "I don't agree because…."
- If you hear children making discriminatory comments, don't silence them. Use the opportunity to correct their misconceptions.

Understanding Racism

Racism is the explicit or implicit belief that race accounts for differences in character and capabilities and that some races are superior to others (Merriam Webster, n.d.). It is often associated with discrimination and prejudice. Racism harms our society by creating hurt, fear, and divisiveness. *Systemic racism* refers to ways that racist ideas are built into the systems in our society; for example, in hiring practices, the court system, and the media (Woods, 2020). This gives unfair advantages to some groups of people while disadvantaging others.

In reality, there is essentially no such thing as racial difference; everyone in the world shares about 99.9% of their genes. Ideas about racial differences are socially constructed to justify colonization and oppression. For this reason, the American Academy of Pediatrics calls racism a "socially transmitted disease" (McCarthy, 2019).

Research tells us that children develop their attitudes toward race from an early age and that the preferences they show reflect the characteristics of the adults around them (see Bar-Haim et al., 2006). According to the American Academy of Pediatrics, children begin noticing race-based differences as early as six months and are already beginning to internalize racial biases by the ages of two to four (Trent et al., 2019). By the time they reach kindergarten, children are likely to have the same attitudes about race as the adults in their culture, and make the same assessment of high and low status groups (Dunham et al., 2008). Because children form their attitudes about race and other aspects of diversity at an early age, it is essential that ECEs take an active role in understanding and combating racism and discrimination.

Antiracism protests have highlighted the issue of racism in Canada. In response to protests in 2020, the Canadian Human Rights Commission (2020) issued a statement saying that "the belief that there is little to no racism in Canada is in itself a barrier to addressing it" (para. 1) and that

> [n]ow is the time for all Canadians, but especially non-racialized Canadians, to listen, learn, and reflect on how White privilege and systemic racism contribute to injustice and inequality in this country. We need to look inwards and challenge our biases, fears, assumptions, and privilege. We need to have difficult and uncomfortable conversations. (para. 6)

Canada has a long history of systemic racism: the removal of Indigenous children from their homes to attend residential schools; the "head tax" on Chinese immigrants; the refusal to accept Jewish refugees on the MS *St. Louis* in 1939; the internment of Canadian citizens of Japanese descent during World War II; the bulldozing of Africville in Halifax, Nova Scotia, in the late 1960s; and immigration policies that made it difficult for people of colour to come to Canada, revised only in 1976, are just a few examples.

We see evidence of racism now when we examine statistics on poverty or rates of incarceration and child welfare interventions in which racialized minorities are far overrepresented. These point to systems that advantage some groups and disadvantage others. Systemic racism refers to the social structures that make these kinds of inequalities possible.

One of the difficult things we have to do in order to understand racism is to look into our own experiences and attitudes. The term *cultural humility* refers to an attitude and habit of both looking deeply within ourselves and opening ourselves to discovering the realities of others. It's equivalent to saying to another person, "I don't understand, but I'd like to" (Hook et al., 2015).

? WHO AM I?

ASSESSING PRIVILEGE

Some of us come from a position of privilege that others do not enjoy. The privileged position or way of life is considered to be "normal" and allows people to benefit from the power and resources in society. The questions below may help you to assess the privilege that you possess.

Privilege is something that you didn't earn or even ask for, but have anyway just because of who you are and the circumstances of your life. You may be so used to it that you don't even recognize it. Privilege has to do with factors such as race, gender, sexual orientation, class, income, and religion.

Privilege might look or feel like any of the scenarios in the list below (McIntosh, 1988). Read the list and count the number of scenarios that are true for you.

- I feel comfortable walking alone at night.
- I am able to show affection for my romantic partner in public without fear of ridicule or violence.
- I come from a supportive family environment.
- I am able to easily find the hair products I need or cosmetics to match my skin colour.
- I have never been diagnosed as having a physical or mental illness or exceptionality.
- I was born in Canada.
- I am reasonably sure that I would be hired for a job based on my ability and qualifications.
- I get time off for my religious holidays.
- I am able to make mistakes without people attributing them to my race/ethnicity or gender identity.
- I am not afraid to call the police when trouble occurs.
- I have never been bullied or made fun of, especially for something I can't change.
- I do not or would not have to educate my children to be aware of systemic racism for their own daily physical protection.
- I am able to go shopping without being afraid of being followed or harassed.

How many scenarios were true for you? If they were all true, imagine what it would be like to not have those privileges. If the scenarios above were not all true for you, we invite you to use this exercise, to the extent that you are comfortable, as a springboard to discuss how having privilege—and not having it—affects your life.

You will find various questionnaires and exercises on the Internet to help you assess your privilege and start conversations. (We recommend the many adaptations of the "Privilege Walk" exercise.)

Working for Social Justice

What are the things that we, as educators, can do to work for a society where each person is treated fairly? Avoiding stereotypes and labelling and combating discrimination and racism are important goals to work toward. However, our ability to work effectively toward an equitable society begins with our own self-awareness.

Build Self-Awareness

Building self-awareness is an ongoing process. It can be interesting to come to understand ourselves better, but it can also be painful to discover the unconscious biases that we hold. However painful it might be to recognize, our society is structured in ways that advantage some segments of the population and disadvantages others; the Assessing Privilege exercise gave you a sense of the position you occupy in this unequal society and the privileges and disadvantages that position entails.

However, understanding bias may be more complicated than we think. For example, research suggests that our own racial biases come into play when we judge children's emotions. Halberstadt et al. (2020) found that prospective teachers showed racial bias when they were judging whether children were angry. Though this study focussed on anger, it makes sense that this bias could hold true for other emotions, especially given that cultures vary in the ways they demonstrate emotion.

In a further example of racial bias, Head Start (2020) reports that African American children in the United States are almost twice as likely to be expelled from preschool as other children, while White and Latino(a) children are expelled more than five times as often as Asian American children.

Since we know that children are building their attitudes about race and other human characteristics early in their lives, we need to be very aware that they are learning from the ways they see us interacting with other children, families, and our co-workers. Becoming aware of our privileges and disadvantages as well as our biases helps to ensure that our decisions and interactions are fair, and that we model fairness for children.

Be Informed

Try to learn more about historical events and current issues related to privilege, oppression, racism, and social justice. It is your responsibility to actively seek out this information; people struggling under the weight of oppression should not have the added burden of educating you about their struggle. Develop your own consciousness about issues of racism and injustice. When it's appropriate, you could talk about these issues with children.

Be Open to Possibilities

We need to be open to the possibility that others have different experiences of the world, that they make sense of it in different ways, and that they may respond to the world differently than we do. Exploring these differences can be very interesting and can open up new possibilities for ourselves. We can encourage children to have this same sense of wonder and to make an effort to understand others' perspectives.

Include Everyone

Make sure your playrooms reflect the children and families they serve; show them that they belong and are valued by including culturally appropriate items and toys, posters, music, routines, and so on. (See Chapter 9 for an account of one centre's experience with making their environments more reflective of the cultures of the families they serve.)

Be Ready to Talk

Remember Josh's playroom from the beginning of this chapter? Josh knows that it's natural for children to notice differences and want to talk about them. Let's look at another example in which he respectfully encourages this kind of exploration:

> Kima is new to the room. When she arrives, she immediately attracts a lot of attention because she uses a wheelchair. The children have many questions about why Kima can't walk: "What's wrong with her legs?" "Why does she have that wheelchair?" Josh encourages them to talk directly to Kima, so they turn to her with their questions. Kima explains that her legs don't work and she needs the chair to move around." "Awesome!" 5-year-old Khalid exclaims. "How fast can you go?"

If Josh had shushed the children in his playroom or changed the subject, he might have suggested to Kima and the rest of the class that there was something shameful about her difference. Instead, she quickly became an accepted member of the group, even envied for her transportation advantages.

People often think that children shouldn't be exposed to problematic issues like discrimination and racism; however, they are inevitably exposed to issues of racism and injustice in the media and in their communities. Young children are unlikely to understand scenes of violence that they see on television or elsewhere, but they do pick up on the emotions they see and hear—fear, anger, or a sense of urgency. They might show their uncertainty or distress in their play or their artwork. Be ready to sensitively respond and give them an opportunity to talk about what is bothering them. If you sense that a child is upset, it's okay to ask them how they are feeling.

Emphasize the Value of Difference

In his playroom, Josh consciously instills a message about the beauty of difference. As educators, we can look for opportunities to recognize the unique strengths of individual children and the advantages of the diversity they represent. The ECE and her sister who wear hijabs are able to tell the children what a hijab is and why they wear them. The child whose high activity level in the playroom can be problematic can demonstrate a cartwheel in the playground.

We can encourage children to find many different ways to solve problems and perform tasks by asking questions like, "How many different ways can you do this?" We can recognize their unique responses and use the opportunity to emphasize that thinking outside the box can spawn discoveries and inventions.

Use Books to Prompt Discussion

Out on the playground of her child care centre, ECE Fatima diffuses a conflict:

> Fatima notices that two older children are teasing 3-year-old Adam, who lives in a family with two fathers. "You don't even have a mom," one of them taunts. Adam looks tearful and Fatima intervenes. "Everyone has a mom," she says, "but Adam lives with his two dads. There are lots of different kinds of families." Later she tells educator Sam, who works with the boys, about the incident. Sam decides that she will find a book about different family configurations to read and discuss with the children in her room.

Storybooks offer a great opportunity to talk with children about diversity and justice. Point out examples of racism and stereotyping. Choose books with characters of many ethnicities and races. Include lots of discussion. With young children, this might simply mean pointing out features: "This girl has brown eyes and curly hair." This can be a chance to ask questions and find out what children already think. The goal is to let children know that it's okay to talk about race, ethnicity, and other aspects of diversity.

Children need to see themselves, their families, and their friends represented in books. With older children, books about real-life leaders who share their ethnicity can help to instill a sense of pride in their heritage. Books like Sheneeza Kanji's *Amazing Canadian Kids! What They're Doing to Make a Difference!* (Authorhouse, 2012) and Janet Wilson's *Our*

Heroes: How Kids Are Making a Difference (Second Story Press, 2014) show them that young people and people of any background can bring about big change. Books can also help to show the strengths of difference. *Frederick* (Dragonfly Books, 1973) by Leo Lionni is one of many books that show that characters who are different can make valuable contributions.

Appendix B includes books with messages about diversity and books with characters from many different ethnicities and cultures.

Help Children Become Allies

Books, puppets, and storytelling can be used to help children work out ways to respond to problematic situations. For example, you can use puppets to enact a situation where a character is being bullied and ask children how they would respond to it. Discussing these scenarios can help them be prepared to act if they are bullied or if they notice someone else being bullied.

AVOIDING BIAS IN CHILDREN'S BOOKS

Children's books send messages to children about how they and their families are viewed in society. They also tell them how they should view people who are different from themselves. For these reasons, it's important that we choose children's books that send positive messages about various types of diversity. We can also choose books that encourage children to stand up for justice and help them deal with difficult issues, such as bullying. Here are some guidelines (Canadian Children's Book Centre, n.d.; Derman-Sparks & Edwards, 2009):

- Choose books that are appropriate to children's interests and understandings.
- Make sure your book collection includes a balance of books about specific family compositions, ethnicities, religions, abilities, classes, lifestyles, and gender and sexual identities.
- Look at the relationships among the characters in a book. Who takes the leadership roles? Do the "good" characters come from a variety of backgrounds? Are some characteristics acceptable and others not? Does someone have to change in order to be accepted?
- Check the illustrations. Are the characters depicted as real people, or are they stereotypes?
- Look for books about children and adults creating change or acting to correct injustice.

- Consider the language used in a book. Ensure that it is gender inclusive and not demeaning to any group of people.
- Be sure that books give a realistic picture of how people live today. If you are reading folk tales or legends, ensure children can understand that they were written or told in the past.
- Check that the book collection depicts a variety of settings and environments (e.g., urban and rural, various cultures).
- Ensure the books provide a basis for discussion about diverse perspectives and problem-solving.

Figure 3.1. We all need to feel like we belong

|||||||||||||||||||||||||||||||||||||||||||||||||||||||||||||||||||||||||||||||||||||||||||||||||||||||||||||||||||||||||||||||||||
TAKEAWAYS

Children learn their attitudes toward others from a very early age, which makes the work of ECEs particularly important. Social justice work begins with helping children to be open to difference and interested in learning from it. For you as an educator, the first step, and one that will be ongoing throughout your career, is to cultivate your self-awareness. Uncover your unconscious biases and stereotypes and consider how they influence the work you do with children. Take opportunities to talk with children about issues of fairness. There are many children's books with diverse characters and messages about diversity that you can use to support discussions with children (see Appendix B).

An intercultural approach allows us to benefit and work with differences in ways that help us all to build relationships and learn from one another. Chapter 4 will explain the concept of *wise practice*—combining the best of early childhood practice with the best of cultural practice—and show how intercultural dialogue can support this process.

|||||||||||||||||||||||||||||||||||||||||||||||||||||||||||||||||||||||||||||||||||||||||||||||||||||||||||||||||||||||||||||||||||||||||||||||||||

REFLECTION AND DISCUSSION

- This chapter emphasized the importance of self-awareness: understanding your own attitudes and biases so you can truly model acceptance and appreciation of diversity. This is a good time to take stock. What have you learned about yourself and how will that impact your work with children?

- How might you respond to each of the following situations in a way that teaches fairness and consideration? (You could try role-playing these scenarios.)

  › Hana bounces into the room and does a twirl. "Do you like my new dress? We bought it last night." You notice that Chloe is watching with a sad expression. You know that Chloe's mother struggles to feed her children and that there is no money for new clothes.

  › Anton emerges from the dress-up area bedecked in jewels and flounces. Two of the girls say, "You can't wear that, Anton. You're a boy."

  › Dana, who is Black, is sobbing in a quiet corner of the room. When you ask her what's wrong, she says, "They won't let me play. They said I'm dirty."

  › Justin paints a green elephant and Liam says disdainfully, "Elephants aren't green. You don't know anything!"

- How could you use children's books to respond to each of the above situations? Check Appendix B for a children's book that might be useful in each situation.

4

Developing an Intercultural Lens

Our life becomes richer and deeper for
having encountered differences.
—*H. NED SEELYE*

LEARNING OUTCOMES

When you have read this chapter, you will be able to answer these questions:

- What do we mean by the terms wise practice, ethnocentrism, and unconscious bias?
- Why is intercultural practice important?
- How does intercultural dialogue support wise practice?
- How does recognizing our unconscious biases help facilitate intercultural practice?

Introduction

In Chapter 1, we explored what it means to be an ECE—what the work is like and what it means to be a professional. In this chapter, we'll turn an intercultural lens on this work and develop the concept of intercultural practice more fully. The chapter explores the idea of *wise practice*: the best of cultural practice combined with the best of early childhood practice (Goodfellow, 2001)—and shows how an intercultural dialogue supports wise practice. In order to engage in wise practice, or any intercultural dialogue, we must first address our own ethnocentric

43

tendencies. Self-reflection helps us uncover and examine the conscious and unconscious biases that contribute to ethnocentrism and opens us to new possibilities and perspectives.

AN EYE-OPENING EXPERIENCE FOR MARY LYNNE

Years ago, I was invited into a child care centre to observe, give feedback, and support their staff for an upcoming licensing visit. They cared for children from 3 months to 5 years of age and all of the educators and most of the children were from the Somalian community.

During my time in the room with the oldest children, a 4-year-old girl told an educator, "That boy hurt me!" At the time, I thought it was odd that she didn't use his name. Then I began to notice no one used children's names and that educators addressed all children as "baby." I was wondering how they might go about creating a playroom community when children did not know each other's names.

At lunchtime, I observed children sitting as adults stood and circled the tables breaking off pieces of sandwich and putting them in children's mouths. I often heard them urging children to eat, and when all the children were finished eating, the educators cleared the tables and used wet paper towels to clean each child's face. I wondered how licensing officers might view these practices.

I was intrigued. When staff and I met to converse, I shared what I had noticed and invited the educators to tell me about these particular practices. I learned that in the villages they came from in Somalia, all adults were responsible for all children; they were all "mothers" to each child, even if they were not from the same family. The community as a whole took responsibility for all the children and saw them as their own babies. Therefore, they told me, calling children "baby" was an expression of their love for and close relationship with each child. I also learned that most of the educators and families at the centre experienced food insecurity both back home and in this new country. Food was precious and was not to be wasted. They were all worried about children getting enough food. I noticed that almost all of the children didn't object to being fed or having their faces washed by an adult— even the 5-year-olds—and was told that this way of feeding and looking after children was common in children's homes so they were used to it. Mothers showed their love for their children by doing things for them like dressing them, feeding them, and cleaning them.

"Discovering" Cultural Difference

For Mary Lynne, an experienced ECE instructor and one of the authors of this book, the visit she describes in the story above was a pivotal experience—one that showed her that culture goes beyond the external trappings of food, fun, and fashion to the understanding that people can look at the world in completely different ways, and that no one way is right or wrong. She described the visit as "an 'ah-ha' moment: I had been looking at their practice from the lens of the individualist orientation that predominates in North America, and they were acting from a collectivist, kinship-based perspective as lived in their cultural community." She also understood the dilemma this posed when educators and families from diverse cultures were expected to adopt mainstream "Western" standards of practice. "It is little wonder," she said, "that they were having challenges meeting licensing standards; these are two very different world views."

It's been said that our own culture is as invisible to us as water is to a fish. Until we bump up against a difference that challenges our cultural ways of thinking, we tend to take for granted that everyone thinks as we do. Working as a mentor in early childhood programs, Mary Lynne was concerned with helping the programs provide sensitive, responsive care. This program was certainly doing that; it responded to the needs of children by providing consistency between their experiences in their homes and in their child care. What it wasn't doing—and the area that was causing it difficulty in meeting licensing requirements—was following narrow "Western" expectations for child care programs. This was one of the experiences that led her to embrace a "wise practice" approach to negotiating cultural differences.

? WHAT DO YOU THINK?

Imagine you are faced with the dilemma that Mary Lynne encountered: needing to provide guidance to a child care centre that serves a non-Western cultural community to help them meet licensing requirements. What would you suggest?

The Evolution of Wise Practice

In 2012, Carole (the other author of this book) was hired to conduct an action-research-based project to find ways to prepare immigrant and refugee child care educators to pursue Canadian postsecondary studies in ECEC. This "bridging program" was structured as a reciprocal learning process: mentors learned about cultural knowledge that educators brought to their work and educators explored the unfamiliar Western expectations they were encountering in the child care centres where they were employed. The 18 educators who participated over the two-year course of the project were excited about this opportunity to have their expertise recognized and used to enrich ECEC practice.

Mary Lynne joined this project as a mentor in its second year. After it ended, she continued to work with the educators at the Intercultural Child and Family Centre in Edmonton, Alberta, to find ways to use their cultural knowledge to appropriately respond to the culturally diverse population of children and families at the centre. This involved ongoing dialogue and discussion with both the educators and the families. It's this process of negotiation and exchange that is at the heart of wise practice: practice that combines cultural strengths with Western expectations for high-quality care (Goodfellow, 2001).

What might wise practice look like? As an example, let's take a look at ECE Samantha as she works with a child, Hamsa, in her playroom:

> Samantha sits beside 3-year-old Hamsa at the lunch table. Hamsa's family recently arrived in Canada. He is not only new to the centre but also new to the world of child care as well. The lunchtime routine in Samantha's centre supports the development of children's self-help skills by presenting food family style in bowls on the table so children can serve themselves. Hamsa sits and stares at the bowls but does not take any action, even after Samantha invites him to serve himself by gesturing how to do so with the spoon. Samantha guesses that he probably does not serve himself at home and so she asks if he'd like "a little or a lot?" using her hands to show these amounts. When he does not respond, she places a spoonful of stew in his bowl and asks, "More?" showing him another spoonful.
>
> Samantha models by eating a spoonful of stew from her bowl and smiles as she gestures for him to eat as well. Hamsa continues to stare at the bowl. Samantha then uses his spoon to offer him a bite, which he reluctantly eats. She continues offering him bites and makes a mental note to find out how he eats at home: Does he feed himself? What utensils are usually used at home? Does he use utensils or his hands? This will be valuable information as she decides how to support practices from home while also introducing him to routines at the centre.
>
> Samantha spends the next few days feeding Hamsa; she wants him to feel comforted in this new setting, so she begins by copying what she has learned is done at home: he is fed by an adult. Eventually she begins to set two spoons at his place: one she can use to feed him and one that is available for him to use on his own. There is no need to rush him; she trusts that when he is comfortable, he will pick up the spoon himself seeing that this is what Samantha and the other children do.

Approaching this situation in this way is fairly new for Samantha, but she has learned that bridging two cultures takes time and understanding. She recognizes that Hamsa's home practices are important to him and his family and that the ethic of caring that they convey is valid and should be respected. At the same time, helping Hamsa develop his self-help skills will facilitate his success in a culture that values independence. Samantha avoids approaching Hamsa's situation with an either/or solution, opting instead to incorporate both perspectives without implying judgments about either.

Intercultural Dialogue

Samantha understands that wise practice needs to involve close communication with Hamsa's family. She wants to understand values and practices that are important to them and to learn about the hopes they have for their children. At the same time, she will have the opportunity to talk with them about practices at the centre so they will be comfortable with the experiences their son is having. This is an *intercultural dialogue*: a mutually respectful communication between persons from different cultures. She knows that this exchange can help to build understanding and a closer relationship.

An intercultural dialogue requires that each party be genuinely open to listening to and learning from the other. We could represent this process graphically as a bridge in which the individuals who begin at either end are able to meet in the middle.

Let's imagine the dialogue that might have taken place before the scenario described above: Hamsa has just begun attending the child care centre. When his mom, Farah, comes to pick him up on his third day, Stephanie asks if she has a few minutes to chat:

Stephanie: *I've noticed that Hamsa isn't eating at lunchtime, and I'm worried that something might be bothering him about our food or the way we eat.*

Farah: *Yes, he's very hungry when he comes home.*

Stephanie: *Has he said anything about what might be bothering him?*

Farah: *He did say, "I can't eat," but when I asked him why he wouldn't say anything.*

Stephanie: *We had soup for lunch today. Do you have soup sometimes? [Farah nods] How do you eat it?*

Farah: *I take a spoonful and if it's hot, I blow on it to cool it. Then I feed it to him.*

Stephanie: *I think I understand. He's used to you feeding him, but at the centre we try to encourage the children to eat by themselves.*

Farah: *But how do you make sure they get enough to eat? In my culture, we always feed the children. We might feed him even after he begins going to school. That's how we show care for him.*

Stephanie: *I'm afraid we can't feed all the children. They do learn very quickly to use the spoon to feed themselves.*

Farah: *I don't like it that he won't be able to get food unless he learns to feed himself.*

Stephanie: *No, we sure don't want him to be hungry. How about if I start by feeding him but give him a spoon as well. Then when he's ready, he can use it to feed himself. We'll make sure that he gets lots of finger foods as well so he won't be hungry.*

Farah: *I know that you have to follow your rules so that sounds like something to try.*

Stephanie: *Let's talk again tomorrow when you come and I'll let you know what he has eaten.*

Farah: *Okay.*

Interculturalism recognizes that we are all different; we come together with worldviews that are often disparate. Intercultural practice opens us up to learning about and from others, and about various possibilities for thinking and being. It helps us resolve puzzling situations. However, this is a *practice*—it doesn't happen automatically. Certain conditions foster a positive intercultural exchange:

- Ample time and opportunity for openly sharing perspectives
- Participants who are self-reflective and open
- A relationship of trust in which participants know their ideas will be respected by others in the exchange

Intercultural practice is deeply rewarding, not only because it facilitates responsive environments for children and families, but also because it builds a culture of learning, respect, and mutual appreciation.

Barriers to Interculturalism

One of the barriers to interculturalism is our tendency to be *ethnocentric*—that is, to believe our cultural worldview and practices are the best and that other ways of being, thinking, and doing are unwise or inferior. Often, ethnocentrism is linked to *unconscious bias*. Although conversations around unconscious bias have been going on for years, the Black Lives Matter protests during the summer of 2020 brought the concept into sharp relief for many. In the midst of widespread anti-Black racism demonstrations, there were also widespread conversations about racism and unconscious bias. Many people opened their eyes to the fact that certain beliefs, language, actions, and sociopolitical conditions that they had taken for granted are, in fact, harmful to people of colour, and had to reckon with the fact that the very taken-for-grantedness of these things indicated the presence of biases within themselves that they were previously unaware of or had avoided addressing.

Our conscious or unconscious biases can pertain to all kinds of diversity—languages, customs, abilities, religions, gender, and behaviours. Biases are revealed when, for example, we

- Don't provide access to facilities and activities for people with exceptionalities
- Assume that females are more able than males to care for children
- Fail to meet a new English language learner partway by learning a few words in their language
- Distinguish between "boys' toys" and "girls' toys"
- Assume that everyone should celebrate the same religious holidays (e.g., Christmas) that we do
- Avoid doing a school task with a classmate from another culture or race

Ethnocentrism serves us in several ways. We tend to be most comfortable with people who we believe are like ourselves. We have a sense of belonging. We have a way to pass on traditions that are meaningful in our culture. On the other hand, ethnocentrism encourages us to make broad generalizations that may well be inaccurate. It is divisive and encourages negative attitudes. It promotes narrow ways of thinking, limiting our perspectives and choices. The idea that some ways of being are "more advanced" or "more civilized" than others has long been a rationale for colonizing and dominating other peoples.

The first step, then, in moving toward practices that are fair to everyone is working to get past ethnocentrism—to be open to the fact that other people's ways of being and doing can and do have value, and that they make sense given the particular events and circumstances associated with them.

As we mentioned in the Chapter 3, the term *cultural humility* refers to engaging in self-reflection and discovery in order to be open to the realities and perspectives of others. This allows us to build relationships that are honest and trustworthy (Yeager & Bauer-Wu, 2013). Given the diversity of children, families, and colleagues that you will encounter in early childhood programs, openness to exploring differences is important. Self-awareness and reflection enable us to identify our own conscious and unconscious biases so they don't become a part of our interactions and decisions.

Exploring Attitudes about Differences

A tendency to favour one thing over another is called a *bias*. Biases can be positive or negative; for example, we may have a bias toward certain kinds of foods or activities. Most often, though, biases have to do with stereotypes—for example, assuming that boys are better at sports than girls, but girls are better at music.

We all have biases. Like stereotypes, biases are a kind of "cognitive shortcut" that help us quickly make sense of the world. Usually, these biases are shaped by the experiences, values, and beliefs we hold, as well as by the influence of our friends, family, and education.

Biases can be conscious or unconscious. If we know that we tend to make assumptions about particular beliefs, lifestyles, or groups of people, we are more likely to recognize those assumptions when we are in situations that might trigger them. When we recognize our biases, we can put them aside, reduce their impact on our decision-making, and be open to people and experiences that could possibly change our views. However, when we are not conscious of our biases, they can limit our ability to learn about other ways of being, form relationships with those different from ourselves, and make decisions based on many perspectives and possibilities.

It's important that we work to become conscious of our biases relating to the many different aspects of diversity that we might encounter. You are likely to encounter many kinds of diversity in your work as an ECE. Being honest with yourself about your biases makes it less likely that you will allow them to unconsciously interfere with the relationships you form and the decisions you make.

? WHO AM I?

What conscious and unconscious biases do you hold? Here are a few questions to help you think and talk about your biases:

APPEARANCE

- Do you prefer certain physical characteristics, such as hair colour, skin tone, height, weight, and body shape?
- Are there mannerisms that bother you?
- Are there particular types of clothing or head coverings that make you feel wary or uncomfortable?

AGE

- Do you feel that some individuals have certain beliefs, responsibilities, or capabilities because of their age?

FAMILY STRUCTURE

- What is your picture of the "ideal" family?
- Do you believe that lone-parent families have more challenges than two-parent families?
- What are your views on same-sex parents?

SOCIOECONOMIC STATUS

- Do you believe that children who live in poverty are less likely to have happy childhoods?
- Do you believe that children from higher-income families tend to be spoiled?

RELIGION

- Do you believe that some religions or forms of spirituality are better than others?
- How do you feel about persons who profess to have no religion?
- Do you associate certain actions or values with particular religions?

LANGUAGE

- Do you believe that individuals who speak with an accent are less intelligent?
- How do you feel about sexist or racist language?

ABILITIES

- How comfortable do you feel around people who have physical or intellectual exceptionalities?
- Are there particular ways you feel you should talk or act with individuals with exceptionalities?

ETHNICITY, RACE, AND INDIGENOUS ANCESTRY

- What assumptions do you make about people of particular races or ethnicities?
- What assumptions do you make about people of Indigenous ancestry?
- Do you have specific ideas about the foods people of different ancestry eat? the clothes they wear? their customs, beliefs, or lifestyles?
- What are your feelings about persons who come to Canada as immigrants or refugees?

GENDER IDENTITY AND SEXUAL ORIENTATION

- What are your beliefs about the roles of males and females?
- What assumptions do you make about the way a person's gender identity relates to their sexual orientation?
- How do you feel about individuals who identify as, for example, lesbian, gay, bisexual, transgender, two-spirit, queer, or gender or sexually fluid?

Note: This list is adapted, with permission, from *The Educational Assistants' Guide to Supporting Inclusion in a Diverse Society* by C. Massing, B. Anderson, and C. Anderson, 2020. Copyright 2020 by Brush Education, Inc.

||||||||||||||||||||||||||||||||||||||||||||||||||||||||||||||||||||||||||||||||||||||||||||||||||||||||||||||||||||||||||||||||||||||||||||||||||||||||||||||

TAKEAWAYS

Wise practice involves finding ways to combine the best of cultural practice with the best of early childhood practice. Intercultural dialogue supports wise practice by allowing us to learn about another perspective and come to an understanding that incorporates the best of both views.

Intercultural practice has many dimensions, but it begins with your own self-awareness. Reflecting on the unconscious and conscious biases you bring to your work helps you to avoid taking those biases into your relationships and decisions.

In Chapter 5, we'll turn to a discussion of physical development, focusing on brain research and its implications for understanding and working with children.

||||||||||||||||||||||||||||||||||||||||||||||||||||||||||||||||||||||||||||||||||||||||||||||||||||||||||||||||||||||||||||||||||||||||||||||||||||||||||||||

REFLECTION AND DISCUSSION

- Can you think of a time when your taken-for-granted ideas were challenged by a view that was quite different? What did you take away from that experience?

- Think about a time when you had a discussion with someone who had a quite different perspective than you did. What was that conversation like? What was the outcome? Did you feel like the discussion helped to build a better relationship?

PART II

Development and Wellbeing

How We Grow: Bodies and Brains

*We see how early childhood experiences are
so important to lifelong outcomes, how the
early environment literally becomes embedded
in the brain and changes its architecture.*
—ANDREW S. GARNER

‖‖

LEARNING OUTCOMES

When you have read this chapter, you will be able to answer these questions:
- What are developmental milestones and how are they helpful?
- What does brain research tell us about the kinds of relationships children need for optimal brain development?
- What do we mean by "executive function"?
- How can we help to build resiliency?
- What are the consequences of extreme long-term stress?
- How can we recognize and respond to child abuse or neglect?

Introduction

While children grow in the context of their environment, there are other factors that determine the persons they become. Have you ever marveled at how two children who have grown up in the same family can become such different people? Even identical twins develop their own unique identities.

In this chapter, we'll explore the factors that affect growth and development. We'll see that some areas of development are predictable, while others vary with environment and heredity. The debate about the relative influence of nature (biology/heredity) and nurture (environment) has continued through many decades. Recently, neurobiology has taught us more about the interactions between nature and nurture and has alerted us to the importance of a responsive environment to foster optimal development—in particular, brain development.

Diversity in Development

In Chapter 2, you met some of the children in a preschool playroom: Dakota, Jack, Joey, Cassidy, Matija, and Emily. You learned a bit about the environments in which they were growing. Now we'll find out a little more about some other aspects of their development.

- Dakota is tall and slim, with dark eyes and hair. He is well-coordinated and excels at active sports. Dakota has a deep connection with nature and is able to identify a number of the plants he sees when he goes on walks. He is a sensitive child who likes to help others.
- Jack is smaller than many of the children his age. He has sandy hair, hazel eyes, and a winning smile. The educators have noticed that Jack has a little difficulty following complex directions. He has also been a bit slower than average in accomplishing milestones like learning to walk and talk.
- Joey is a bouncy child with a great deal of energy. He loves gym time and enjoys playing active games. He looks so much like his father that people often comment on the resemblance.
- Cassidy's blonde hair and blue eyes hint at her Scandinavian heritage. She loves music and likes to play her favourite songs over and over. Cassidy has autism and is learning to say a few words.
- Matija has dark curly hair and sparkling black eyes. He is just learning English, but his outgoing, sunny personality makes it easy for him to connect with people. He is fascinated with math and can readily do two-digit calculations in his head.
- Emily has red hair, green eyes, and an abundance of freckles. She is a bit chubby, and other children have commented on this. Emily is teaching herself to read and is happiest when she is ensconced with a book in the reading area.

The children are all different in their interests, abilities, and physical characteristics. How are we to understand these differences?

Assessing Development

One way to understand differences is through developmental assessment. The children are all similar ages. Their physical characteristics show us a diversity in height, weight, appearance, and motor abilities. We also see a diversity of cognitive abilities: Matija excels in math. Jack has difficulty with following complex directions. Cassidy has language delays related to her autism and has difficulty reading social cues. Emily has an affinity for reading and doesn't pay a lot of attention to other children right now. As we look at this group of children, we might wonder: What is "normal," and when is there cause for concern? Moreover, if something *isn't* normal, what can we do about it?

Developmental Milestones

You have probably seen developmental charts that show the ages at which children can be expected to perform certain skills—walking, saying a few words, or waving goodbye, to name a few. These skills are known as *developmental milestones.* Parents, educators, and health professionals use these milestones to assess whether a child is proceeding normally in their development—this is, at a similar rate and in a similar way to most other children.

Even though all aspects of development are interrelated, we tend to divide them into categories, and this is often reflected in developmental charts. Common categories include the following:

- **Physical development**: Gross or large motor development (arms, legs, and torso) and fine or small motor development (hands, fingers, wrists, feet, and toes)
- **Cognitive development**: The ability to use thought processes such as remembering, problem-solving, and decision-making
- **Language development**: The process of learning to understand and communicate with language
- **Social development**: Learning to interact effectively with others
- **Emotional development**: The ability to recognize, express, and manage feelings and have empathy for the feelings of others

Not all charts are the same. For example, social and emotional development are closely linked, and the two categories are often referred to together as socioemotional development. You will also find that some charts and assessment instruments add other categories, like creative development or cultural development.

Children may reach developmental milestones at different ages, but they all tend to follow similar sequences in their physical development.

They crawl or creep before they walk; they walk before they can hop on one foot; they reach for toys before they can do puzzles. Understanding these sequences can be very helpful to you as an educator. If your observations show that children have achieved a particular milestone, you can better predict what the next one might be and, if necessary, provide them with some support in reaching it. In the playroom we've been learning about,

? WHAT DO YOU THINK?

You will find many milestone charts online. Take some time to explore them. What categories are used? What similarities and differences do you find among the various charts? What are some benefits or challenges of using some charts over others?

we see this happening with Jack. Educators have learned to "chunk" instructions into smaller pieces so that he can follow them. This means, for example, that when they ask the other children to get ready to go outside, the educators will ask Jack to go to his cubby, then they ask him to take off his indoor shoes and put on his boots, then to put on his jacket, and so on.

Developmental norms must also have been useful for detecting Cassidy's autism, and this assessment has made it possible for her, and for the child care centre, to access a consultant who helps guide educators in their work with Cassidy. If your observations show that a child is deviating substantially from the norm, make a point of observing and documenting the child's behaviour. If, after careful observation, you believe there is cause for concern, discuss the matter with your supervisor, who can decide whether or not to bring the matter up with the family.

However, it's important to be tentative in interpreting deviations from the "norm" that the developmental charts define. The developmental charts usually used in Canada were created based on "norms" associated with mostly White, mostly middle-class children. As we've mentioned, children reach milestones at different ages –but when these milestones are reached may depend on a child's environmental circumstances, including their culture. The sequence of developmental milestones may also be influenced by culture and other environmental factors (Huang, 2018; Rogoff, 2003). Different cultures have different child-rearing methods and also different expectations about the skills that children should develop and the ages at which they should develop them. Think, for instance, of Barbara Rogoff's research with Mayan and American children (see Chapter 2, p. 21): Rogoff found that Mayan children were made part of the community early in life and expected to "pitch in" more than children in American families. As a result, Rogoff concluded that

Mayan children reached certain milestones ahead of American children: for instance, they participated independently in household activities.

Rubin and Menzer (2010) discuss social goals that families encourage in different cultures. As one example, they mention that Western cultures interpret socially wary behaviour as shyness or social incompetence while East Asian cultures see the same behaviour as a sign of social maturity and accomplishment. You can imagine that children would receive quite different messages about the same behaviours in the two cultures: behaviours that would be encouraged in one may be discouraged in another. Similarly, developmental assessments will interpret a behaviour differently depending on the culture in which the assessments were developed.

The Academy of Pediatric Physiotherapy (2018) documents differences in physical development between different populations. They note, for example, that the gross motor skills of infants in Jamaica, Kenya, Mali, Nigeria, and Uganda are particularly advanced because of culturally based handling and positioning practices and the belief that walking fosters independence and allows children to become part of society. This is just one of a number of examples the Academy provides about cultural differences in physical development. It cautions physiotherapists that families often retain their cultural beliefs and practices after they move to new countries and cultures, so practitioners should be cautious in applying Western-based assessment tools to every child and every situation. The same caution would apply to educators and others making developmental assessments.

The Nature Versus Nurture Debate

In each of our descriptions of the children in this playroom, we included hair and eye colour. This is because these are characteristics that are obviously inherited: they are "natural," or genetic. Other characteristics may be influenced more by the environment in which the children have grown, or the way the children were "nurtured"—Dakota's love of nature, for example, or Emily's enjoyment of reading. Other traits may derive from a combination of both genes and environment: both nature *and* nurture.

Studies to determine the relative influence of nature (genes) and nurture (environment) in human development are considered to have begun over a century ago with the work of Francis Galton (1822–1911). Galton used twin studies (i.e., studies that compare the development of identical twins who were raised in different families apart from one another, or the development of a set of twins compared to that of other members of the same family) and family histories to try to determine whether human traits such as intelligence or criminality were the result of nature or nurture.

Galton believed he had determined that nature was more influential than nurture. Beyond having now been shown to be incorrect, the belief that all human traits are biologically heritable, and that nature trumps nurture in every case, has proven to be dangerous. Galton's ideas laid the foundation for *eugenics*: an ideology and set of practices that encourage people with traits that are deemed "positive" to have children and discourage or inhibit childbearing among persons with traits deemed "negative" (Tabery, 2014). Eugenic and related beliefs about "natural" inferiority and superiority underlie terrible injustices such as Hitler's program of racial cleansing, discontinuation of funding for social programs for Black families in the United States in the 1970s, and forced sterilizations of mentally disabled and Indigenous individuals in Canada and elsewhere.

Brain research now provides an answer to the nature/nurture debate: both are important. Let's consider first how the brain develops, then look at how genes and experiences interact to shape the brain.

INTRODUCING...ERIK AND JOAN ERIKSON

Erik Erikson (1902–1994) is well known for his theory of psychosocial development and for coining the phrase *identity crisis*. Although in the literature these ideas are typically associated with Erik Erikson alone, he acknowledged the role of his wife, Joan (1902–1997), as an active collaborator in this work; in fact, she continued his work after his death.

Erik Erikson's childhood was confusing, and this may have been the reason for his interest in how people develop their identity. He was born in Germany and grew up as tall, blonde, blue-eyed, and Jewish. He felt that he didn't belong to either Jewish or Gentile communities. He grew up not knowing who his father was because his mother refused to tell him—a situation that probably only added to his sense of unbelonging.

Erik met his Canadian-born wife Joan when she was studying dance in Vienna. Later, as Hitler rose to power, the couple and their two children moved to the United States. It was at this point that they changed their name from Homburger to Erikson (much to their children's relief, as they were tired of being called "Hamburger").

Erikson's theory of personality maintained that each stage of life is characterized by a specific psychological struggle that needs to be resolved if the individual is to move successfully on to subsequent stages. He identified the developmental stages as progressing from trust through autonomy, initiative, industry, identity, intimacy, generativity, and integrity. Joan Erikson later added a ninth and final stage in which an individual revisits each of the earlier stages.

As part of his research, Erikson spent time studying the cultural life of the Sioux in South Dakota and the Yurok of northern California. These studies contributed to his conviction that the environment in which a child grows is critical to their self-awareness and identity.

Erikson's theories have been criticized as applying more to males than to females and as focusing more on the early stages of development than the later ones. The sequence and timing of the stages he proposed have also been questioned. Still, the Eriksons' work was ground breaking and is highly regarded as a basis for understanding the contextual nature of children's identity development.

How the Brain Develops

Human brains begin to develop before birth and continue that growth into adulthood. Neuroscientists tell us that in the early years of life, the brain makes more than a million new neural connections every second. These connections are then "pruned" to make them more efficient. This process of connection and pruning happens in a prescribed order, with sensory pathways (e.g., vision, hearing) developing first, followed by language and higher cognitive functions.

The brain is most "plastic" early in life; that is, it has the flexibility to adapt to a wide range of environments and interactions. For example, infants are initially able to recognize sounds from all languages. Within their first year, however, their brains become more specialized to the specific patterns of sounds they hear spoken, and they begin to lose the ability to recognize the sounds in languages they hear less often or not at all. The "windows" for language learning are still open, but brain circuits become increasingly "pruned" as years progress, making it more and more difficult to develop new circuits.

Genes and experiences interact to shape the brain as it develops. This is seen in the language example above: our experiences of language interact with our inherent brain architecture, specializing it to the languages we hear. Other types of experiences can affect this architecture, as well. Scientists identify what they call "serve-and-return" relationships between children and their caregivers as critical to the brain developmental process. Serve-and-return interactions occur when young children reach out to adults (serve), for instance by smiling, babbling, and gesturing, and adults respond (return) in a similar way. An adult's consistent failure to respond appropriately, or their consistent failure to respond at all, has a negative effect on the child's brain architecture (Center on the Developing Child, 2007; National Scientific Council on the Developing Child, 2004, 2005/2014).

On the flipside, supportive relationships and consistent routines help to develop biological systems, including brain circuits, that promote healthy, lifelong development. Cognitive, language, physical, and socioemotional health are all interconnected and lay the foundations for future success in school and adult life.

Building Executive Function

Below are excerpts from a learning story of ECE Nirmali's practice that Mary Lynne wrote to her, reinforcing her sensitive manner in which she carried out the diapering routine. (Learning stories are discussed further in Chapter 15.) As you read this, think about how Nirmali's interactions with each child supported their executive function skills:

> Nirmali, you played peek-a-boo with Noah on the change table; you put the cloth over his eyes and then pulled it away looking right at him. Noah laughed and had a great big smile on his face. I am sure that he really enjoyed this playful episode. Getting this kind of individual attention in group care is a gift to each child!
>
> When it was Kashif's turn for a diaper change, you stood behind him as he skillfully climbed up the table shelves using them as stairs. He is learning to do it by himself, and you gave him the opportunity to prove it while you were close by for support if needed.
>
> It was Niko's turn to have her diaper changed. She got to be a part of the process when you offered her the chance to hold the clean diaper until you were ready for it.
>
> You let her know what you were doing by respectfully saying, "I am going to clean your bum now." You continued to talk to her and you also sang to her. Niko did the actions, clapping after the song was done. Both of you seemed to enjoy this special time together!
>
> **Importance:** You connected with each child whose diaper you changed; you took time to make each child feel cared for in a very special way—it is no wonder that children in that room are drawn to you! Diaper changing can be so much more than just a routine to be performed, and it is reassuring to see you use it as an opportunity to

> build relationships with individual children. You show how much you care in every interaction.

In her feedback to Nirmali, Mary Lynne affirms Nirmali's interactions with the babies during diapering as a way to connect with them and build relationships. Brain research suggests that such responsiveness has tremendous value to the development of executive function.

Just as an air traffic control system at a busy airport ensures that all the planes at the airport are on the correct runways and proceeding safely, executive function skills—for example, making plans, setting goals, paying attention, switching gears, and managing our impulses—help our brains to control many things at once. These are skills that contribute to success at school and throughout our lives.

While some part of executive function is genetic, experience and practice have the greatest influence on the development of these skills. Responsive parents or caregivers who provide focussed attention during the early months and years of a child's life help build that child's executive function skills. Routines, role-playing, and games that encourage imagination, following rules, and controlling impulses support children in building these skills (Center on the Developing Child, 2021). If children don't get the attention and support that they need from their relationships with adults and from their environment, executive function may be delayed or even fail to develop.

Developmental Risk Factors

Biological and environmental factors both affect the development of the brain. Some specific factors inhibit or risk inhibiting healthy brain development. In the lists below (Kaiser, 2020), you'll notice that trauma, though it is an environmental risk factor, has a separate category; this is because of the profound influence it has on children's behaviour and learning.

Biological Risk Factors

- Temperament
- Genes
- Complications of pregnancy and birth
- Substance abuse during pregnancy
- Neurological delays
- Emotional and behavioural disorders
- Gender
- Serious medical conditions

Environmental Risk Factors

- Family factors and parenting style
  › Abuse, neglect, domestic violence parents
  › Loss of a loved one
  › Harsh parenting style
  › Parents suffering from mental illness, addictions
- Poverty and the social conditions surrounding it
  › Poor nutrition, housing, and/or medical care

Trauma

- Displacement or refugee trauma
  › Not being part of the mainstream culture or language
- School or community violence
  › Being bullied or rejected
- Natural tragedies
  › Natural disasters, pandemics
- Intergenerational trauma
  › Impact of residential schools

The Effects of Stress and Trauma

We are writing this book in the midst of the COVID-19 pandemic. Schools and child care centres have been closed and are now gradually reopening. Many children have been deprived of social interaction with their peers and, even now, are being taught not to get too close to their playmates and to be careful about what they touch. Home environments may be tense as parents struggle to balance child care and work, and worry about finances and future employment. No one really knows what effect this disruption will have on children's brains and functioning.

What we do know, however, is that when children experience extreme and long-lasting stress, particularly when they have no buffering relationships, it can weaken their brain architecture in ways that prevent social, emotional, and cognitive capacities from developing to their full genetic potential. Stressful situations cause the adrenal gland to release the hormone cortisol. Where stress is extreme or long term, the excess cortisol can affect the hippocampus, a part of the brain that is responsible for converting short-term memories into long-term memories (Center on the Developing Child, 2007, 2011; Kaiser, 2020; Pickens &

Tschlopp, 2017). We call the psychological effects of severe and/or long-term stress *trauma*.

Trauma may be a response to a recent or past event. It can also be intergenerational—that is, its effects can be passed on through generations. Children whose parents or guardians have experienced trauma may adopt those parents' or guardians' ways of coping. Healing from trauma and adapting to trauma can take many forms, which can be more healthy or more problematic, depending upon individual circumstances and resilience.

The nature and severity of damage that stressors cause depends on the length, intensity, and timing of current and past stressful experiences and whether the child has safe, stable relationships with persons who can offer support. Obviously, the child is at greater risk of experiencing detrimental effects of trauma when they live with repeated abuse, neglect, poverty, and parental depression (Center on the Developing Child, 2007; National Scientific Council on the Developing Child, 2020).

SAROYA'S STORY

Saroya was 3 ½ years old when she and her father moved to Canada to join Saroya's mother, who has been studying here for her PhD. For two years, Saroya's grandparents had been caring for her in her home country while her father worked and her mother studied abroad. Now, the family was reunited at last, but both of Saroya's parents had to work. Just hours after her three-day journey to Canada, Saroya's mother brought her to our child care centre. Confused and jet-lagged in this environment that was so unlike home, Saroya cried heart-wrenching sobs and shudders for days.

The educators were kind and did everything they could think of to help, but the crying wouldn't stop. One of the educators, Sara, asked Saroya's parents to teach her a few words of Saroya's home language. The educators tried to help Saroya engage with other children. As the crying continued, the educators, and everyone else within ear-range, began to feel desperate.

Slowly, though, Saroya quieted. She attached herself to Sara and only cried when she was separated from her. Her family adjusted their schedule to correspond with Sara's shifts. Saroya followed Sara everywhere—to the kitchen to pick up food trays, to the storage room for supplies—and even, to Sara's dismay, to the bathroom.

Encouraged by Sara's patience and empathy, the children in the playroom began recruiting Saroya to be the baby in their house play. They would lay her on the "bed" and cover her with a blanket. As Saroya began to take a more active role in the play, she picked up more and more words of English. Sara slowly distanced herself and was finally able to leave the playroom without her little tagalong. After about four months, Saroya was actively involved with the other children and learning more English words every day. By the time she left the centre at age 5 ½, she was a leader in the room.

Building Resilience

Saroya's story recounts the experience of a child who came through Carole's child care centre and had to adjust to a new and stressful situation. Reflecting on this story, Carole outlines some of the many stresses Saroya would have had to manage when she arrived at the centre:

> What must it have been like for her to be taken away from her caring grandparents and brought to see a mother that she remembered only slightly? What must it have been like to come to a place where she couldn't make herself understood except by crying, where the faces, the food, the routines, and expectations were unfamiliar? Where, since she arrived in November, even the weather was very unfamiliar and probably a bit scary?

More than a story of struggle and stress, though, Saroya's story is one of a young child learning to become resilient with the encouragement of her responsive parents and a group of supportive ECEs. Sara, in particular, made an extra effort to make Saroya feel welcome by learning a few words in her language and responding to her need to form a secure attachment.

Resilience refers to our ability to adapt positively and quickly in the face of adversity. When we are confronted with a stressful situation, our bodies and brains react with an adrenaline rush and an increase in stress hormone levels and heart rate. When these systems are activated in young children, a supportive adult can help buffer these effects, allowing the child to manage their stress and return to normal. This helps children develop healthy and capable stress response systems. In other words, it helps them become resilient—able to bounce back from difficult situations.

THE RESILIENCE GAME

Harvard University has developed an online resilience game that you will find very useful (and kind of fun!) in understanding negative and positive factors that can affect individual children. The game also looks at how policy initiatives can support children's wellbeing.

 To play the game, visit https://developingchild.harvard.edu/resilience-game/.

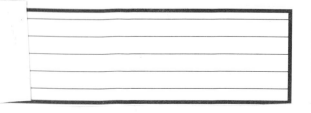

Neglect and Abuse

As an ECE, you have close contact with children and families. If things aren't going well for families, you might be one of the first people to detect a problem. It's important that you know the signs of neglect and abuse and that you know how to respond appropriately should you suspect either.

The Government of Alberta (2021) provides useful definitions of neglect and emotional, physical, and sexual abuse, along with the warning signs to watch for. See a summary of this information in Appendix C.

Responding to Neglect or Abuse

You probably will encounter situations of neglect or abuse sooner or later in your career, so it's very important that you be prepared to deal with them appropriately. Take responsibility for finding out who to contact should you suspect neglect or abuse. In most provinces, this will be the Child Protective Services (CPS) department of the provincial government. In some provinces, it will be the Children's Aid Society. In smaller, isolated communities, police might be the first responders to cases of serious abuse. Some Indigenous communities may have their own child protection agency.

Every province and territory will have legislation mandating the reporting of neglect or abuse. If you believe that you are seeing signs of abuse or neglect, or if a child tells you they are being abused or neglected, you have an obligation to follow up. Carefully document any relevant signs or discussions and take these to your supervisor. If you feel strongly that your supervisor isn't taking appropriate action, you may need to make a report yourself.

If a child discloses abuse or neglect to you, listen calmly. Tell the child they have done the right thing in telling you and that they have done nothing wrong. Acknowledge what the child might be feeling (i.e., "That must have been confusing for you" or "It sounds like you were pretty scared when that happened"). Let the child know that you will have to tell your supervisor what they have told you. Carefully document what the child has said and share it with your supervisor immediately.

To protect the child and the integrity of the investigation, do not talk to the child's parents or guardians about the allegations. Don't probe for details or ask the child to repeat their story to your supervisor or anyone else. Having to repeat the story can be hard for the child and can make the process more difficult later.

Cultural Considerations Regarding Child Abuse

Cultures vary in their beliefs about what practices with children are considered to be abusive. For example, a survey by the International Society for the Prevention of Child Abuse and Neglect (Gray & ISPCAN, 2012) found that only 53% of respondents worldwide considered physical punishment to be abusive. In our discussions with our multicultural health broker (MCHB) advisory group, we heard that physical punishment is used in many cultures and that newcomer parents are sometimes at a loss for alternative methods for discipling their children.

Some traditional practices such as cupping (an alternative therapy that involves creating suction on the skin with heated cups) may appear abusive to people who are unfamiliar with the practice (Ward et al., 2018). Differences in child-rearing customs can be confusing to newcomer families who find that their usual ways of disciplining their children are no longer considered acceptable in their new country.

It's important that we, as ECEs, work to understand the child-rearing practices and beliefs of all of our families. (Often this information is gathered as part of the intake process.) An intercultural dialogue allows for sharing parenting practices: you can learn about guidance strategies that are used in the home and describe the approach followed in your program. This is also an opportunity to sensitively and respectfully share the norms and expectations of the larger Canadian society with respect to child guidance.

As we have discussed, you are required by law to report to child welfare authorities if you suspect physical or sexual abuse, neglect, or emotional abuse. You may hesitate to make this call for fear that the children will be taken from their families. This outcome is, however, generally a last resort (Ward et al., 2018), and it is nonetheless your legal responsibility to make the report.

||||||||||||||||||||||||||||||||||||||||||||||||||||||||||||||||||||||||||||||||||||||||||||||||||||||||||||||||||||||||||||||||||||||

TAKEAWAYS

Assessments of developmental milestones can tell us when a child is lagging in areas of development. These assessments are usually based on European or Euro-American standards. Because cultures vary in the priority they give to areas of development and in their child-rearing practices, such assessments must be used sensitively and carefully.

Both nature and nurture contribute to the persons we become. Interactions with parents or caregivers are key to the development of healthy brains. Positive, nurturing interactions build strong brain circuits, while threatening ones weaken circuits. These foundations are laid in the early years of life.

While brains can be changed and strengthened later in life, making these changes becomes progressively more difficult.

Chronic stress and trauma can affect brain development and body systems in ways that have lifelong negative consequences for mental and physical health. However, relationships with caring adults can help to mitigate the effects of stress and trauma.

Abuse and neglect are forms of trauma that can have long-lasting effects. ECEs have an obligation to document and report suspected or disclosed abuse and neglect. It is important to have an intercultural lens towards these issues, too. Although you are required to report child abuse according to the standards of your own jurisdiction, it is important to know that parenting practices differ from culture to culture. Intercultural dialogue can facilitate sharing information about parenting practices and communicating the norms and expectations of Canadian society.

REFLECTION AND DISCUSSION

- Which aspects of the person you've become can you attribute to the genes you inherited? which to the environment in which you were raised? which to a combination of the two? (If you have a sibling, thinking about the differences and similarities between you will help you to answer this question.)

- What impact have your experiences as a child had on your development?

- How will your understanding of brain development impact your interactions with children?

- How have you, as an adult, responded to the coronavirus pandemic or another national or international crisis? How did it affect the wellbeing of children that you know?

6

Supporting Social and Emotional Wellbeing

Every day, in a hundred small ways, our children
ask, "Do you hear me? Do you see me? Do I matter?"
Their behavior often reflects our response.

—*L.R. KNOST*

IIIIIIIIIIIIIIIIIIIIIIIIIIIIIIIIIIIIIIIIIIIIIIIIIIIIIIIIIIIIIIIIIIIIIIIIIIIIIIIIIIIIIIIIIIIIIIIIIIIIIIIIIIIIIIIIIIIIIIIIIIIIIIIIIIIIIIIIIIIIIIII

LEARNING OUTCOMES

When you have read this chapter, you will be able to answer these questions:

- Why is work in ECEC often called a "practice of relationships"?
- What are some characteristics of an environment
  that helps to foster warm relationships?
- Why are listening skills important?
- What are some cultural factors we should consider
  when interacting with children and families?
- What are some ways that we can support children's
  social and emotional wellbeing?

Introduction

Healthy, positive relationships are essential to our wellbeing. We all need to feel supported, connected, and valued. We want to have people to turn to when times are tough. Research tells us that people who have satisfying relationships and a network of social supports are healthier, happier, and live longer ("Health benefits of strong relationships," 2019). As well, we know from brain research that the relationships children have in their early years are critical to their healthy development and to their future success in school and adult life.

This chapter suggests ways to build warm, secure relationships with children, but also with families and co-workers. It will list characteristics of an environment intended to foster such relationships. Attentiveness and careful listening seem to be important skills for fostering feelings of security, trust, and affirmation. However, families differ in their expectations of children and in the ways that they interact, so it's important that educators be sensitive to possible differences.

An Environment for Relationships

It's sometimes said that ECEC is a practice of relationships. Our relationships with children, with families, with colleagues, and even with our profession is at the heart of everything we do. We work to create an environment where children have a sense of belonging and where they feel safe, valued, and competent. We can have the same goals for families and colleagues.

An environment of warm, safe relationships allows children to take the risks they need to take in order to learn and to express themselves. Such an environment lets children know that even when they push the boundaries, they will be met with calm, caring responses from educators. It lets families and educators know that they are valued members of a team that is working to provide the best possible experiences for children.

The interactions we have with children and families in this environment are critical, but the physical space and equipment, and the experiences we facilitate, also contribute to a positive social and emotional environment. Here are some of the things you might see in such a setting:

Interactions with Children

- Educators warmly welcome children and their families.
- Educators listen attentively to children and comfort them when they are in distress.
- Educators inspire trust by keeping their promises to children.
- Educators show they value children's activities by paying attention and providing descriptive feedback.
- Educators help children learn to understand and manage their emotions and to "read" the emotions of others.
- Educators help children develop empathy through modelling and storybooks.

- Educators help children develop positive social skills, such as how to initiate play or deal appropriately with conflict situations.
- Children are helped to understand the impact of their behaviours on others.

Interactions with Families

- Educators make time to get to know all families.
- Families are welcome in the room.
- Educators and families share information about children's activities and needs.
- Families are encouraged to share their cultural practices, and these are treated with respect.
- Families are actively engaged, whenever possible, in sharing culturally affirming activities and resources for play.
- Educators actively and creatively mediate between the families' cultural ways of raising children and mainstream early childhood practices.
- Departure times are pleasant for children and families. This is a time when educators and children can share information about the day.

Staffing and Staff Considerations

- Staffing and staff schedules support long-term, secure relationships between educators and children.
- Educators are chosen in part to reflect the cultural identities of the children in the program.
- Educators model a respectful, cooperative tone in their interactions with one another.
- Educators use self-reflection to uncover biases and assumptions that might influence their interactions with children and families.

Physical Environment

- There are places where children can be alone as well as places where they can be together.
- There are cozy places, such as a reading area with a rug, sofa, and/or rocking chair.
- There is a place in the playroom that invites family members to sit and watch.
- The cultures of the children are reflected in the room (this includes broad dimensions of culture, including ethnicity, class, gender, abilities, religions, and other characteristics).
- There are enough materials and equipment to minimize conflict among children.

Programming

- Educators observe children carefully and provide experiences that build upon their interests and strengths.
- Materials and experiences are organized in ways that allow all children to participate.
- Routines and activities help children feel challenged and successful.
- Routines and transitions are calm and orderly.
- Children have choices and opportunities to feel ownership over the room and its activities.
- Expectations for behaviour are clear and consistent, and are stated positively (e.g., "Touch the baby's head gently" or "Please hang your coat in your cubbie").
- Educators involve children in developing and discussing the guidelines so children understand why the rules are important.

Children flourish when they grow within a web of warm, responsive relationships. This list shows many of the characteristics of such an environment. Your sensitivity and caring will contribute a great deal to this environment, but there are also skills that will increase your effectiveness. The first and perhaps most important of these is listening.

Listening with Full Attention

We all believe that we are good listeners. Whether or not this is true, there is one thing we can say for sure: it is difficult to be a good listener all of the time. Most of us are familiar with the experience of only half listening to someone who is speaking to us. Often, we do this because we are distracted by other thoughts: What are we going to make for dinner this evening? Who will pick up the dog from the vet? Other times, we distract ourselves by thinking about what we want to add to the conversation, as soon as we have a chance. Truly listening requires that we focus our full attention on the other person and what they are saying. The ways people show attention vary from culture to culture but might include making eye contact, leaning toward the other person, mirroring their emotions, nodding, or using sounds or words like "Mm-hmm," "Yes," or "Aha" to encourage the other person to continue.

For children, the opportunity to express ideas can be a springboard to problem-solving or to new creative ventures. Listening to children with your full attention tells them that their ideas and feelings have value and builds their confidence in their abilities. It also supports a relationship of trust and caring between you and the child.

Listening to Nicholas

Years ago when I was visiting a student on practicum, the children were playing in the gym as I sat on the stage gathering observations of my student's practice. I noticed a little boy who seemed quite upset. I watched him speak with an educator and then turn away with tears in his eyes. I smiled at him, and he came over to sit beside me on the stage. We began a conversation:

Me: *You look pretty upset...*

Child: *He called me poop.*

Me: *Oh no, it's not much fun when you get called names, is it?*

Child: *No.*

Me: *Ah, I bet it hurt your feelings, eh?*

Child: *Ya. My mom calls me Nicholas.*

Me: *I guess you wish he'd call you Nicholas, too?*

Child: *Ya. In the classroom he calls me Nicholas, but in the gym he calls me poop.*

Me: *Hmmm, I wonder what to do about that...*

Child: *I'm gonna just sit here for a while.*

Me: *Okay, Nicholas.*

Later, I spoke to the educator, asking what was happening for this child. She told me, "He's just a sensitive child. I told him to just ignore the other boy." Hers was a somewhat typical educator response to a child's strong feelings; it is one I have heard frequently from adults—parents, teachers, and educators alike. I wonder to this day why it seems so hard for adults to acknowledge children's feelings. All Nicholas needed was an adult who perhaps understood what he was going through.

> ### ⍨ WHAT DO YOU THINK?
>
> The next time a friend or family member is speaking to you, notice if you are really listening. Try practising attentive listening behaviour. Do you notice a difference in the way the speaker responds to you when you are fully attentive? Do you notice a difference in how the speaker feels? What does this tell you about the importance and power of listening?

> ### ⍨ WHAT DO YOU THINK?
>
> What do you think it meant to Nicholas, the child in the story, to be actively listened to? Can you remember a time when you were in distress or had a problem and someone really listened? How did it feel?

Active Listening

"I wonder," Mary Lynne ponders in the story above, "why it's so hard for adults to acknowledge children's feelings." Reflecting on this question, we thought maybe it's because we adults are too busy or too distracted to make space for this kind of acknowledgment. Perhaps we are even afraid of the feelings we might feel ourselves, were we to acknowledge what the child is feeling. Whatever the reason, it seems like we often try to put an end to the distressing feelings with pat responses like "Just ignore him," "We are all friends in day care," "Put your tears away," or "You're not bleeding; you'll be okay." What we can see in Mary Lynne's story, though, is that acknowledging a child's feelings, as Mary Lynne did on the stage, helps the child to feel supported and understood. In this scenario, this paved the way for Nicholas to work through the problem on his own.

Notice the particular ways that Mary Lynne responded to Nicholas: She smiled at him to invite him into a conversation. When he responded, she acknowledged his feelings: "You look pretty upset…" She said this in a tentative way because she didn't want to make assumptions about his feelings. When he told her the problem he was facing, she acknowledged his feelings again: "It's not much fun when you get called names, is it?" "I bet it hurt your feelings, eh?" "I guess you wish he'd call you Nicholas, too?" Notice the questioning tone in these statements: Mary Lynne is still checking to see if her assumptions are correct, and making space for Nicholas to correct her if they are not.

Finally, Mary Lynne invites Nicholas to problem-solve by asking, "I wonder what to do about that?" It's important to notice that she didn't move directly to problem-solving. She knew that in situations where emotions are running high, people are often not ready to find solutions. They first need to know that their feelings are understood.

The extra moments that Mary Lynne took to listen to Nicholas let him know that he was not alone and that an adult cared about what was happening to him. With this validation, he was able to take charge of his situation and decide what to do: "I'm gonna just sit here for a while." The way that Mary Lynne spoke with Nicholas, acknowledging his feelings, is called *active listening*.

Active listening is an important skill for ECEs. It is a technique that grows from genuine concern. The premise is that the speaker is the expert on their own experience. The listener contributes to what the speaker is saying by checking to see whether their interpretation of the speaker's message is correct. When they do speak, therefore, the listener uses a tentative, questioning style.

Active listening is just one way for us to engage more effectively with another person by paying special attention to the conversation and focusing on genuine understanding of the other person rather than just on responding to them.

Years ago, Thomas Gordon (1970) introduced us to something called the *language of acceptance*, which involves responding compassionately to children who have strong feelings. The language of acceptance includes active listening as well as three other skills:

1. **Listen with full attention**: This sends a powerful nonverbal message of responsiveness and might encourage a child to share what is happening for them. Consider the body language and facial expression that might accompany listening with full attention.

2. **Door openers**: Door openers are invitations for the other person to speak. They may encourage a reluctant child to talk to you about what is happening, especially when used with a tone of acceptance and encouragement. "Can you tell me more about..." or "Do you want to talk about that?" are examples of door openers.

3. **Acknowledgment responses**: When a child is speaking, we can signal our interest and understanding by using acknowledgement responses such as "Uh huh," "Hmmm," and "I see." These minimal responses signal our attentiveness to what is being said.

Figure 6.1. Heather listens with full attention to Ethan

Intentional Interactions and Decisions in Practice

In ECEC, educators have to make decisions about how to guide inter-actions and mediate conflicts. Just like in active listening, slowing down and trying to really understand the situation can help us to make good decisions about how we respond to children. When we are intentional in the ways we engage with children, we make a conscious decision to respond to the child thoughtfully and skillfully rather than just "reacting."

Chelsea, an ECE, told us about her experience helping a child—Terran—navigate a choice about his toy spider. As you read, think about how Chelsea decided to manage this situation, and why.

> Children were getting ready to go outside and 4-year-old Terran clenched a small plastic spider in his hand, wanting to take it with him into the playground. Educator Chelsea approached him and explained her worries about taking it outside: it might get lost and if it got dropped, a younger child might find it and put it in their mouth, caus-ing them to choke. Today, none of this mattered to Terran, and he held onto the spider more tightly, insisting that he have it with him. Chelsea acknowledged just how much Terran wanted to have the spi-der and then asked for Terran's ideas on how he might keep the spider safe while he is outside. Terran decided that he would get his "Work in Progress" emblem (a laminated photo of him holding a sign saying "Work in Progress"), place the spider on top of the photo, and stow it in his cubbie until he came back inside.

When Chelsea responded by acknowledging Terran's feelings and tell-ing him that she understood how much he wanted the spider, Terran became open to engaging in the problem-solving process with her and came up with his own solution.

Chelsea might have just told Terran that he couldn't bring the spider with him and taken it away. Instead, she made an intentional decision about how she was going to respond. When asked to share the thinking that led her to making the decision to respond to Terran in the way she did, Chelsea said:

> I remembered how I felt as a child when something I was attached to was just taken away. I wanted to empower him so he knew that he was in control. I knew it was important for him to make the decision, and I wanted him to feel that way. I knew he was capable if I just gave him the chance.

The decision that Chelsea made was based on her beliefs about children and the importance of engaging them in problem-solving. She made an intentional decision to respond to him thoughtfully and professionally—and with compassion.

Communicating across Cultures

Earlier in this chapter, we mentioned that listening behaviours can vary across cultures. For example, in some cultures, including a number of Indigenous cultures, avoiding eye contact is a sign of respect. However, in mainstream Canadian culture, avoiding eye contact has often been interpreted as a sign of guilt, inattention, or indifference. There is a growing awareness about such cultural differences in nonverbal communication, but miscommunications do happen. As you can imagine, such misinterpretations could have very negative consequences.

Families and cultures vary widely in the ways they communicate and interact. Areas that might lead to misunderstanding include norms about physical touch and personal distancing, the kinds of problems that can be discussed outside the family, showing respect to elders and those in authority, the amount of time spent getting acquainted as opposed to getting to the point in a conversation, and so on.

Knowing about possible variations in interaction styles can help us in our relationships with families. Because children learn these styles from their families, this knowledge can also assist us in knowing how children might be interpreting our interactions. As an example, one cultural broker in our advisory group commented, "Ours is a trusting and warm culture, with lots of hugs and kisses...Western culture is very cold." If children are used to lots of hugs and kisses, will they think they aren't appreciated when they are in an environment where this doesn't happen? This example shows us why it is important for us to become aware of family and cultural norms.

Child Guidance, Behaviour, and Culture

Expectations for behaviour are culturally constructed and come out of the experiences and expectations held in each family. Without conversations with families about their values and beliefs related to behaviour and guidance, we may default to assuming that we all hold the same things as important. For example, while you may take for granted that children of any gender be treated the same, some families may have different role and behaviour expectations for their male children than they do for their female children. As well, some families may not acknowledge genders other than male or female. Understanding what is valued in each child's family plays an important role in being culturally responsive. Conversations about goals for children might begin as soon as families register their child at your centre. You can explain guidance and behaviour practices at the centre during these conversations.

Consider the example below of a group of educators learning about the hopes parents at one child care centre had for their children's behaviour. While you read, think about the hopes that surprised the educators involved, and those that didn't.

> In order to gain some insight into families' goals and aspirations for their children, our centre hosted a parent event focusing on this topic. Gathered with parents around a big table drinking coffee and eating dessert while the children were cared for in one of the playrooms, educators posed the simple question, "What do you want for your child?"
>
> In this intimate setting of just a dozen parents, the educators heard a variety of responses:
>
> - I want my child to have friendships.
> - I want my child to know about other cultures and be accepting.
> - I want my child to be ready for school.
> - I want my child to be kind.
>
> These responses confirmed what the educators suspected; however, there were also some surprises. One father wanted his child to have the kind of relationship with him that he did not have with his own father as a result of the trauma experienced from residential school. When one mother told the educators, "I want my child to obey," there were some head nods from other parents who added that they wanted their children to be respectful and to listen to adults.

WHAT DO YOU THINK?

What do the educators' feelings of surprise tell us about the educators' own perspectives and expectations?

As educators, it is important to recognize that, just like the parents in the story above, we have varying goals and expectations about children's behaviour and how to respond to it. Even though we may all have the same ECEC postsecondary training, we have had different experiences growing up, and these can affect the ways we respond to children's behaviours. Until we stop to reflect, we may not even be aware of how our personal experiences, emotional triggers, expectations, and biases impact our work. Take, for example, Ani's experience:

> Ani and her teammates are upset because a 5-year-old boy, Albert, refuses to listen to them. In observing his interactions with his parents, they notice that his father is dominant, and his mother always defers to him. They wonder if Albert has learned that he doesn't have to listen to women. Upon reflection, Ani admits that it's hard not to feel resentful when Albert treats her dismissively.

Ani discovered that she resented Albert's behaviour; this resentment was affecting the way she interacted with him. By becoming aware of her reaction to Albert, Ani can better understand and respond professionally in her interactions with Albert. By becoming aware of her own triggers and the way in which they impact her work as an educator, Ani has taken a vital first step in becoming an educator who learns to respond intentionally and skillfully to situations that occur in a typical child care day.

Working with Conflicting Expectations

When we asked about strategies for dealing with the conflicting expectations of parents and child care centres, the MCHB advisory group recommended the following: "The parent knows most about the child and can give the most guidance about how to deal with their child."

We've seen that different families have various hopes and wishes for

> **WHO AM I?**
>
> Being aware of our own biases helps to keep them from entering into our interactions with children. Our biases develop over time, and through our personal experiences and the expectations others have had for us.
>
> Consider your own experiences:
>
> - What behaviours were expected of you by your family when you were growing up? in school? by the community?
> - What values are important to you now?
> - How are these expectations and values reflected in your own expectations for children's behaviour?

their children and different ways of interacting with them. We've seen, too, that this might be puzzling for children who find themselves in child care centres that operate under different cultural norms. One of our MCHB advisory group members, an immigrant from an African country, related that when her parents came to visit, their behavioural expectations were so different from those her Canadian-born daughter was used to that her daughter asked, "Why are you confusing me?" Children are resilient, but it certainly must be difficult for them when they are asked to navigate several sets of expectations at once.

Consider the following example:

> Adam is playing enthusiastically at the water table and splashing water on the floor. Educator Sheila approaches and says, "I see that there's lots of water on the floor and I'm worried that someone might slip on it and hurt themselves." Adam ignores her. Zaira, another educator, explains that Adam's family's culture doesn't use a lot of words to express their expectations. They would probably say, "Adam, stop splashing."

How might you convey your concerns to Adam, while also considering the guidance approach he is used to hearing at home? As professionals, we need to find the best ways to integrate the hopes, norms, behaviours, and wishes of the children and families at our centres with our own early childhood practices. Again, respectful intercultural conversations can help us untangle conflicts, understand differences, find mutually acceptable ways to deal with challenging behaviours, strengthen our relationships with families, and help children through the confusing landscape of conflicting expectations.

MAKING TIME STAND STILL

"She made time stop with every interaction," said my daughter, a mother of young children and an early childhood educator in New Zealand.

My daughter and I often talk about the nature of the interactions that adults have with children. We become dismayed and discouraged when we hear educators using their "teacher voice" and ordering children about, telling them to "put away their tears" and "sort themselves out." But this time, our conversation was different. My daughter was describing a beautiful interaction of presence and attention.

She said, "Observing in an infant playroom in Aotearoa, New Zealand, I was struck by one particular teacher's interactions with a 5-month-old child as she changed his nappy (diaper). She looked into his eyes, spoke to him about what she was doing, and waited for his responses—every time—before she proceeded. This meant pausing halfway through the diaper change when she noticed that he needed time to kick his legs and pausing again when they poked their tongues out at each other, blew raspberries, and laughed together. There was no rush. She set the pace by listening with full attention to his nonverbal cues. Her whole body conveyed her calm, unhurried presence; that made it feel like time was standing still." I imagined what child care would be like if all ECEs made time stand still.

Every Child Is Different

As members of the MCHB advisory group reminded us, "Every child is different. Every child has a development plan." This is an understanding that we, as ECEs, share. Because each child is different, there are no formulas for supporting the development of a particular child, or dealing with their challenging behaviours. What, then, can guide us in supporting children's social and emotional wellbeing?

In this chapter, we've learned a number of skills that help us listen, adapt, and respond to the needs of individual children. First of all, we can *be present* for children and practice active listening. We know we need to slow down and focus fully on children when we interact with them so we can be thoughtful and intentional in our interactions.

Closely tied to being present is *connecting* with children to build their trust and feelings of security. Everything we say and do sends a message about who they are and how important they are. Mary Lynne's daughter described a powerful example of this in the story above. Nicholas's story is another example. As we saw with Nicholas, we connect with children when we acknowledge what they feel and want. We can also use descriptive feedback ("You made a very careful outline around the lion") rather than praise ("You're such a good artist") to show children that we are really paying attention and value their efforts.

We can *help children to learn* socially acceptable behaviours through our own modelling and by providing guidance and support. We can anticipate and prevent negative behaviours as much as possible. When an undesirable behaviour occurs, we can let the child know why we are concerned. For example, "I'm worried that something will get broken when you throw the ball indoors."

We can *include children in problem-solving*. Questions like, "Can you think of a way to...?" "I wonder what we can do?" "How could we make it better?" and "What would work for both of you?" support children's learning and their senses of competence. We can allow children to maintain some control over their decisions by offering choices. For example, ask, "What works best for you: putting away the blocks or the animals?"

We have seen that we need to build close *relationships with families*. We need to value the intimate knowledge families have of their child and respect their suggestions. If these suggestions conflict with professional standards, we must work with the family to find solutions that are acceptable to all.

Finally, we must be *self-reflective*, identifying any biases we might have that could enter into the situation and evaluating our responses. For any situation, we can ask ourselves about the way we respond:

- Does the way I respond give the child positive messages about themselves?
- Does it build the relationship between us?
- Does it model how I want a child to behave?
- Does it help the child develop inner control and give them new information for next time?
- Did it result in a favourable outcome for both of us?

TAKEAWAYS

Warm, secure relationships are critical to children's healthy development. The physical environment and the interactions we have in it can build a network of relationships that allows children to feel that they belong and that they are valued and competent. Being attentive to children and paying close attention to their words and feelings is a critical skill for ECEs.

Families differ in their expectations of children and in the ways that they interact, so it's important for educators to be sensitive to possible differences and find ways to work with families to ensure that children have the best possible experience.

Every child is different, so there is no formula for dealing with difficult situations. However, there are approaches that will help us: being present and connecting with children; extending their learning by modelling, explaining, offering choices, and encouraging problem-solving; involving families; and being self-reflective.

||||||||||||||||||||||||||||||||||||||||||||||||||||||||||||||||||||||||||||||||||||||||||||||||||||||||||||||||||||||||

REFLECTION AND DISCUSSION

- One way to give children more control over their lives is to offer them choices. However, sometimes what is offered as a choice is really a threat. In the statements below, which would you say are choices and which are threats?

  › You can behave or go sit on the chair.

  › Do you want to wipe up the water on your own or would you like my help?

  › Do you want me to put your name on your picture or is that something you want to do?

  › It's your choice: play nicely here or don't play at all.

- Giving descriptive feedback tells children that you are really paying attention to them and value their efforts. Which of the following statements are examples of descriptive feedback?

  › You gave some markers to Amy and now she can draw too!

  › You put the lids on all the markers. Now they won't dry up.

  › Nice sharing!

  › Thank you for helping Joshua open his granola bar.

  › Good job!

PART III

Creating Engaging Environments

7

Routines, Rituals, and Transitions

We need rituals because they help guide us,
keep us feeling grounded and balanced, and
give our lives a rhythm we can dance to.
—*DR. DEEPIKA CHOPRA*

LEARNING OUTCOMES

When you have read this chapter, you will be able to answer these questions:
- What are rituals and why are they important
  in early childhood settings?
- How can rituals contribute to routines and transitions?
- What are some ways to make routines and transitions
  effective, pleasurable, and special?

Introduction

Routines and transitions make up a large part of the day in early childhood programs. Because of this, we need to think about how we make them not only effective, but also fun and even special.

Routines are the things that have to be done during each day, like eating, napping, cleanup and washing up. Transitions occur when we move from one activity to another.

Rituals are special actions that help us navigate stressful events as well as enhance aspects of our daily routines and transitions. Rituals can deepen connections and relationships. Rituals are magical and children look forward to them with anticipation. They contribute to a warm and safe environment where children experience a sense of belonging and wellbeing.

Routines

> It's Tomas's first day in the program and he's finding it very difficult. As he sobs for his father, ECE Susie kneels to make eye contact, puts her hand gently on his shoulder, and acknowledges how he might be feeling: "You miss your Papi, don't you?" Susie pauses, making space for Tomas to respond if he wants to. Then she adds: "First we'll have snack, then we'll play outside, and then your Papi will come."

Knowing the order in which the day will proceed can help relieve children's stress and anxiety. It helps children to have a sense of control over their lives and can allow them to wait more patiently for expected events—like Dad coming to pick them up.

The schedule of a day in child care is composed of many routines: arrival, snack, cleanup, lunch, nap time, and so on. Posting a schedule can help children anticipate what will come next. For instance, children could help you organize photos or drawings representing the various parts of the day and attach them to a string with clothespins (Figure 7.1). That way, you can rearrange them if there is a change in plans on a particular day.

Here are some things to think about when you are planning for routines in your playroom:

- **Consider the children's ages.** For example, some older children may not need a nap, so you will need to plan how you will accommodate them while other children sleep. Infants have their own biological schedules. They will need individualized schedules; trying to get them all to eat and sleep at the same time will be frustrating for you and them. Once children are toddlers, they will benefit from consistent times for eating.
- **Balance quiet times with active times.** Often, children find it difficult to slow down and rest even though they need to. Having a consistent rest time (along with sleep rituals such as a story, music, back rubbing, or a book to read on their cot) will help them relax and recharge.
- **Keep the routines consistent.** Doing things in the same order each day helps children know what to expect. If it's necessary to deviate from the schedule, it's best to warn the children in advance.
- **Consider how to adapt to children's individual needs.** For example, a child who has difficulty settling down to nap may need

Figure 7.1. One way to represent the daily schedule

to be with an educator in another area of the room or outside of the room.

When they are approached thoughtfully, routines offer wonderful opportunities for growth and learning. In this toddler room, the educators are willing to take the time to allow children to participate in a meaningful way in the lunchtime preparations and cleanup:

> Visitors to the toddler room are surprised to see these young children busy setting up for lunch. They wipe the tables, arrange the plates and glasses on them, and dish their food from the communal serving bowls. After lunch, each child scrapes any remaining food from their

plate into the compost bin and puts their dishes and utensils on a cart to be taken to the kitchen. The educators, who work alongside the children, understand that this is an important time for the children to learn many valuable skills and to develop feelings of competence and independence.

Routines can be considered as things that just need to be done, or they can be approached as opportunities for learning. In this toddler room, the children are encouraged to take ownership over the proceedings and are proud of their ability to contribute. They are learning cooperation, caring for others, problem-solving, and numeracy skills (i.e., one-to-one correspondence as they set one plate and one glass on the table at each placemat). The educators involve the children in caring for the compost bin, so they are learning about nature: they explain that "worms eat the food we have left and they make dirt."

WHAT DO YOU THINK?

Attitudes towards time vary among cultures. Some cultures tend to be more time-conscious, while others have a more fluid or relaxed approach to time. There has been a suggestion that removing clocks from the playroom might lead ECEs to focus on making decisions that respond to children's behaviours rather than to the hands on a clock (Wein & Kirby-Smith, 1998). What do you think about this approach? What might be some benefits of this approach, and what might be some challenges?

Transitions

Transitions mark the end of one experience and the beginning of another. This might involve moving from home to the child care centre, or it might mean moving from one activity to another in the course of the day. In this section, we'll focus on transitions during the day.

Transitions can be difficult. In this example, Andreas does not want to move on from his current activity:

> During playtime outside, 3-year-old Andreas is making ditches in the sand box and pouring water into them. When the educator announces that it's time to clean up and go outside, he yells: "No, I won't! I won't go inside." He continues to yell and scream while the ECE tries to persuade him.

Like Andreas, children may be engrossed in a project that they don't want to leave. (Can you blame him? It sounds like great fun!) As well, some children need more time than others to prepare themselves to move from one activity to another.

What can you do?

- **Think about your schedule.** Is your schedule allowing enough time for children to become fully engaged in their play? If children know that they are going to have to move on soon, they might not bother to enter into complex play activities.
- **Think about compromises.** Consider whether it's possible to make accommodations for children who haven't had enough time to finish their play activity. For example, two children who are building a dollhouse from blocks might be able to leave their construction and go back to it later in the day.
- **Show that you understand.** Say, for example: "It's really frustrating when you're working on something great and you have to stop in the middle of it." Then engage them in problem-solving: "Can you think of a way that we might be able to save this so you can come back to it later?"
- **Warn children well in advance of a transition.** Give children time to prepare themselves for a transition. Walk among them calmly as they play and quietly tell them that it will be time to change activities soon.
- **Plan time for transitions.** Think about allowing more time between activities so children don't feel rushed.
- **Plan for as few transitions in the day as possible.**
- **Avoid wait times.** Think about whether it's necessary for everyone to make the transition at once; for example, can an educator be outside and receive the children there as they are dressed and ready to come out? Do all of the children need to go to the washroom at the same time? Could one educator read a story while the children go one by one to wash up for lunch?
- **Make sure that children have something to do during wait times.** Perhaps you can sing with them or read a story.
- **Acknowledge smooth transitions.** Notice and comment using descriptive feedback when children manage transitions well. Say, for example: "Jonah, you put away the blocks very quickly. Thank you!"

Since a good part of the child care day is made up of routines and transitions, it's important to plan carefully for them to make them unhurried and pleasant for all. Think about possibilities for learning, and take advantage of opportunities to chat with children individually.

RETHINKING CIRCLES

In Western culture, many early childhood programs have moved away from whole-group circle times on the grounds that children shouldn't be forced to sit if they aren't interested in the story, song, or "show and share" that is happening in the circle. However, as educators in our MCHB advisory group pointed out, the circle is an important symbol in Indigenous cultures, and circle activities are a time for showing respect, sharing together, and seeing one another. As such, they can be valuable as a transition time. These comments highlight the difference between the goals of independence in Western culture and of interconnectedness in Indigenous and many other cultures. How might you accommodate these two world views in your program?

Helping Children Navigate a Stressful Transition

The COVID-19 lockdowns were especially stressful transitions for everyone, including children. Educators and families had little opportunity to prepare children for the upheaval of the pandemic. Many centres tried to stay in touch with children and families during the time the centres were closed and the children were at home. Coming back to their child care programs after the lockdown was difficult for both families and children. Families were fearful about the safety of themselves and their children. Some didn't understand the procedures that were necessary to keep everyone safe. Requirements varied from centre to centre, and from one jurisdiction to the next. At some centres, families were required to enter the building one at a time, fill out a health questionnaire, or have their temperature checked at the door. Children came back to stripped-down playrooms, fastidious sanitation procedures, and often to the absence of a beloved educator or a favourite friend.

Programs found various ways to ease the transition and help the situation feel as normal as possible. Because families were unable to spend time with their children in the playroom, one centre began the day outside so that families could connect with each other and with their children. Picture-rich learning stories (discussed further in Chapter 15) that described children's play and learning helped families see how their children were faring during the day and reassured them that educators were attentive to their wellbeing. One centre created a storybook featuring a bear that children could follow through the steps of the new daily routine (Figure 7.2). And of course, it was very helpful when children could come back to a familiar educator—someone they knew they could count on to be with them even though their world was shifting in unpredictable ways.

Although these examples come from experiences during the COVID-19 pandemic, they could be used to ease any sort of transition. No one knows at this point what, in the end, the impact of the pandemic will be on children's development. Will months of distancing from friends and family make them fearful of physical contact? Of other people? Of germs? Will the stress that their families are feeling impact their wellbeing in the short or long term? What we do know, from brain research, however, is that the presence of an attentive adult who can support children through this stressful period is critical to their healthy development. As educators, we are in a position to provide reassurance and stability.

Figure 7.2. A story for children about the new health and safety protocols during the COVID-19 pandemic

Rituals

Rituals can be added to routines or transitions. They can be reassuring and calming. Relationships flourish and connections deepen when routine tasks are enhanced by creating rituals.

Morning departures are part of the daily routine at any child care centre. Khadra, an ECE, has a special arrival ritual that she does with Bilan each morning as she arrives and her mother departs:

> When Bilan arrives in the toddler room each morning, Khadra goes to the door, kneels down, and extends her arms, saying, "*Subax wanaagsan!*"—"good morning" in Somali. Khadra wiggles her fingers, and Bilan eagerly leaves her mother and jumps into her caregiver's arms. Bilan's mother smiles and waves goodbye to them both, heading to her classes at the local college. Khadra and Bilan go to the window and wave at her mom as she heads to the bus stop.

Engaging in rituals, particularly during morning departures, reassures children and helps them transition from home to the centre; rituals are predictable and are something that children can depend on. They contribute to feelings of safety and comfort. Rituals reassure children that their child care centre is a place where they are welcome and valued (Reynolds, 2008). Separation can be hard for many of us, but it is especially hard for young children because their greatest need is attachment with important people in their lives. Familiar welcome rituals in the morning set the tone for the day. They support children to cope with the stress of saying goodbye to parents heading off to work. As well as comforting the child, rituals can provide reassurance for the family member having to say goodbye; they know their child is in caring hands. Rituals can also transform an ordinary moment into the extraordinary. Remember Nirmali from Chapter 5? When it is time to change Niko's diaper, Nirmali invited her to hold the clean diaper as she got ready. Nirmali and Niko sang a favourite song together during the diaper change. By carrying out this routine task in an intentional way that is both familiar and special for Niko, Nirmali created a ritual that allows Niko to build her trust in Nirmali.

In one preschool playroom, educators decided to collaborate with children's family members to create special, recorded rituals:

> In the preschool playroom, educators were intrigued when they noticed that the father of twin girls said goodbye to each girl in a different way. They began to look more closely at the ways other family members said goodbye to their children each morning, and this led to a project on documenting goodbye rituals by observing, taking photos, and describing what they saw. Educators asked for feedback from families on what they had noticed and invited them to record a goodbye message that children could listen to during the day. Tran's father recorded a message for him in Korean. Misha's auntie and older sister each recorded a goodbye to her. Evan's mothers recorded themselves singing Evan's favourite song.

These educators know that acknowledging the goodbye rituals between children and their families recognizes that these practices are important. Educators' documentation of these special moments invited conversations about other family rituals and also led to staff in the infant room connecting with their families about sleep-time rituals to help make nap a special time for these young children. What if families recorded a sleep-time message or sang a familiar lullaby? This is the magic of ritual.

Routines and rituals overlap when ECEs handle routines in a thoughtful way and are willing to take the time to make them special. Mealtimes, nap time, and toileting offer excellent opportunities for one-to-one times with children. They can become times for building relationships as well as for learning.

Routines and rituals can also offer important opportunities for intercultural learning (Figure 7.3). Why not include snacks and meals inspired by the cultures of the children and educators in your playroom?

Figure 7.3. Snack time: Experiencing cultural ways of eating

? WHAT DO YOU THINK?

Figure 7.4. Devin enjoys his lunch

Knowing the mess he is likely to make, would you let Devin eat his lunch this way? Why or why not?

|||||||||||||||||||||||||||||||||||||||||||||||||||||||||||||||||||||||||||||||||||||||||||||||||||||||||||||||||||||||||||||||||

TAKEAWAYS

Rituals at home and in child care give children a sense of belonging and make mundane activities special. They help to build relationships and relieve stress. While rituals are defined as meaningful practices that focus on the experience of a task, routines are actions that are a part of our shared daily activities such as eating, sleeping, and washing hands. Consistent routines help young children feel secure and in control of their days. Transitions can be as simple as moving from one activity to another, or they can involve a drastic change. In either case, educators need to approach them thoughtfully so children can feel as prepared as possible.

|||||||||||||||||||||||||||||||||||||||||||||||||||||||||||||||||||||||||||||||||||||||||||||||||||||||||||||||||||||||||||||||||

REFLECTION AND DISCUSSION

- What are ways to carry out cleanup routines that engage children's participation?

- What are ways to reduce the waiting time when children are transitioning to play outdoors?

- What are some of the ways that you, as an educator, can help children feel secure in a time of change?

- Consider routines that occur on a regular basis with children and their families in your program. How can you transform some of these into rituals that children come to anticipate and treasure? How might the everyday be made magical?

- What are some of the rituals that are meaningful to you in your own life? What role do they fill?

8

Play Is Learning...and More!

You see a child play and it is so close to seeing an artist paint, for in play a child says things without uttering a word. You can see how he solves his problems. You can also see what's wrong. Young children, especially, have enormous creativity, and whatever's in them rises to the surface in free play.
—ERIK ERIKSON

||||||||||||||||||||||||||||||||||||||||||||||||||||||||||||||||||||||||||||||||||||||||||||||||||||||||||||||||||||||||||||||||||||||||||||||||||||||||||||||

LEARNING OUTCOMES

When you have read this chapter, you will be able to answer these questions:
- How would you define play?
- What are some terms used to describe different types of play?
- How does play support children's development?
- What are some ways that educators can support play?
- What are some cultural differences in attitudes toward play?

Introduction

Children's play has been of huge interest to theorists throughout the last couple of centuries, and the work of cognitive psychologists has linked play firmly to children's learning. This is why the idea of learning through play has become firmly entrenched in Western ECE practice. In this chapter, we'll elaborate on this critically important concept by looking at the characteristics of play and the ways that various aspects of development are supported by play. We'll look at Parten's stages of play, a common way of categorizing play into developmental stages; consider categories that are used to describe various types of play; and discuss the role of the educator in supporting play.

Then we'll consider some cultural perspectives with regard to play and learning. We will explore the impact these might have for adults working in early childhood programs.

Let's begin, though, by looking beyond the concept of play as learning to think about the wonder of play—the undefinable qualities that make play such a special part of our lives and our memories.

The Magic of Play

Theorists regard play as the key to children's development and learning, and a great deal of research has been done to define play, to identify different kinds of play, and to understand how play benefits children. When we recall our own childhood play and listen to others' stories, though, what emerges is a sense of how very special play is to us, beyond whatever developmental advantages it might carry. Indeed, some writers consider play as a spiritual activity that can nurture and heal our souls (Lewis, 2019). Take a look, for example, at these stories of childhood play:

> One of my favourite places from when I was 6 until about 10 was the local junkyard. There were a lot of machine parts and other junk lying around and I remember trying to make a car out of them.
>
> —ABDIEL

> Back home, the coffee ceremony is very important for us. After school when we came back with my friends and my siblings, we went outside. We made some mud, and with mud we made a coffee cup and coffee maker, and we had a celebration. And we had popcorn and we made some plates. We made a house with mud, we made bread, and we collected leaves and made some sauce…I really enjoyed those times.
>
> —SARA

> I had a cousin who was my age and we would do a lot of things together. On weekends, the whole extended family would get together at my grandparents' house. My cousin and I liked to hang out in the front closet—it was our private space. My grandmother's fur coat hung in there and we liked to rub our faces against the soft fur.
>
> —MILA

> My friends and I would ride our bikes down the trails, down into the river valley, and poke around down by the river. There was a rumour that someone had been murdered down there so that, along with the

fact that our parents had told us not to go there, made it especially interesting. We were sure that we'd find buried treasure. Or maybe a skeleton.

—ALEX

We see glimmers of this magic quality in these stories. Being in the junkyard sparks ideas about what could be made. Mud and leaves stand in for cooking utensils and ingredients, allowing Sara and her friends to recreate a social experience that is special to the adults. We can sense that being in the dark closet away from a crowd of people gives two young girls a feeling that they are in their own private world. The risk of exploring forbidden territory is heightened with imaginings of danger and possible treasure.

Sara's story is typical of stories told by immigrant educators when reflecting on their childhood play experiences. Many spoke of playing outside with natural materials and with little adult supervision. It's interesting to note that the other stories also made no mention of adult participation or supervision. Perhaps part of the magic of play is a sense of independence and opportunities to take initiative.

? WHO AM I?

Describe your favourite place to play when you were a child. What was it like? What smells, sounds, or even tastes do you remember? What did you do there and who did you do it with? What feelings do you remember? (If possible, write this reflection down and share it with others.)

Studying Play

In the second half of the nineteenth century, Euro-American philosophers and activists began to "discover" childhood as a unique and important life stage. Children were no longer to be considered as miniature adults. Having "discovered" childhood, experts of the time began to focus intensely on making sense of play. It was obvious that play was a very important activity—children play in every culture and have done so throughout history. The fact that young animals also play made the area of study even more compelling. Surely, they thought, there must be some important purpose for play.

Theorists came up with a variety of explanations. No single explanation provides an overarching, universal explanation of the purpose of play, but each of these explanations may well touch on an aspect of the answer. Friedrich Schiller (1759–1805), for instance, speculated that play serves purposes such as getting rid of surplus energy (see Bentley, 2009). Motitz Lazarus (1824–1903) postulated that play provides people with relaxation or recreation. G. Stanley Hall (1884–1946) thought of play as a way of eliminating inappropriate primitive instincts. Karl Groos (1861– 1946) theorized that play was a means of practising skills that would be needed for later survival.

One of (if not the) most influential psychological theorists of the nineteenth and twentieth centuries, Sigmund Freud (1856–1939), saw play as an activity that allows children to express their feelings and work through negative emotions. His daughter Anna Freud (1895–1982) extended these ideas when she theorized that play helps children cope with overwhelming anxiety. These psychoanalytic theories formed the basis for play therapy.

In ECE, the cognitive theories of developmental psychologists Jean Piaget (1896–1980) and Lev Vygotsky (1896–1934) have been very influential. Both saw children as active learners and understood their interactions with the larger environment to be critical to learning. But they, too, differed in certain aspects of their explanations of play. While Piaget envisioned the child as a solitary learner who constructs understandings individually, Vygotsky believed that children develop through their social interactions.

INTRODUCING...JEAN PIAGET

The principle goal of education in the schools
should be creating men and women who
are capable of doing new things, not simply
repeating what other generations have done.
—JEAN PIAGET

Jean Piaget (1896–1980) is considered to be a principal founder of child psychology (Smith, 1980). He was one of the first to recognize that children's thought patterns are different from those of adults.

Piaget was born in Switzerland in 1896. He was interested in the natural sciences from an early age and published his first academic article—about mollusks—at the age of 15. He became interested in child development in his early twenties and continued to pursue that interest throughout his career. Much of his research was based on sensitive observations and questioning of his own three children.

Piaget's approach can be described as constructivist. He understood children to be active learners—"little scientists"—who *construct* their understanding of the world based on their explorations of and interactions with it. As his words show, constructivism has implications for the role of the adult in children's learning:

> [I]f something is not acquired by experience and personal reflection it is acquired only superficially, with no change in our thought. It is in spite of adult authority, and not because of it, that the infant learns. Hence it is to the extent that the intelligent teacher knows when to step down as a superior and to become an equal, when to engage in discussion and to require proof rather than merely to make assertions and compel morally. (Piaget, 1977/1995, p. 204)

According to Piaget, when children encounter new information that doesn't fit with the ways they have developed to make sense of the world (their cognitive structures), they will handle that information in one of two ways:

1. **Accommodation:** They will reorganize their previous thinking to make the new information fit.
2. **Assimilation:** They will make the new information fit with their existing cognitive structures.

Piaget suggested that cognitive development occurs through four stages, and he attached ages to those stages:

1. **Sensory-motor stage (0–2 years):** Children use senses and motor skills to explore and learn about the world.
2. **Preoperational stage (2–6 years):** Children add language, symbolic thinking, and imagination to motor skills as means of exploring the world. Their thinking is egocentric, and they have difficulty with complex, abstract thought.
3. **Concrete operations stage (7–11 years):** Children can think logically about concrete events but have difficulty understanding abstract concepts. They understand conservation and can perform mathematical operations (e.g., with numbers, mass, and volume).
4. **Formal operations stage (12 years–adulthood):** Children and adults are capable of abstract reasoning (e.g., about morality).

From an intercultural perspective, it is important to recognize that Piaget's work has been criticized for the small size of his sample and the fact that the children he studied were all of similar backgrounds. Critics also maintain that Piaget underestimated the ages he assigned to different stages of cognitive development.

However, it is equally important to note that his work has been replicated in a number of different cultures. The basic cognitive processes that he identified have been found to be applicable, although the details, such as the age at which children demonstrate specific abilities, vary depending on what was valued in a particular culture (Babakr et al., 2019; Cherry, 2020).

Despite these discrepancies, Piaget's work is still widely respected and supports a focus on learning through exploration, the manipulation of objects, and, for older children, the manipulation of ideas.

INTRODUCING...LEV VYGOTSKY

It is through others that we become ourselves.

—*LEV VYGOTSKY*

Lev Vygotsky (1896–1934), like Piaget, has made huge contributions to our understanding of children's learning. The ideas that these theorists began formulating over a century ago have been a source of constant study and inspiration.

Lev Vygotsky was born the same year as Piaget—1896—in Orsha, a city in western Russia. He earned a law degree and studied in various other subjects before he entered the Institute of Psychology in Moscow in 1924. He was awarded a doctorate in absentia in 1925 while he was recovering from tuberculosis. In the 10-year period before his death in 1934, he published six books on topics in psychology. However, his work was slow to reach the West and only began to be influential in the 1970s. Despite his tragically short life, Vygotsky has had a strong impact in the fields of education and psychology.

Vygotsky saw children as active learners who develop their understanding through hands-on experiences. He emphasized that children learn through social interactions and through their culture. Vygotsky's thought can be described as *social constructivism*.

Vygotsky saw language as playing an important role in learning. In part, this is because it allows knowledgeable others to transmit information to children. For Vygotsky, however, it is also because language is a part of the process of maturation: the egocentric speech of young children is transformed into silent inner speech as children mature.

Vygotsky developed the concept of the *zone of proximal development* (ZPD), describing it as the difference between what a child can do without help and what they can accomplish with assistance from a more knowledgeable person. This guidance could be provided by an adult or a peer; the important thing is that it occur during the sensitive period in which the child is open to assistance (i.e., the ZPD) when they are faced with an intriguing challenge. The support that enables children to move to the higher level of skill or understanding is called _scaffolding_. Like the scaffolding that surrounds a building as it is being constructed, the idea here is that this support will be removed when the child no longer needs it.

Play creates situations where the child is challenged to move to a higher level of learning. In Vygotsky's words,

> play creates a zone of proximal development of the child. In play a child always behaves beyond his average age, above his daily behavior; in play it is as though he were a head taller than himself. As in the focus of a magnifying glass, play contains all developmental tendencies in a condensed form and is itself a major source of development. (Vygotsky, 1978, p. 102)

In play, children can learn through imitation and collaboration as well as through more intentional forms of guidance.

Despite Vygotsky's emphasis on the sociocultural context of learning, Rogoff (1990) maintains that his theory is not culturally universal. Scaffolding depends heavily on verbal instruction, which may be an unfamiliar way of learning in cultures that focus on learning through observation and practice.

What Is Play?

Theorists have developed many different definitions of play, but there seems to be general agreement on some characteristics (Rubin et al., 1983):

- **Play is fun.**
- **Play is intrinsically motivated.** There are no obvious external rewards.
- **Play is process-oriented.** You are not striving for a particular final result.
- **Play is freely chosen.** No one tells you that you have to play, or that you have to play in a particular way.
- **Play involves active engagement.** You are fully involved in the play and giving it all of your attention.
- **Play is nonliteral.** Play can involve imagination and make-believe.

WHO AM I?

As we've seen, play is vital for child development. However, children aren't the only ones who play. Play is important for adults, too! Think about your life today. What activities do you enjoy as an adult that meet some or all of these criteria for play?

Describing Play: Parten's Stages

In 1932, Mildred Parten developed a system for classifying children's involvement in play that was intended as a progression from less to more sophisticated levels of play. She observed that, as children grew older and had more opportunities for social interaction, they tended to move from solitary and onlooker play to associative and cooperative play.

Parten identified six stages of play:

1. **Unoccupied play**: The child isn't actually "playing," but looking around at things that are happening, playing with their own body, moving or remaining still, or following an adult.

2. **Onlooker behaviour**: The child is content watching other children at play.

3. **Solitary independent play**: The child prefers to play by themselves and doesn't appear to be interested in interacting with other children.

4. **Parallel play**: Children occupy a space near others but seldom share materials or toys. They might talk, but each has their own conversational strain.

5. **Associate play**: Children play in close contact and may share toys or materials with one another, but each considers their own viewpoint to be the most important one.

6. **Cooperative play**: Children take turns, share, and allow some children in the group to serve as leaders.

We can argue, from experience, that this progression isn't universal—sometimes, for example, a child's ability to choose solitary play marks a higher level of awareness than when they follow along with the group—but the descriptive terms that Parten uses to name her stages are very useful as a way of describing different play relationships. For instance, it isn't unusual to hear ECEs mention that a child prefers solitary play or that they are engaged in cooperative play.

Some other terms that you will hear used to describe children's play include the following:

- Object play, sensory play, exploratory play
- Construction play, constructive play
- Physical play, sensorimotor play, rough-and-tumble play
- Dramatic play, sociodramatic play, fantasy play, make-believe play, symbolic play
- Games with rules, competitive play

Play and Development

When we talk about child development, we often divide it into categories. We do this as a matter of convenience, but it's important to remember that all areas of development are intertwined.

We briefly described areas of development in Chapter 5, but we'll review them here so you can think about ways that play contributes to growth in each of the areas:

- **Cognitive development**: How children think and figure things out
- **Socioemotional development**: The combined social and emotional aspects of development, including the ability to establish positive relationships and express and manage emotions
- **Physical development**: The ability to use and control one's body using both gross motor skills and fine motor skills
    › Gross motor skills involve the larger muscles in the arms, legs, and torso that we use to walk, throw, run, and so on. These skills also relate to reaction speed, balance, strength, and body awareness.
    › Fine motor skills have to do with dexterity and the use of the fine muscles of our hands and wrists.
- **Cultural development**: The process by which children learn the behaviours and traits that are valued in their culture; an important part of developing identity
- **Language development**: The process by which children learn to understand and communicate using language; closely related to cognitive, physical, and cultural development; occurs best in a nurturing, language-rich socioemotional environment

Play allows children to discover, explore, and solve problems at the level that is appropriate for them. Think back to play stories that began this chapter. What types of learning could have been occurring for Abdiel, Sara, Mila, and Alex during their play?   _ _ reflection

Abdiel, for example, was engaging in cognitive and creative processes and developing both fine and gross motor skills as he explored the junkyard and figured out how to build a car out of parts he found there.

Alex, on the other hand, was using gross motor skills to ride his bike down into the ravine. Once the children arrived at their destination, they had to make decisions about what and how to explore. These decisions required social skills, including negotiation and compromise. The children certainly exercised their imaginations and probably increased their vocabularies as they exchanged pirate lore and speculated on the murder

Table 8.1. Developmental Learning through Different Play Areas and Activities in Child Care Centres

MUSIC AND MOVEMENT ACTIVITIES	ART ACTIVITIES	PLAYING WITH BLOCKS
• Artistic expression • Creative movement • Language development • Prereading skills (e.g., hearing rhythmic patterns) • Physical fitness • Cultural awareness • Fine motor skills	• Creative expression and imagination • Sharing and cooperation • Fine motor skills • Self-esteem and confidence • Math and science concepts (e.g., sorting, classifying) • Science concepts (e.g., change of state) • Patterns, symmetry, and balance • Decision-making and problem-solving • Perseverance • Visual–spatial skills • Cultural awareness	• Science concepts (e.g., gravity, stability, weight, balance, inductive reasoning, interaction of forces, properties of matter) • Math concepts (e.g., depth, width, height, length, measurement, volume, area, classification, one-to-one correspondence, shape, symmetry, mapping, equality [same as], and inequality [more than, less than]) • Art concepts (e.g., patterns, symmetry, balance) • Symbolic representation • Interdependence of people • Mapping, grids, and patterns • Prereading skills (e.g., shape recognition, differentiation of shapes, size relations) • Language skills • Cooperation and respect for others' work • Dramatic play • Feelings of competence • Autonomy and initiative
OUTDOOR PLAY	COOKING	LOOKING AT BOOKS AND BEING READ TO
• Gross motor (large muscle) skills • Balance and control • Learning about one's own strengths and abilities • Physical fitness • Imagination	• Competence and independence • Math skills (e.g., counting, estimating, measuring, fractions) • Fine motor skills • Nutrition • Science concepts (e.g., change of state) • Cause and effect • Sensory awareness	• Vocabulary • Listening skills • Symbolic representation • Interest in reading • Imagination

Table 8.1. *Continued*

PLAYING WITH MANIPULATIVES	SAND AND WATER PLAY	DRAMATIC PLAY
• Fine motor control • Math skills (e.g., sorting, classifying, counting, patterning, sequencing) • Shape and colour discrimination • Abstract thinking	• Math concepts (e.g., fractions) • Science concepts (e.g., volume, weight, physical properties) • Hand–eye coordination • Cause and effect • Acceptable ways to release emotions • Success experiences	• Concentration, attentiveness, and self-control • Imagination • Planning and sequence • Flexibility and creativity • Empathy for others • Cultural awareness • Abstract thinking • Problem-solving • Figuring out the adult world
SNACK TIME PARTICIPATION	CLEANUP	
• Fine motor skills (e.g., pouring, spreading) • Competence and independence • Social skills • Nutrition • Risk-taking (i.e., as they try new foods) • Cultural awareness	• Sorting, matching, organizing, and classifying • Language skills (e.g., through labelling) • Self-discipline • Following directions • Cooperation • Feelings of competence, independence, and responsibility • Enhanced self-esteem	

that was said to have occurred. They also engaged in risk-taking; risky play can help children challenge themselves, test limits, develop confidence, and learn to judge and make decisions about risk.

Another way to look at the developmental potential of play is to consider possible learning that is happening at each of the play areas and activities that we typically find in child care centres (Table 8.1).

It's easy to see why play is considered to be critical to children's learning: all aspects of development are enhanced by play. What does this mean for the role of educators in supporting children's play?

The Adult's Role in Children's Play

As an ECE, you can help children grow and learn by interacting with them in their play. Certainly, you will want them to know that you are interested in their play and understand it as a valuable activity. You can also watch for ways to further their learning by extending their play. The roles that you might take in children's play include the following:

- Observing and documenting play
- Participating in play
- Intervening in play
- Extending play

Observing children's play will help you learn about their skills and understanding, and will determine the role you should take in order to support the play. Documenting the play, perhaps in the form of a learning story (see Chapter 15), will allow you to revisit it with the children and share it with parents and other educators.

If you choose to take part in the play, be careful not to take it over. Follow the children's lead and take on the roles that they assign you.

If children are having difficulty resolving interpersonal issues that arise in their play, you can enter into the play to help them get back on track. You should only intervene if necessary, though; children need opportunities to practise problem-solving and conflict resolution.

You can also "extend play" based on your observations of the play by adding new props, as ECE Rahwa does with Genet, a child in her playroom:

> Rahwa notices that 3-year-old Genet has been poking at the red tissue paper and logs in the sand table, stoking it as if it were a fire. Genet is humming to herself while repeating the words, "Cooking, cooking, cooking on the fire." Quietly, Rahwa gathers some craft sticks and playdough from the shelf with art materials and sits down on the floor beside Genet. Rahwa begins to squeeze the playdough, asking, "Genet, do you want to make food for your fire?" When Genet enthusiastically responds, "Kebabs!" Rahwa begins to wrap the playdough around one of the sticks and Genet follows her lead. They engage in conversation about making chicken and beef kebabs, and which ones Genet's family eats at home.
>
> Genet holds the sticks over the "fire" as another educator, Senait, offers her a "grill" to lay on the tissue. Genet understands exactly what to do and places her kebabs on it, turning them as they cook. When they are done, she offers them to Rahwa who pretends to eat. The two of them chat as they enjoy their kebabs. Then, Genet begins to offer them to her playmates.

Rahwa began by being an observer of Genet's play. She carefully watched what the child was doing and listened to what she was saying. You'll notice that Rahwa did not take over the play, but engaged Genet in conversation to find out what she would like to make. Rahwa and Senait both facilitated Genet's play by finding objects and materials to support what Genet was doing. Finally, Rahwa was a participant in Genet's play as she role-played eating kebabs. Rahwa's involvement let Genet know that what she is doing is valuable, giving her the opportunity to persist in her play and develop the plot line further.

Cultural Perspectives on Play

Roopnarine and Davidson (2015) remind us that views that understand play to be developmentally valuable have Euro-American roots. Play may not have the same significance in all cultures. We see this difference in viewpoints, for example, when families complain that their children are "just playing" at child care centres and ask ECEs to spend some time teaching the children to read or do math. We also need to be aware of the fact that play does not take the same form in all cultures, and that there are cultures and circumstances in which children do not have the luxury of playing because they are expected to work to help support their families.

These varying views of play mean that all adults may not see their role in play the same way. Most of the immigrant and refugee ECEs who participated in Carole's bridging program (discussed in Chapter 4; see p. 45) remembered carefree play in their early years. This play was often in the outdoors and occurred without intervention or oversight from adults. The ECEs made a distinction, however, between play and learning. Learning meant school and school meant sitting quietly and listening carefully.

? WHAT DO YOU THINK?

Prochner et al. (2016) describe various ways that immigrant students in field placements respond to the expectation that they will play with children. The students reported that they would not think of sitting on the floor with children or playing with them directly, but found various ways to accommodate the expectation nonetheless. One of these was to incorporate "academics" in the play. Prochner et al. provided the example of Amita, a former high school teacher, who described her interaction with a young child, Coco:

> I noticed Coco was watching the blocks. I went close to him and sat on the floor to play with him. Then we started to make a tower. We counted the blocks and helped each other say "my turn" and "your turn." Coco was very much interested in making a tower and crashing the tower. We talked about the pictures on the blocks and the difference between smaller and bigger things.

I learned about the child. He has different qualities and interests. He can learn when I show him examples [how to roll the playdough, learning about shapes and size]. He can develop these skills through different types of play. I only need to guide and teach him. If I converse with him, he can develop his language skills [saying "roll, roll" "triangle"]. (p. 57)

Amita's interactions, as described here, are sensitive and relational. She has integrated play and instruction with the intention of supporting this young child's learning. Do you think her approach enhances or detracts from the child's play? Is this play, and does it matter if it's not?

TAKEAWAYS

The idea that children learn through play has long been at the core of early childhood practice. Theorists have worked to define the purpose of play, different types of play, and how and what children learn through their play. In some cultures, however, play is seen as separate from learning and this has implications for how the adult might view their role in children's play.

REFLECTION AND DISCUSSION

- Earlier in the chapter, you described one of your favourite places to play when you were a child. Now, consider your play in relation to the theories of play that you've learned. How would you classify your particular kind of play? What might you have been learning from it? What role, if any, did adults have in your play? How might your childhood play impact your work with children?

- As an ECE, how would you respond to a parent who is unhappy that their child is "just playing" and asks you to do more academic work?

9

Creating Environments for Play

LEARNING OUTCOMES

After you have read this chapter, you will be able to answer these questions:
- What are some key considerations in planning a play environment?
- What is the value of a culturally responsive environment?
- What are some considerations in planning an environment that reflects the diversity of children and families in a playroom?
- Why are relationships with families vital in creating a responsive environment?

Introduction

Loris Malaguzzi, the father of the well-known Reggio Emilia approach, emphasized that the environment plays a central role in the process of making learning meaningful. So important was this notion that Malaguzzi defined the environment as "the third teacher" (Gandini, 2012, p. 339), alongside parents and educators. As educators, we have a responsibility to provide environments with carefully selected materials that engage children in wonder, discovery, and exploration. The children play an active part in this design process because ECEs are constantly changing the environment to respond to children's evolving interests and learning. As Fraser (2012) says,

> A classroom that is functioning successfully as a third
> teacher will be responsive to the children's interests, provide

opportunities for children to make their thinking visible, and then foster further learning and engagement. (p. 67)

As an ECE, you can plan carefully to provide children with joyful opportunities to play. This chapter outlines basic principles for creating environments that stimulate positive interactions and deep engagement during play. From there it looks at some of the changes that were made in one child care environment in order to make it more truly reflect the children, families, and educators who inhabited it.

INTRODUCING...REGGIO EMILIA

Following the devastation of World War II, the people of Reggio Emilia, a small town in Italy, set about rebuilding their lives and their society. Their strong desire for a free and equal society led to many cooperative movements. The women of Reggio Emilia were instrumental in building a system of preschools in the area.

Loris Malaguzzi (1920–1994), a local primary school teacher, was deeply invested in helping to build a strong future for the children and families of Reggio Emilia. He studied psychology in order to learn more about young children and became a leader in the parent cooperative program. Malaguzzi's involvement eventually led to the Reggio Emilia movement in ECE.

Today, Reggio Emilia has just over 35 preschools, and their system of education is known through much of the world. International networks sponsor study tours of the centres and host conferences and seminars. The Reggio Emilia experience prompts educators and families to consider important questions about our views of children, the nature of learning, and the purpose of education.

The Reggio Emilia approach is characterized by the following:

- A view of children as capable and competent, full of potential, and having equal rights to adults. Their voices, thoughts, and opinions are considered to be just as valuable as those of adults.
- A focus on children's relationships with parents, teachers, the community, and other children
- A strong emphasis on the visual arts, in keeping with Malaguzzi's conception of the "100 Languages" of children, beyond spoken language
- Recognition of the importance of the classroom environment in learning, and a characterization of the environment as the "third teacher," after parents and educators
- An expectation that the adult's role is to help children reach their potential

- Documentation of children's work as a way of making their learning visible
- Project work where children make choices about what they will explore and work with their teachers to investigate and make meaning of their work
- Avoidance of standardized tests, in accordance with a focus on who children are now rather than who they may become

Although early childhood programs in many countries have adopted a Reggio Emilia approach, it's important to remember that Reggio Emilia reflects a particular historical, cultural, and political context that might not fit with all local conditions. While we may not accept all aspects of the approach, at the very least it reminds us of the need to value children and families, and provokes us to think about ways to best support our individual children and communities.

Planning the Physical Environment

Architects, urban planners, and decorators tell us that our physical environment has a profound effect on our behaviour and our feelings of well-being. Colours affect us in different ways; for example, a bright colour tends to energize us, while a light neutral colour tends to be calming. For this reason, many child care centres have moved away from bright colours with Disney-themed decorations to neutral tones that showcase the children's work. Similarly, many centres are replacing brightly coloured plastic toys with materials such as tree stumps, pine cones, tree branches, tree cookies, and stones. An environment rich in textures and interesting objects creates a valuable play experience.

It makes sense that children will work and play best in an environment that is calm and harmonious. A comfortable environment helps children who are stressed or who are just getting used to the program to feel safe. When you are creating an effective and nourishing environment for play, it is important to consider how time, the space itself, and the materials in it contribute to the overall environmental experience.

Time

Think about a time when you've considered working on a favourite hobby. Maybe you wanted to paint a picture or work on a craft. Would you have even begun if you knew that you were going to be interrupted in a few minutes? Children need time to become deeply engaged in their play activities. The daily schedule should include long periods of uninterrupted play and, where possible, provision for children to come back to activities that they haven't had time to finish. Time needs to be flexible and adapt to what children are telling you through their actions. For example, when a child or children are deeply engrossed in play inside, offering them the option to go outside a bit later than usual may give them the time they need to finish what they are doing. Conversely, if some children are anxiously running or wandering in the playroom, this may be the signal that it is time for them to go to the gym or playground for some active pursuits.

Space

The schedule should allow for both active and quiet play. Active play requires plenty of space; unfortunately, most child care playrooms can't accommodate highly active play, so be sure that there is provision for active play in a gym or outdoor space. The playroom should accommodate both small and large groups. Cozy spaces where one or two children can huddle provide security and privacy, while an area where the whole group can comfortably gather promotes group cohesion and teaches valuable lessons about respecting one another's space.

Messy play (e.g., water, sand, crafts) should be located near a water source and on a floor surface that is easily washed. The reading area, on the other hand, should have cozy pillows and rugs to invite relaxation. Areas should be clearly defined with paths that lead through the room but are not so straight that they encourage running. The block area should be large enough for complicated structures and enclosed enough that the block play won't be disrupted by children passing by.

Materials and Equipment

There should always be enough materials and equipment that children have choices; for example, if there are 16 children in a playroom, there should be at least 32 play spaces available. For instance, your materials could allow for 4 children at a time to be playing with the blocks, 4 in the house area, 6 working on a special project, 6 using various manipulatives, 4 in the water table, 4 in the sand, and 4 listening to a story in the reading area.

Toddlers don't usually have the social skills to share their toys, so if you are working with that age group, you can head off disputes by having several of each toy available.

Store materials neatly near the areas where they will be used and encourage children to take pride in keeping their work area tidy. Attractive containers can add to the aesthetics of the space. Labels, in words and/or pictures, help children know where items go. Materials should be stored where they are easily accessible to children, including children who have limited mobility.

Most playrooms are equipped with the following:

- Blocks and block accessories
- A water table
- A sand table
- A reading area with cozy seating and/or cushions
- Tables for activities and lunch
- Shelves and bins for storage
- Manipulatives (e.g., loose parts, small blocks, and figures)
- A housekeeping area (which may be converted for other purposes, e.g., a restaurant, hairdressing salon, store)
- If there is space, a loft and/or climbing apparatus

Think about materials that would encourage imaginative play; for example, you could include vehicles and multicultural person figures in the block area, or perhaps pictures of interesting buildings. An area with readily available recyclable materials such as boxes of various sizes, paper rolls, yarn, plastic containers and lids, and other throwaways, along with tape, glue, and staples for fastening, can encourage both creativity and recycling. Dress-up clothes or pieces of fabric with interesting accessories can spark role-play, and a house area with kitchen accessories can encourage children to take on family roles.

Many centres make prop boxes or bags that are geared to specific jobs or roles. Some typical prop box themes include hospital, fire station, florist, grocery store, garden, restaurant, and office, but the possibilities are limitless. Often, parents are able to donate items from their households or place of work to create such prop boxes. Try to include cultural materials that reflect the lifestyles of families in the playroom.

An important thing to remember is that the playroom, and the space and materials in it, should be flexible and respond to the interests of the children. Maybe this means setting aside an area to build a spaceship big enough for two children to share, a marketplace, or a campsite where children can reenact a recent camping experience that one of them has enjoyed. Older children will be able to actively engage in the process of planning the environment and activities, while younger children will show you through their actions what they want and need.

INTRODUCING...MARIA MONTESSORI

*The goal of early childhood education should be
to activate the child's own natural desire to learn.*
—MARIA MONTESSORI

Maria Montessori (1870–1952) was the first woman in Italy to graduate in medicine from the University of Rome. After having endured hostility from professors and other students because of her gender, she graduated with honours. While working at the psychiatric clinic at the university, she became interested in the educational challenges of children who were intellectually disabled. Her interest expanded to the education of all children, and in 1907, she opened the first *Casa dei Bambini* ("Children's House") for preschool children in a slum district of Rome and began to develop her own pedagogy. Her writings soon attracted international interest, and the Montessori method became popular throughout Western Europe and in many other countries, including India, Mexico, New Zealand, and the United States. Montessori travelled widely, giving lectures and training teachers.

As a result of her observations and work with children, Montessori came to believe that children's spontaneous activities showed their individual program of development. The goal of education, therefore, was to encourage autonomy and self-motivation by allowing children to choose their own activities within a carefully structured environment.

Montessori discovered that children would become deeply engaged when they were working with concrete materials, so she designed simple, attractive materials to teach concepts and skills. She also observed that young children had a strong interest in arranging their environment—for example, by straightening tables and shelves. Her pedagogy called for classrooms with child-sized furnishings and practical activities such as sweeping floors and washing tables. Later, she extended her program of education to older children.

Maria Montessori continued her work until her death at the age of 82. What she was able to discover and accomplish in her lifetime is remarkable, especially considering the times in which she lived. She gave educators a new understanding of children's development and learning, and her influence is still seen in the Montessori programs throughout the world.

Unfortunately, not all programs that call themselves "Montessori" are equal: they sometimes lack proper resources because Montessori materials are expensive, and educators may not have accredited Montessori training. Some critics also question whether the methods—for example, the expectation that each material will be used in a prescribed way—are still applicable in modern society. What do you think?

Environments and Materials that Create Wonder

> What sort of environments support wonder and wonderful things and experiences? Wonder is not hard to do; group living is hard to do, particularly with children. Group living leads to institutionalization which drives wonder underground. (Greenman, 1993, p. 32)

Even though Jim Greenman wrote this almost 30 years ago, his sentiments are valid to this day. Children (and adults as well) do best in environments that are not only designed with their developmental capabilities in mind, but that are also aesthetically pleasing and culturally relevant. Rich in natural materials, beautiful items, inviting aromas, objects that play with light, living things such as plants, and invented spaces, such environments promote exploration, creativity, and divergent thinking. As educators, we have a responsibility to provide environments with carefully selected materials that engage children's wonder, discovery, and exploration.

In the quote above, Jim Greenman refers to the stress of "group living with children"—that is, being together in a group for many hours a day, week after week—and alludes to its potential negative impact on wonder. Greenman cautions that wonder is also killed by lack of standards for quality, educator stress and fatigue, and an unchecked insistence on tidiness, as well as disarray and messiness (1993). Many of us in the field of early childhood tend to be collectors. We collect boxes and containers of all shapes and sizes, ribbon, wool, rocks, twigs, buttons, and all kinds of recycled items that eventually get transformed into "beautiful junk" or *loose parts*.

Loose Parts

The "theory of loose parts" was first introduced in 1971 by British architect Simon Nicholson as a way to encourage creativity and richness in the environment. Nicholson (1971) claimed, "In any environment both the degree of inventiveness and creativity, and the possibility of discovery, are directly proportional to the number and kind of variables" (p. 30). This is why we are seeing more loose parts in ECEC settings, as many centres move away from single-use commercial toys. Chapter 11 provides examples and further discussion of loose parts.

Figure 9.1. Creating wonder and beauty

MESS AND STRESS? LEARNING TO WORK WITH LOOSE PARTS

When we opened our new centre, new children came into playroom environments that were already fully set up; they were rich in beautiful loose parts, natural materials, and open-ended materials. However, after the first few days, educators expressed frustration about the disarray in the rooms and the volume of loose parts that had to be put away during cleanup, and especially at the end of the day. Children had been dumping baskets of loose parts on the floor and tables and then walking away; some of the younger children were throwing them around the room.

Upon reflection, we began to recognize that these kinds of materials were new to most of the children. We realized that we had not introduced children to loose parts and that they may not have a sense of how to use them or of their possibilities for play. As a result, we decided that educators would be intentional about role-modelling ways to manipulate, organize, and experiment with these materials—not that they would direct children's play but that they would introduce children to the possibilities for design, testing their theories, classifying, and so on. In addition to guiding children in the possibilities for using loose parts, educators decided to cut back on the number of loose parts in playroom, keeping only those that were of interest to the children as they were introduced to them.

But what to do about the younger children throwing the loose parts all over the playroom? Educators decided to support this "play urge" or "schema" (in this case, the trajectory schema, which is all about tossing items), by creating places to throw and providing soft loose parts such as bath puffs. This way, children could practise and master throwing in a safe way, and the mess could be contained.

The Importance of Decluttering

While this ability to be resourceful is certainly an asset in any program, and while these kinds of materials promote creativity, discovery, wonder, and play in children, loose parts also pose the dilemma of storing all our collected treasures. As Mary Lynne's story above demonstrates, however, by approaching loose parts reflectively and intentionally, you can discover strategies that reduce clutter, facilitate cleanup, and promote children's exploration.

When these items end up in our playrooms, we may not notice the accumulation of materials and papers on shelves and countertops or the cardboard boxes packed with all our resources and extra materials stored above cupboards. Although we may become accustomed to this kind of clutter when it is in the environment every day, it can add visual weight or heaviness to the playroom; that is, it may impact the ability to focus and process information and create too much stimulus on the senses. Monitoring and eliminating clutter in the environment is an ongoing process if we want items of wonder to be a focus in the playroom. A strategy that was employed periodically at one centre involved the director taking photos of cluttered shelves, window ledges, counters, and cupboards in playrooms and engaging in reflection with educators on their impact on wonder.

Figure 9.2. Avoiding clutter

Miriam Beloglovsky (Beloglovsky & Spahn, 2021) has responded to educator concerns about the cleanup of loose parts by noting that learning to put them away is part of a process of teaching children to work with them. Cleanup reinforces the idea that materials are easier to find when organized. Educators can also reframe how they look at cleanup time, moving away from its being a chore to its being a valuable learning experience. When educators avoid rushing the cleanup process, they can participate playfully with children to put away loose parts and engage their cooperation and ideas; in essence the work of cleanup transforms into play. When we invite children's help by asking, for example, "Hmmm, I am not sure where this piece should go. Martine, what do you think?" children get to be experts in the playroom and will often willingly participate with us to put materials away.

Beloglovsky and Spahn also discuss the need to organize loose parts for accessibility and engagement, noting that the kind of containers we choose for storing loose parts can send messages about where they go. For example, they suggest using a metal bucket to store metal loose parts such as screws, nuts, and bolts. Woven baskets can be used for natural items like pine cones and twigs, and clear containers for other loose parts (Beloglovsky & Spahn, 2021). In this way, the environment speaks to children and lets them know where things belong.

Culturally Responsive Environments

While loose parts invite investigation and inquiry, they can also contribute to a familiar home-like atmosphere in the playroom when we include baskets, containers, dishes, bowls, and fabrics that reflect the cultures of educators and children who work and play there daily. A collection of beautiful bangles may remind some children of the bracelets worn by family members for special occasions. Adding buttons donated by

Figure 9.3. Loose parts can have personal meaning

families to the centre's collection might evoke memories of baby clothes and favourite pajamas when we invite families to share the story of the button they are donating. ECEs can also take part in these donations. The collection of gold and silver buttons in Figure 9.3, for example, includes buttons that came from an educator's father's regimental uniform; they evoke fond memories and stories from her family.

Cultural items add beauty and interest to a play environment. They tell children and their families that the child care centre is a place where they are welcome and, at the same time, introduce them to aspects of different cultures. Familiar vessels, cooking utensils, tools, and artwork in the playroom are comforting, affirming, and make it easier for children to engage in pretend play. Cultural items should be carefully chosen to authentically reflect the home environment and the experiences of the children. Consulting with families is critical to make sure that cultural items are familiar and used in ways that are culturally appropriate.

Figure 9.4. Materials that reflect the cultures of those in the playroom

Transforming Our Environment to Reflect Culture

The Intercultural Child and Family Centre (ICFC) in Edmonton, Alberta (one of the centres from which many of the stories and experiences in this book have been drawn), is committed to finding ways to become truly intercultural—to look beyond music, clothes, and food to discover and respond to the culture of children and families at a deeper level. Mary Lynne, who was a mentor to the ICFC program and is an author of this book, and Jasvinder Heran, ICFC Executive Director, wrote about their early experiences creating playroom environments that reflect interculturalism.

ICFC's participation in a pilot of *Play, Participation, and Possibilities* (Makovichuk et al., 2014), the then newly developed curriculum framework for early learning and child care in Alberta, led them to wonder how to create playroom environments that reflected the children, families, and educators. In the article, Jasvinder reflects,

> I looked around the toddler room as if for the first time and took in the row of Fisher Price high chairs along one wall, six cribs lined up along another wall, and two change tables in the centre of the room. To my dismay, I realized that this was a room that screamed "custodial care" and it did not speak to the cultural diversity of our centre's families and staff. Any artifacts that represented culture were hanging from the ceiling or up high on a bulletin board where children couldn't see them. We realized right then that we had some work to do on our playroom environments. (para. 2)

Educators began small by transforming the house centre into a place that looked like home. Inspired by that space, they quickly moved on to creating playroom environments that reflected the diversity of their child care community. Most of the plastic storage bins and commercial single-use toys were donated and replaced with natural materials and real items such as copper pots and pans, wooden spoons, and items of beauty and cultural significance, much of which was purchased from second-hand stores or donated by staff and families.

Transformations of the playroom environments to reflect the cultural backgrounds of the community played a major role in ICFC's journey towards interculturalism. The intercultural transformation of the playrooms also encouraged a transformation of certain daily practices, including documentation of children's learning and play. This included the use of learning stories (discussed in Chapter 15):

Figure 9.5. Initial transformation of the preschool house area included adding a homemade low table, ethnic fabrics, pictures depicting spices and dishes from Ethiopia and Eritrea, wooden bowls, babies of all colours, and cultural clothing and footwear.

> Some of our most memorable learning stories have been titled "My mom's bread is thin," a comment from children's conversations while making an Ethiopian bread called *himbasha*; "We eat like this at home," a comment from a child upon seeing a lunch of *mesir wat, tikel gomen*, and *injera* served on a communal plate on the floor; and "Safwan understands Somali," an insight by an educator when she realized a toddler who seemed non-responsive and non-verbal reacted to instructions spoken in Somali.

All in all, the process was powerful for children, families, and educators alike. The full article, "Culturally Responsive Practice at the Intercultural Child and Family Centre," describes the process and thinking that went into the decisions in more detail, and is included in Appendix D with the permission of the Canadian Child Care Federation.

AN ENVIRONMENT FOR INCLUSION
Children and families need to feel welcomed, valued, and comfortable in a child care program. Children need to be able to access a variety of activities regardless of their ability. The next

time you are in an early childhood playroom, check for these aspects of inclusion:

- Are there interesting activities and resources that promote multisensory experiences (i.e., seeing, hearing, touching, tasting, smelling)?
- Are natural materials and loose parts an important part in the program?
- Are photos of the children and their families displayed in the room?
- Are there dolls that represent major ethnic groups? Is there a balance of male and female dolls?
- Do coloured paper, crayons, and playdough represent a variety of skin tones?
- Are materials accessible to all children of all abilities, or are there items that some children can reach and use but not others?
- Are appropriate supports and equipment in place for children who have exceptionalities?
- Are there items that would be familiar to children from their home environment?
- Do dress-up clothes represent the cultural background of children and educators in the playroom? (See Chapter 11, "Rethinking Dress-Up Clothes," p. 153)
- Are families' home languages represented? For example, do educators speak the languages or make the effort to learn a few key phrases in each? Are greetings posted in various languages?
- Do pictures, posters, and books
  › Show children and adults of various ethnicities and abilities?
  › Avoid the use of stereotypes?
  › Show a fair balance of men and women doing similar jobs, both inside the home and outside the home?
  › Include stories about different cultures and abilities?
  › Show pictures of older people engaged in a variety of activities?
  › Show familiar items from the children's home cultures?

TAKEAWAYS

The environment in which children spend their days has a huge influence on their learning and behaviour. Environments that encourage play require careful planning with respect to aspects such as space, time, and materials. They should be inviting and well organized and should inspire wonder and discovery. Thoughtful consideration is needed to ensure that environments are inclusive: that they reflect and respond to the abilities, interests, and experiences of the children who inhabit them.

REFLECTION AND DISCUSSION

- What is the space in which you are most comfortable? What makes it comfortable?

- If you were to choose an artifact that reflects who you are, what would it be?

- Read the article "Culturally Responsive Practice at the Intercultural Child and Family Centre" in Appendix D. What sorts of physical changes were made to the playroom environment at the Intercultural Child and Family Centre? Why do you think educators made these changes?

- Every playroom and every family is different. Think about a playroom that you know and the children and families in it. What elements respond to the unique needs and cultures of the children? What more might be done? How do educators seek cultural input from the families?

- If you are able, spend some time in an early childhood playroom and notice what the artifacts, posters, play props, and books tell you about the group of children and families that inhabit the space. Then, check your impressions with one of the educators in the room. What things might you add or take away to more accurately reflect those children and families?

Children and Nature

I was warmed by the sun, rocked by the winds
and sheltered by the trees as other Indian babes.
I can go everywhere with a good feeling.
—GERONIMO (1829–1909)

‖‖

LEARNING OUTCOMES

When you have read this chapter, you will be able to answer these questions:
- How do children benefit from spending time in nature?
- What are some of the societal changes that have taken us away from our connection to nature?
- Why might some children and adults be fearful of nature?
- How can Indigenous perspectives inform our relationship with nature?
- How can we help children connect with nature?

Introduction

Recent years have seen increased concern about what Louv (2005) calls "nature deficit disorder"—the cost of our alienation from nature. This chapter explores how time spent with nature benefits children and how our society has become increasingly disconnected from nature. The bond that Indigenous Peoples of Canada have historically had—and many still have—with nature is very different from the Euro-American, industrialized relationship between humans and nature. Given the current stresses on our environment, it may be especially important to consider this connection and find ways to help children have a closer relationship with nature.

ADVENTURES AT THE CRICK

When I had a sleepover with my cousin Dianne, we used to spend the whole day with her brothers and a couple other neighbourhood kids at the "crick"—a creek near her house. My family lived on the sixth floor of an apartment building, so I always looked forward to a sleepover and a day at the crick.

Off we would go down the street and across "the big road" to splash, dig, and reroute the water flow by building dams with everything we could find—stones, branches, and anything else that was nearby. The crick wasn't very deep, so one of our projects often involved digging down to make a pool that one or two of us could lie in to cool off. We spent a lot of time figuring out what tools we could use to dig since we didn't have any of the plastic shovels or buckets that my own children have. Sometimes, we found a discarded can or piece of fender to dig; other times we sent someone back to the house to sneak a couple big spoons from my aunt's kitchen.

We figured things out at the crick: rubbing mud on a mosquito bite stopped the itch, adding sticks to a dirt dam strengthened the structure, lining the bottom of a pool with stones made it less slippery and slimy, and diverting the course of the stream didn't last very long. Mostly, we all worked together on a big project, but sometimes Dianne and I picked a variety of wildflowers and weeds and created pictures on the ground with the petals and leaves. In the late afternoon, we usually made ourselves "beds" to rest on from reeds, grass, and leaves. We searched the sky for clouds that looked like something, calling out to each other when we made a discovery. I remember the sounds of stones skipping across the water, birds chirping, and a lot of splashing.

We rarely went back home for lunch, choosing instead to preplan and bring a sleeve of crackers and some peanut butter with us. When one of us found a pop bottle in the ditch near the big road, we hiked to the store to redeem it for a popsicle; it took a lot of negotiating to decide on the flavour and then divide it between all of us!

When we heard my aunt calling from the front porch, we knew it was time for dinner. Reluctantly, we headed back home, often still wet and covered in mud. A bathtub with warm water and lots of soap awaited us; the girls got to bathe in it first and then the boys got the leftover murky water. It's just the way it was back then.

As I recall these times, I realize that my own children didn't have these same experiences except perhaps for times when our family went camping. I wonder how much they would have loved the sense of adventure that came out of a day at the crick.

Nature, Identity, and Wellbeing

Some theorists believe that children are born with a natural sense of relatedness to nature. Many researchers have found that children's regular contact with, and play in, nature builds an affinity for nature and a desire to protect the environment (White, 2006). The fact that they are attracted to animal characters in books and tales set in nature is seen as evidence of this (White, 2006). Sobel (1996) wrote that building upon children's empathy with the natural world should be the main focus for children aged 4 through 7 years.

In Chapter 2, we looked at two similar sociocultural "ecological" perspectives of development, one developed by Urie Bronfenbrenner (1994) and another by Blackfoot Elders (Lindstrom et al., 2016). Heerwagen & Orians (2002) suggest that these sociocultural views of child development are inadequate and that a truly ecological perspective should also include a relationship with the natural and biological world. Certainly, the 2020 coronavirus pandemic has shown us how nature impacts us and our development at every level, from the individual child through to the broadest levels of influence. However, we don't need to be in the midst of a pandemic to experience nature's influence on our identities and wellbeing.

Research confirms the benefits of connecting with the natural world. It is well known that being in nature and/or interacting with animals is beneficial to our mental health. As Chawla et al. (2014) report, time spent in nature can help children develop capacities for problem-solving, focus, critical thinking, and decision-making. Children can learn lessons in resilience; for example, changing seasons show that nature is resilient and that children can respond in resilient ways by dressing for the weather (Gifford & Chen, 2016).

Studies also show how experiences in nature can help relieve anxiety and depression, combat obesity, promote physical wellbeing, and establish a healthy relationship with food (Gifford & Chen, 2016). Environment-based education has been shown to enhance creativity and promote fantasy and make-believe play (Louv, 2005). As an added bonus, when we, as adults, interact with children in nature, we, too, can experience it again through their eyes.

Hewes (n.d.) points out that the outdoors provides opportunities for noisy, physically active play and risk-taking that are unavailable indoors. Outdoor play provides chances to develop physical skills such as balance and coordination and to manipulate loose parts such as twigs, pine cones, and stones. It also offers chances to negotiate the unique social situations that arise in active play.

A Montreal study of immigrant and refugee children's interactions with nature during a camp experience found that children formed caring responses to nature, were protective of the plants and animals they encountered, and had conversations and friendships with plants and animals (Hordyk et al., 2015). Some children who initially had ambivalent

Figure 10.1. Taking risks outdoors

reactions—for example, to snails and dirt—came to be comfortable and interested in exploring further. The children appeared to relax physically and emotionally in the natural environment of the outdoors. Social and linguistic barriers lessened; aggression and anger diminished. Some children had specific sensory experiences—sounds, tastes, smells, sights— that reminded them of home.

Immigrant children face many stresses as they and their families negotiate a new culture with unfamiliar foods, languages, and institutions. In their study, Hordyk et al. (2015) suggest that the immigrant children who were allowed to develop profound and nourishing relationships with nature found security in those experiences, which helped them foster friendships and express often-difficult emotions.

THREE VOICES ON CHILDHOOD AND NATURE

I grew up on a small farm that was quite isolated. We raised cattle, pigs, and chickens, and of course, we had cats to keep down the mice, and a dog, Tilly. I was the eldest, so it was my job to bring the cows in for milking every evening. Tilly and I would head off through the barnyard in the general direction where we thought we could find them, then listen for the cowbell to locate them exactly. I can still remember what it was like to wind along narrow paths through trees and bush, past spongy swamp areas with marsh marigolds in the slough. I didn't always enjoy this job, especially if it was raining or if the neighbour's bull had gotten loose and was somewhere around, but there was a sense of adventure and certainly of responsibility. Tillie and I were all by ourselves, making our way through the wilderness.

—CLARE, AGE 70

When I was small, we lived on an acreage outside of the city. There were a lot of trees and wild vegetation. I remember catching frogs and climbing trees. One of the things I loved to do was to pack a small lunch and walk down the road half a kilometre or so until I was out of sight of the house. I'd have my picnic and then head back home. I was probably about 5 or 6 at the time. We moved into the city when I was 10. The main reason we moved was that we were driving back and forth every day for school and work, as well as swimming and ballet lessons. It was too busy and we really didn't have a lot of time to be at home.

—TRACEY, AGE 46

I like to go to the park with my mom. My favourite thing is to play on the monkey bars with my friends. And I like playing games and listening to stories on my iPad.

—CAMI, AGE 5

Figure 10.2. The joy of being in nature

Our Disconnect from Nature

Take a look at the three stories above. We selected these stories as a way of illustrating changes over time that theorists believe have served to distance us from nature. These include the move from rural to urban environments, increased vigilance and involvement on the part of parents, the play spaces we provide, and the influence of technology.

Until very recently, many children grew up intimately connected with nature. You can see this in Clare's story, and in Tracey's description of her earliest years. Nature wasn't something that was "out there" but an integral part of their lives. In Tracey's life, however, we see the shift from relaxed explorations of nature to a busy lifestyle that prompted a move to an urban setting.

In Tracey's early memories, we also see a degree of freedom that parents now would be reluctant to permit. White (2006) points to a "culture of fear" in which concerns about safety prevent parents from allowing their children to play outdoors unattended. Louv (2005) cites an American study of how far from home children are allowed to roam on their own. The study showed that by the 1990s, this radius had shrunk to a ninth of what it was in 1970 (cited in Louv, 2005, p. 123). The desire to keep children inside has led to more structured activities that, in turn, cut into the free time that children have to imagine and explore.

The nature of playgrounds is another factor in children's separation from nature. A playground where monkey bars are the main attraction hints at the sterile nature of playgrounds that are built for ease of supervision and without an understanding of children's needs. Both indoor and outdoor environments are highly regulated in order to keep children safe and healthy. For example, health standards for the use of water tables are often so stringent that some educators might limit their use.

In Cami's comments, we see the pervasive influence of technology. Cami may be more likely to be exposed to "nature" on the screen than in the hands-on way that has meaning to young children. Along with distancing her from nature, the time she spends with technology is time that is not available for her to explore the real world.

All of these factors have combined to separate us from the natural world or even, as White (2006) suggests, cause us to fear it. This separation, especially in developmental years, may hinder us from recognizing our dependency on nature or the benefits we can derive from interacting with it.

Fear of Nature

The term *biophobia* refers to a fear of the natural world. There are a number of reasons that parents and children may develop such a fear. Children hear stories about dangerous wild animals or about natural disasters such as earthquakes or floods. Sometimes they mimic adults' fears of spiders, snakes, or worms.

Some fears are realistic and help protect children from danger. We probably don't want young children to be wandering unaccompanied beside a rushing river, for example. It is also important to consider those who have had different experiences of nature than our own. For example, newcomers to Canada may have had previous experiences where "the woods" held genuine danger. They may have come from countries where it was unsafe to play in the dirt or in the water or where there is limited water for drinking and for washing soiled clothes.

Winter may be an unfamiliar experience for newcomers to Canada and may be another cause for fear. They might quite rightly worry about their children's safety in the cold. Educators who come from warm countries may be reluctant to allow children outside in the winter, even though time outside is considered important. Indeed, even parents and educators born and raised in Canada may fear the cold! Early childhood programs can help by ensuring that families know how to dress appropriately for the weather and by organizing clothing exchanges to ensure that families have access to warm clothing. Some centres offer organized winter fun days to introduce families to some of the sports and activities that people enjoy in the winter.

We want children to enjoy and appreciate nature, so it is important to think about how we approach topics of environmental preservation. Research suggests that, while an attachment to the land encourages people to take responsibility for preserving it, children need to build this attachment through personal contact and hands-on experiences. Exposing children to environmental concerns too early, before this attachment has formed, can have a detrimental effect. Because the issues are so complex and abstract, children may tend to be overwhelmed and block them out (Louv, 2005, p. 133).

Indigenous Connectedness with Nature

As we become aware of the devastating effects that human activity is having on the Earth, it seems vitally important that we teach children to love and respect nature. Indigenous worldviews may provide us all with clues as to how we can accomplish that goal in ways that are appropriate to children's development and that won't frighten or immobilize them.

First of all, it's useful to understand that there are fundamental differences between Indigenous and Euro-American ways of looking at the world. Euro-American worldviews tend to see humans as the most important creatures, and the land and its resources as there to serve our needs. In contrast, Indigenous worldviews tend to see all things and creatures, including humans, as equal and related. The land is sacred, and humans have a responsibility to respect and preserve it.

In a presentation at the 2018 conference of the Canadian Association for Young Children, Monique Gray Smith spoke of "weaving" Indigenous ways into the curriculum. She suggested very simple ways to teach children to respect the land, the water, and the air, which are sacred elements in Indigenous teachings. Let's take a look at how ECE Alexis integrates these ideas into her playroom:

> Alexis points out that wholeness with nature is part of her Indigenous identity: "The land and sea, and the creatures in it, are a part of who we are. We are connected to all of nature and feel that we have a responsibility to look after it," she explains. You can see this ethic reflected in Alexis's playroom as the children carefully empty any water left in their glasses after lunch into the plants in the room and compost the food that's left on their plates.

We can help children connect with the land by spending as much time as possible outside with them. When children can be outside in bare feet, they can feel connected to the earth. Alexis's practice of encouraging children to use the water they don't drink to water the plants is one way to show respect for water. We can also play with water in ways that

Figure 10.3. A provocation with moss and yarrow

are respectful, perhaps by using natural materials and vessels to see the movement of the water and its properties. The air is a third element of nature that we can consider. Monique Gray Smith (2018) describes storytelling as "the gift of the wind." She suggests that we can help children learn to take deep breaths to gain control in times of stress or high emotion. Starting the day with gratitude and breath is centering and relaxing.

It seems that one of the ways we can help children learn to value nature is to slow down and appreciate it ourselves. When we see humans and nature as interdependent, we can value the gifts that it offers and convey that appreciation to children.

Helping Children Connect with Nature

As we have seen, giving children opportunities to experience and care for nature has many benefits. Nature or forest schools are built upon this premise. However, many of our early childhood programs lack access to natural spaces, so we need to be creative in building opportunities to connect with nature.

First of all, we can take stock of what is around us. Do birds fly past, or bees buzz nearby? These are sounds of nature that children can be encouraged to notice. Perhaps you could involve the children in making a bird feeder or a bee house to encourage these visitors to come by more often. Maybe you can observe an ant hill and research how ants organize their colonies. Worms wiggling through the soil provide the same opportunity. Sometimes it's just a matter of paying attention to the everyday things: the wind blowing through the trees, cloud formations, sunsets.

Here are some other ideas:
- **Adopt a tree** and observe it through its yearly changes. You could document these changes in photographs or drawings.
- **Plant a garden** so that children can have the experience of nurturing plants and seeing them grow to produce food.
- Take the children on expeditions to **pick up trash** in the neighbourhood.
- **Grow herbs indoors** and use them in cooking or to make teas.
- **Care for animals.**
- Provide and read many **books about nature.**
- Carefully and respectfully **observe errant bugs** that stray into the room. (Never reveal your own fear of spiders!)
- **Set up an aquarium** where you watch tadpoles turn into frogs.
- **Hatch chicks or butterflies.**

- **Keep an ant farm.**
- **Listen to nature sounds.**
- **Celebrate International Mud Day** on June 29th.
- **Make compost.**
- **Build a terrarium** in a mason jar or larger container. Add dirt, stones, and small succulents or little ferns.
- **Build a dinosaur habitat** in the dirt.
- **Make mud pie sculptures.**
- **Dig for worms.**
- **Have a treasure hunt** in the dirt. Children can use small shovels to find "treasures" that you've hidden.
- **Make rubbings** of different kinds of bark or of other natural objects.
- **Support collections of natural materials** that children find on the ground (such as rocks, cones, bark, and leaves).
- **Study the parts of a flower,** and explore how seeds spread.
- **Gather seed pods** from plants in the fall, sprout the seeds in wet paper towels, and plant them.
- **Create a creature** from found natural materials. Build a habitat for it.
- **Decorate stones.**
- **Bring natural elements inside.** Water, sand, and dirt can be poured and measured. Snow brought inside offers a sensory experience and also allows children to observe a change of state as it turns into a liquid. You could even go on to boil the water to show how it turns into a gas.
- **Freeze blocks of ice** in ice cream pails. Colour the water with paint or food colouring, if you like. Use the blocks of ice to build a structure outside.
- **Freeze objects in ice** for the water table. Children can use tools or utensils to free them, or they can watch them appear as the ice melts.
- **Display objects from nature**—for example, a hornet's nest, feathers, fossils, or a bird's nest. Have microscopes available for close examination. You could include pencils and papers and encourage the children to make drawings. Loose parts such as stones, seashells, leaves, twigs, and pine cones can be displayed in baskets and made available to use.
- **Display artwork or artifacts from tree branches** suspended from the ceiling.

Figure 10.4. A hands-on experience with nature

Encourage children to think of themselves as scientists. Make sure that they have magnifying glasses, cameras, pencils, and paper to explore closely and document their findings. Teach them to observe carefully and keep notes about what they see. Ask questions that invite them to observe and share their observations.

||||||||||||||||||||||||||||||||||||||||||||||||||||||||||||||||||||||||||||||||||||||||||||||||||||||||||||||||||||||||||||||||||||||||||||||||||||||

TAKEAWAYS

Children may not spend as much time in nature as they once did, but connection with nature is very important to their physical and emotional well-being. Moreover, children learn to respect and care for nature when they have the time and opportunity to have intimate, hands-on experiences with it. There are many things we can do—indoors and out—to help them learn to be comfortable in nature and to take care of it. Our own appreciation and enthusiasm will be key elements in determining children's attitudes and engagement.

||||||||||||||||||||||||||||||||||||||||||||||||||||||||||||||||||||||||||||||||||||||||||||||||||||||||||||||||||||||||||||||||||||||||||||||||||||||

REFLECTION AND DISCUSSION

- What experiences did you have in nature when you were a child? What sights, sounds, and smells do you remember? What was your favourite thing to do outside? What part does nature play in your life now?

- What are some things you can bring from your own experiences in nature to your work with children? Consider both indoor and outdoor experiences.

PART IV

Supporting Creativity, Literacy, and Inquiry Skills

11

Supporting Creative Expression

I really love being human. But some
days I really wish I could be a fairy.
—GRETA, AGE 4

LEARNING OUTCOMES
After reading this chapter, you will be able to answer these questions:
- What are some ways that children can express
  their thoughts and learning?
- How can we encourage creative expression through visual
  arts, music and dance, construction, and dramatic play?

Introduction
Children are naturally creative, and they express their creativity in many different ways. In this chapter, we will explore creative expression through visual arts, movement and music, and dramatic play. We'll look at the value of such play and how we can support it through the materials and experiences we provide and the ways in which we, as educators, respond to children's creative efforts.

DEVIN BUILDS A CABIN
One summer, my husband and I worked with our daughter and her husband to build a cabin near the mountains. Our grandson Devin was 3 years old at the time, and he was with us for the whole process. We

slept in tents, cooked and ate outside, and worked from dawn to dusk on the building.

Devin watched intently as the concrete was poured and levelled, as the walls went up, and as his dad nailed down the roof sheathing. Devin had various construction toys, a pile of dirt that he called his "recycling plant," and odds and ends of lumber to play with. When his great-gramma visited, they collaborated to build a fort around her chair.

Despite a few bumps, it was a glorious summer. Toward the end of August, Devin began to construct his own cabin. He levelled the ground with his toy grader and poured "concrete." His dump truck hauled odds and ends of lumber that would make the walls. Then he was stuck. "What can I use for a roof?" His grandpa found him a piece of plywood that was about the right size and he placed it on top of the structure. "There, it's done," Devin said. "Let's go home."

In building his cabin, it seemed like Devin was expressing everything he'd experienced and learned in an eventful summer. His other message seemed pretty clear, too: "Okay, I've had enough."

Figure 11.1. Devin builds a cabin

Self-Expression as Creative Expression

Loris Malaguzzi said, "A child has a hundred languages" (Malaguzzi, cited in Edwards et al., 2012, p. 3). By this, he meant that children have

? WHAT DO YOU THINK?

Chapter 8 listed some of the things that children can learn from their experiences with art and block-building (p. 106). What do you think Devin might have been learning as he built his cabin?

many ways of expressing themselves beyond just speaking. Dance, painting, music, construction, writing, drawing, and dramatic play can all be ways for children to communicate their feelings and experiences. In the process, they are thinking, solving problems, and trying new ways of doing and seeing things. They are enhancing their confidence, improving their motor skills, and developing concentration and focus. They are using their senses to learn about their environment and connect ideas. If they are with other children in a creative environment, they can be learning valuable social skills.

WHAT DO YOU THINK?

We live in a world of constant and rapid change—technological, climactic, political, and more. Given the unpredictability of the future, what skills and qualities do you think are important for children to develop? What is the place of imagination and innovation in these skills?

Every child is born with imagination and creativity. Children are innovators, experimenters, and inquirers. Jean Piaget and Loris Malaguzzi both pointed out the challenge of hanging onto these qualities as we get older. Even Pablo Picasso, recognized as one of the most creative minds in Western culture, recognized the difficulty of keeping creativity alive! The question is, How can we, as ECEs, provide opportunities for children to express their creativity? Moreover, how can we encourage them to do so?

Other parts of this book provide tips to encourage imagination and exploration. Chapter 9, for example, discusses the importance of creating wonder in child care environments. Chapter 10 talks about extending this wonder and exploration by creating connections with the natural world. Chapter 12 shows that books and storytelling play a critical role in sparking children's imaginations, and Chapter 13 looks at how math and science explorations depend on curiosity and risk-taking. This chapter also focuses on imagination and exploration, and developing these skills through self-expression in the visual arts, music and movement activities, and dramatic play.

Visual Arts

Many of the activities that we do with children fall into the category of visual arts: drawing, painting, photography, sculpting with playdough and other materials, making collages, and constructing with recycled and found materials, to name a few. All of these activities allow children to express themselves creatively as long as the activities meet a few criteria:

- **There is no right or wrong way.** Probably many of us have had the experience of trying to reproduce a piece of art or a craft so that it looks exactly like the one the instructor made. We've also probably had the experience, in such a situation, of feeling frustrated and dissatisfied with our efforts and ourselves. We may even have decided that we never want to try again. As adults, we might be realistic about our abilities and understand that it takes practice, not to mention dexterity, to create a product similar to that of someone more experienced. Children, however, might not have that perspective and may become discouraged about their abilities. Open-ended art experiences—that is, experiences in which children have control over the materials they use and how to use them—support children's creativity, autonomy, and decision-making.
- **The results are original and unique.** If all of the art pieces basically look alike, the children are expressing the adult's ideas, not their own. This might be the place to mention colouring books and sheets: People often defend these activities because they are calming and help to develop fine motor control. However, colouring sheets allow little opportunity for creative expression. In fact, the adult-drawn, cartoon-style pictures in colouring books may inhibit children's artistic development because they feel they should draw in the same simplistic way.
- **The child is able to work independently.** If the activity requires a great deal of adult preparation or assistance, it usually offers little opportunity for children to express their creativity. Avoid any activities that take longer for the adult to prepare than they do for the child to complete, and activities that require constant adult attention to complete.
- **The child initiates and directs the activity.** When the child takes control of the activity, they are able to express their own ideas and feelings. Adults can learn a great deal about the children by observing these self-directed activities.
- **The important thing is the process and experience.** For young children, especially, the end product is not as important as what it was like to do the activity. Rather than asking, "What did you make?" we should ask, "How did you make it?" or just describe what we see.

Supporting Visual Art

Beautiful environments with lots of materials will spark creativity; painting, drawing, modelling materials, and loose parts can be attractively arranged in ways that make them inviting for all children. Well-chosen art pieces from various cultures can add to the environment. Similarly, books with beautiful illustrations can add wonder and provide inspiration. You can also encourage visual art by inviting local artists to paint or sculpt with the children. Maybe your families include artists or have links to artists in the community.

Art centres need to be set up differently for different ages of children:

- **Infants** will probably not have a permanent centre; their materials will be brought out when they are needed and stored out of reach when not in use.
- **Toddlers** might have some materials, like crayons and paper, available to choose and use independently. For safety reasons, materials like markers, preschool scissors, and paint might be stored out of reach and taken out as needed. Toddlers can be encouraged to put their materials away once they are finished.
- **Preschoolers and older children** can have centres with many more materials. These will be accessible to all children, and children will be expected to put their materials away once they are finished with them.

As an educator, your role in supporting children's visual art creation will include the following:

- **Make sure that children have enough time for creating.** If they don't have a chance to finish, find a way to preserve their work for later.
- **Make sure that there is a good supply of materials.** You could rotate them regularly to keep children interested.
- **Show interest in what children are doing.** By observing them carefully, you'll learn about their interests, thinking, and abilities.
- **Assist them,** but only if they ask and only to the extent necessary. When a child asks you to draw something for them, you can tactfully remind them that it's their work that is important.
- **Help them with drying and display,** as necessary.
- **Be respectful of their work.** If you need to write their name on their creations, ask where they would like it (e.g., on the back or front of a drawing or painting.) If you would like to display it, or cut it into a shape to fit with a display, ask for their permission.

Adventures with Paint

Paint is paint is paint, right? Wrong. There are many ways to be creative with paints, surfaces, brushes, and other implements that can diversify

Figure 11.2. A provocation for collage with fabric and paper scraps

and enhance children's creative expression. For instance, by adding different materials to paints, you can create unique experiences that engage all of a child's senses. Table 11.1 offers some suggestions for additions to paint and the effects these additions create.

There are also so many different things to paint, and so many different ways to paint them. Beyond the traditional paper and paint brushes, there are all sorts of surfaces and implements that children can use to paint (Table 11.2).

Practical Considerations

- Be sure to check the safety of all the materials you use. Read the labels carefully.
- Consider allergies and sensitivities. Children may need to wear plastic gloves if materials irritate their hands.
- Dust and fumes from art materials can pose inhalation risks. Choose dustless chalk, liquid or premixed tempera, oil-based pastels, and water-based paints, markers, and adhesives.
- Ensure that children wash their hands after using craft materials.

Table 11.1. Materials to Add to Paint to Create Different Sensory Experiences

MATERIAL	WHAT DOES THIS INGREDIENT DO TO THE PAINT?	WHAT KIND OF SENSORY EXPERIENCE DOES THIS PROVIDE?
Sand	Makes paint gritty	Tactile
White glue	Dries shiny	Visual Tactile (feels smooth)
Essences & extracts*	Smells good	Olfactory
Dish liquid	Helps in cleanup	Olfactory (may add scent)*
Corn starch Wallpaper paste	Thickens paint	Tactile
Add primary colours to each other	Mixing paints creates other colours	Visual (chromatic)†
Add white paint to colour	Mixing paints creates different intensities of colour	Visual (chromatic)†
Water	Thins paint (e.g., for use in a salad spinner)	Visual
Shaving cream* and glue	Makes puff paint	Tactile Olfactory (if shaving cream is scented)
Cold cream	When mixed with powdered tempera paint, makes face paint	Tactile
Baby oil	Marbles paint	Visual

* Be aware of scent allergies and sensitivities.

† Also teaches the science concept of change.

- Be aware that small collage materials and loose parts could pose a choking hazard for some children.
- If necessary, you can use old short-sleeved shirts for paint smocks.
- Avoid using glitter. Children love it, but scientists and doctors point out that it is harmful to children's eyes and skin and pollutes the environment.

Loose Parts

As mentioned in Chapter 9, loose parts are collections of intriguing found, collected, and recycled materials that children can move, combine, line

Table 11.2. Different Painting Surfaces and Implements

PAINTING SURFACES		PAINTING IMPLEMENTS	
• Pieces of cardboard	• CDs	• Straws (i.e., for blow paint)	• Cotton swabs and balls
• Big boxes	• Milk cartons	• Eye droppers	• Plastic mesh
• Shoe boxes	• Tiles	• Kitchen implements	• Dandelion heads
• Paper towel rolls	• Roll ends	• Basting brushes	• Marbles
• Mirrors	• Paper mâché creations	• Paint rollers of all sizes	• Golf balls
• Acrylic sheets	• Clay creations	• Toothbrushes	• Salad spinners
• Overheads	• Egg cartons	• Fall leaves (once they are off the tree)	• Record players
• Plastic shower curtains	• Baby food jars	• Pine cones	• Sponges
• Pieces of cloth	• Paper plates	• Potato mashers	• Chopsticks
• Windows	• Rocks	• Popsicle sticks	• Fly swatters
• Bed sheets	• Wooden picture frames	• Rolling pins with fun shapes glued to them	• Feathers
• Canvas	• Wooden shapes	• Bath puffs	• Strings of beads
• Denim	• Bodies and faces	• Bubble wrap	• Spray bottles
• Tree stumps	• T-shirts		• Spoons
• Tree "cookies" / round circles of wood	• Shells		• Pipe cleaners bent into shapes
• Sticks	• Tin foil		• String
• Styrofoam pieces	• Acetate		• Fingers
			• Feet
			• Corks

up, and use in multiple ways. They provide opportunities for inquiry, innovation, and creativity. They also invite children to test their theories (e.g., about balancing or sorting items) and show educators what children know (e.g., perhaps they arrange blocks and small cardboard boxes to represent the bus shelters and buildings on their bus route to their child care centre). Because many loose parts are often recycled items, they also promote sustainability, are economically feasible, and can be provided in abundance—an added bonus when budgets for play materials are strained. Many loose parts are objects from nature, so they add the richness of the outdoors. Loose parts promote children's development across domains as they are shared, manipulated, described, and organized.

When loose parts are added to the art centre, they spark many possibilities. Moreover, since they do not have a prescribed use, loose parts are open-ended and can be used successfully by all children, encouraging problem-solving, creativity, and divergent thinking (Daly & Beloglovsky, 2015).

Figure 11.3. A collection of loose parts

Table 11.3 shares some suggestions of what to add to your loose parts collection. Of course, the size of materials is an important safety consideration because young children explore their world by putting things in their mouths. It is also important to pay attention to which materials actually spark children's interest.

Table 11.3. Recycled and Foraged Loose Parts

RECYCLED OBJECTS	OBJECTS FROM NATURE
• Boxes of different sizes	• Rocks
• Jars, containers, and lids	• Shells
• Buttons	• Beach glass
• Fabrics	• Plants
• Cardboard rolls (wrapping paper, food wrap; not toilet paper rolls because of sanitation concerns)	• Feathers
	• Tree cookies
	• Acorns
• Paint sample chips	• Seed pods
• Pompoms	• Pine cones of various sizes
• Beads	• Sticks and twigs
• Spools	
• Nuts and bolts	
• Corks	
• Bottle caps	
• Bread tags	
• Yarn and string	

Music and Movement

Children have an inherent affinity for music and movement. If you've spent time with infants, you have probably noticed that even from just a few months of age, they will respond to music by bouncing their bodies, banging objects, and clapping. Meanwhile, parents seem to know instinctively that music can soothe and calm their babies; they rock them and sing to them when they are distressed.

Movement has been called the first language of childhood because it allows children to express their feelings and ideas, explore their surroundings, develop body awareness, and learn to control their bodies. When movement is set to music, as it is in dance, it teaches children to listen carefully and to be aware of the space that they and others occupy. They learn useful lessons about motion and stillness.

Music supports young children's cognitive, motor, and emotional development. It is closely connected to language development, helping them learn the sounds and meanings of words. Children can learn about cultures through their exposure to different kinds of music. Perhaps most importantly, music can affect their mood, bringing them joy when they are feeling down, and calming them when they are anxious.

Even if you don't feel particularly confident about your abilities in music and movement, there are many things you can do to support children's development in those areas. These are critical avenues for children's creativity and self-expression, and it's very important that they are included in each day.

THE ROUND DANCE

When Francine, an ECE who is Cree, introduced a small group of toddlers to round dancing, she noticed Destiny's confidence in showing other children what to do. Destiny smiled as she grabbed Francine's and another child's hand when the music began. Her family was proud that Destiny had led the other children; they did not realize how much she had learned from attending powwows with them.

Supporting Music and Movement

Music can be built into routines so that children know they can expect music at certain points in the day. This may be classical music played at sleep time or a circle in the late afternoon where children sing familiar songs or explore beat by clapping or using simple instruments.

Music and movement don't, however, have to occur as a scheduled part of the day. Spontaneous activities are often the best: perhaps an educator begins to sing an improvised song about something that is happening in the classroom, and the children join in with their own additions. Maybe, in the story above, an educator could bring out a drum to support Destiny's round dance. A child may begin to sing while they are rolling out playdough and, because other children know the song, they join in. An educator may sing and dance playfully with an infant in her arms.

Table 11.4 offers suggestions of how to support music and movement in your playroom.

Dramatic Play

Dramatic play, also known as pretend play, occurs when children take on roles and act them out. They pretend to be something or someone different from themselves and act out the situations and feelings of their characters.

Vygotsky believed that dramatic play was fundamental to cognitive development, involving both memory and attention (1978). Dramatic play allows children to

- Form relationships with others
    › They learn to regulate their emotions in order to coordinate with others and make plans.
    › They learn to consider other perspectives and negotiate and resolve conflicts.
- Sort through difficult emotions by playing out situations that have been upsetting or traumatic
- Develop language skills as children need to communicate with others
    › Taking on a role can sometimes encourage a shy child to speak with others.
- Develop literacy skills as they play out scenarios they have invented (narrative skills) or have heard about from books
- Develop math skills, for example, when totalling up the bill in restaurant or grocery store play

Supporting Dramatic Play

Children's dramatic play tells us about their understanding and their experiences in the world. When they pretend to be medical personnel, truck drivers, teachers, and cashiers, they demonstrate what they know

Table 11.4. Activities to Support Music and Movement

USE SONGS AND MOVEMENT IN GAMES AND ROUTINES	EXPLORE INSTRUMENTS AND SOUND
• Encourage children to use songs and stories as a basis for dramatic play. • Use a song to signal routines such as cleanup time. • Sing songs that allow you to insert children's names in them. • Sing your own silly made-up songs as you move through the day, or make up lyrics to familiar songs. • Collect singing games to play with the children. • Do silly dances with the children. • Encourage children to make up their own songs and rhymes. • To add to movement experiences, provide materials like ribbons, streamers, scarves, hoops, and wristbands.	• Make instruments with the children (e.g., drums out of coffee cans, rattles from two paper plates stapled together). • If possible, have an assortment of rhythm instruments in the room. Xylophones, triangles, and conga drums are fun for children to play. • Encourage children to compare the sounds that different objects make when they hit them with a stick.
INVITE GUESTS TO SHARE MUSIC	**EXPLORE DIFFERENT KINDS OF MUSIC**
• Invite musicians to come to the classroom. Ideally, these would be individuals who would communicate with the children at their level, demonstrate the sounds that their instruments make, and so on. • In some cultures, children are given name songs that tell about their family's hope and dreams for their future. Ask your families about this and if they and their children would be willing to share their song with the group. • Invite families to come to the program to teach children a song in their first language. • Encourage educators to teach children songs in their home language.	• Play various genres of music. Soothing classical music is especially nice at sleep time. • Play music from different cultures; you could ask the families to contribute their favourite pieces. • Encourage educators to teach children songs in their home language.

about different roles in society. When they "cook" in the house area, they show us what they know about food preparation. Their domestic play tells us, sometimes to the chagrin of their families, about their lives at home. By paying attention to their dramatic play, we learn how to best support children and their play.

RETHINKING DRESS-UP CLOTHES

In our attempts to transform our playrooms to reflect the cultures of children, families, and educators in the playrooms, we were faced with a dilemma related to dress-up clothes. We noticed that many of the multicultural dress-up clothes available in child care supply catalogues reinforced cultural stereotypes and were meant for a single purpose; often we could not find anything that related to the backgrounds of our families. So, instead of purchasing commercial dress-up clothes, we opted to provide a variety of textiles that children can use to create capes and shawls, saris, sarongs, and *lungis*, as well as head coverings of all sorts. Lengths of cloth can be fashioned as dress-up clothes for children of any size and shape—and for educators as well! They can be used to wrap and carry babies and adorn a tabletop. The addition of accessories such as jewelry, satchels, bags, and purses, often sourced from our staff and families, rounds out the collection of dramatic play clothes we provide to children.

Here are some ways to encourage dramatic play:

- **Provide enough time** for scenarios to develop.
- **Provide props** that children can use for dress-up. These should include items that represent the ethnicities of the families and educators (who may also be happy to donate these).
- **Display dress-up props** in an attractive and organized manner, and encourage children to put them back where they belong.
- Be prepared to **facilitate the play** if you see that it could be extended with particular props or if the children seem unable to negotiate a conflict. Be careful, though, to give children enough time to work through problems and situations on their own. Sometimes you might tactfully join in as a play partner if the play is stalled or if it seems worthwhile to introduce a new idea.
- **Ask open-ended questions** about the play, such as, "What do you suppose would happen if the zookeeper forgot to lock the cages and all the animals got out?"

Provide as many experiences as you can to give children ideas for their play. These can include field trips in the community or building, stories

Figure 11.4. "Carrying my baby"

or books, or bringing in guests to dance, play music, or do other activities with the children.

Respecting Children's Creative Efforts

Educators are significant people in children's lives, and the way we respond to their creative efforts gives them important messages about their efforts and abilities. Suppose, for example, that you are 4 years old. You have just spent quite a lot of time working on a painting. You used a lot of different colours, and you feel good about how it turned out.

When you are finished, you bring it to an adult and ask, "Do you like my painting?"

Maybe the adult stops what they are doing and looks carefully at your painting. They might notice the way you used your brush to create certain effects or comment on all the different colours you used. Perhaps they ask if you are satisfied with how the painting turned out. This is descriptive feedback.

On the other hand, the adult might praise your work. They might say, "Yes, it's beautiful" or "You're such a good painter!" or, if they are especially busy, just "Nice!" If you are the child in this situation, what message might you take from each of these kinds of responses? Table 11.5 shows some possible interpretations.

Which of these kinds of responses do you think would be the most likely to encourage your creativity? Which would tell you that the adult

Table 11.5. Possible Interpretations of Praise Versus Descriptive Feedback

PRAISE	WHAT A CHILD MIGHT THINK OR FEEL
That's beautiful. Nice! You're such a good painter!	• They like my picture. • Since they like this picture, I'll make my next one just like it. • It's important to please adults. • All my paintings had better be good or they'll think I'm not a good painter.
DESCRIPTIVE FEEDBACK	**HOW A CHILD MIGHT THINK OR FEEL**
I notice that you used your brush to make little swirls in this corner. Can you show me how you did that?	• I made swirls with my brush. I wonder what other effects I could create with the brush.
You were painting for a long time and you added lots of details. (ECE points out some of the features.)	• When I work carefully, I get a result I'm happy with. • I'll try taking more time with my other work.
I notice that you used yellow here and blue beside it. When they mixed together, they made a different colour.	• I made green! I wonder what other colours I can make by mixing colours together.
I think this is the biggest painting you've ever made!	• The adult pays attention to my work!

is deeply interested in your work? Which would encourage you to experiment further?

Praise sends a message to children that adult approval is more important than their own satisfaction. This focus on adult approval tells them that their worth depends on whether they please adults. The result is an ongoing search for adult validation. It limits their creativity by encouraging them to stick to their tried-and-true formula rather than trying new ways to express themselves. It sends a message that it is the product, rather than the process, that is important. It may also imply that success is tied to talent; either you have talent or you don't.

While praise teaches children to rely on external validation, descriptive feedback teaches them to look inside themselves for motivation, purpose, and direction. It encourages them to express themselves by taking creative risks, and it suggests that success results from ongoing efforts and experimentation. To give descriptive feedback, we as educators have to truly pay attention. This shows children that we take their work seriously and that we genuinely respect them and their efforts.

Psychologist Carol Dweck's (2006) work supports the importance of providing descriptive feedback. Her message to parents is equally valuable for educators:

> If parents want to give their children a gift, the best thing they
> can do is to teach their children to love challenges, be intrigued
> by mistakes, enjoy the effort and keep on learning. That way,
> their children don't have to be slaves of praise. They will
> have a lifelong way to build and repair their own confidence.
> (pp. 176–77)

TAKEAWAYS

Children can express their feelings, their creativity, and their understandings through their creative activity in visual arts, movement and music, and dramatic play. As educators, we can facilitate these activities by providing time, space, and materials, as well as through our observation, descriptive feedback, and tactful participation.

REFLECTION AND DISCUSSION

- What creative activities did you enjoy as a child? Do you think these activities would work well in a modern child care context?

- How do you express yourself creatively now as an adult? What function does creativity serve in your adult life?

- Challenge yourself to find a craft
  project online or in a book. Evaluate the activity as to the opportunities it provides for children
  to be creative, make decisions,
  and complete it in their own way.
  How could you adapt this craft to
  be a more creative experience for
  young children?

12

Supporting Language
and Literacy

You are never too old, too wacky, too wild
to pick up a book and read to a child.
—DR. SEUSS

llllllllllllllllllllllllllllllllllllllllllllllllllllllllllllllllllllllllllllllllllllllllllllllllllllllllllllllllllllllllllllll

LEARNING OUTCOMES

After you have read this chapter, you will be able to answer these questions:

- How do young children's language skills develop?
- What are ways to support young children's
  language and literacy development?
- Why is it important to encourage home language?
- Why is language significant to the culture and
  identity of Indigenous Peoples in Canada?

Introduction

Communication is the process by which we send and receive messages. It allows us to exchange information and build relationships. We communicate in many ways: through speech, expressions, and actions; through writing, art, and music. In this chapter, though, we'll focus on language as an instrument for communication and on literacy as the ways in which language is used to communicate through speaking, reading, and writing.

Although we communicate in many ways, the ability to speak, read, and write effectively is highly valued in our society and is basic to school success. Parents are understandably anxious for their children to learn these skills, and ECEs are sometimes at a loss to explain to parents why they are not focusing more on academics and are instead allowing children to "just play."

Once you recognize children's emerging language and literacy skills—including in their play—you can respond to them in ways that are natural and appropriate to each child. This also allows you to provide useful information to families about their children's literacy development and the ways that you are facilitating it.

This chapter also addresses the context of language learning in Canada, where almost 8 million Canadians have a first language other than French or English and over 200,000 people speak one or more of 70 Indigenous languages (Statistics Canada, 2017). This context makes it important to understand the value and significance of supporting families in retaining or reclaiming their home languages.

How Does Language Develop?

What does language development look like? If we were to peek into a playroom at a child care centre, here are some things we might see:

> As Aisha changes his diaper, baby Anthony watches her face attentively, kicks his legs, and babbles excitedly. Aisha mirrors his excitement by widening her eyes, smiling, and mimicking his sounds.
>
> While Carmen helps Anthony get dressed to go outside, she describes each step, "Now I'll put your arm in the sleeves. And now I'll fasten the buttons."
>
> Sofia and her friend Neelam have built a tower of blocks. "Wow! Look how big it is!" Sofia exclaims. "It's higher than the stool."
>
> In the cozy reading area, four children are cuddled with Merak reading a book about space. As they read, the children discuss the pictures, turn back to previous pages, and consider possibilities for the spaceship they plan to create.

Looking at these communication examples, we see a number of different strategies and stages of communication. For example, we can see a lovely example of "serve-and-return" in Aisha's interactions with baby Anthony. He is learning how conversations work: that people take turns with speaking and listening. As we have already seen, these responsive interactions are also critical for brain development and relationship building. Language development begins very early in life; in fact, some research claims that it begins before birth when the fetus begins to recognize their mother's voice and speech patterns. Babies are usually able to understand before they can speak. In the period before they can express themselves in words, they use gestures and vocalizations to make their needs and interests known. When Anthony is hungry, he will probably cry; when he wants to be picked up, he might raise his arms to Aisha.

As children get older, they begin to communicate with words instead of gestures. Usually, children say their first words when they are between 9 and 18 months old. Interestingly, in any language the first words that children speak usually refer to their mother or father. Carmen tells Anthony what she is doing as she helps him dress so he won't be taken by surprise, but she is building his vocabulary at the same time.

Children learn new vocabulary and begin to make more complex sentences until, by age 4 or 5, most communicate easily with other children and adults. This means that they can learn concepts and vocabulary from each other as well as from educators. When Sofia comments on the height of the tower that she and Neelam have built, she introduces the useful concept of "higher than."

Children who have been exposed to books from an early age learn to appreciate them as a source of enjoyment and information. Merak encourages the children to use books to inform their spaceship project. By now, these 5- and 6-year-olds are able to "read" the pictures in the book and to recognize some of the words. They are well on the path to literacy.

 GUIDELINES FOR CHOOSING CHILDREN'S BOOKS
These guidelines use an intercultural lens to help you select high-quality books for your playrooms.
- Is the story interesting to children?
  - › Is it appropriate to the children's age and interests?
  - › Does it have an intriguing plot?
  - › Are the characters believable and appealing?
- Is the language rich and evocative?
- Does the story encourage thought and discussion?
  - › Does it give children something to think about or to question?
  - › Does it lead children to appreciate multiple perspectives?
  - › Could it help children cope with a problem or change in their lives?
- Are the illustrations of high quality and appealing?
  - › Do they reflect the plot, characters, and setting?
  - › Are they artistically pleasing?
  - › Are cultural settings shown accurately?

- Does the story counter stereotyping?
  - › Does it show people from various races, ethnicities, ages, genders, abilities, religions, and lifestyles as capable and worthy of respect? (See also Chapter 3 in this volume, "Avoiding Bias in Children's Books," p. 39.)

Tips for Supporting Language Learning

Language development proceeds best in an environment that is rich with language and with warm, attentive interactions. The educator who cuddles and sings to a child who is obviously sleepy, who collaborates

Table 12.1. Strategies for Stimulating Language Development in Different Age Groups

INFANTS AND TODDLERS	PRESCHOOLERS
• Pay attention to them and respond to their verbalizations. • Describe what they are doing and what you are doing: "You're putting the ball in the box." "I'm going to set the table now." • Point to and name things you are both seeing. • Sing to them. Make up songs to signal routines (e.g., "Now it's time to go to sleep…"). Make up silly songs or songs about them (e.g., "Janie has blue eyes, blue eyes, blue eyes. Kazim has brown eyes, brown eyes…") • Read to them. This should happen in an unstructured way; for example, if you go to sit in the reading area with a book at least one child is sure to join you.	• Talk with children about recent events or what they are doing. • Play word games. • Create group stories, where each child contributes a line. • Encourage their participation while you read. • Read a lot, preferably in small groups or one-on-one so that reading is special rather than a whole group activity that they have to do. • Ask open-ended questions that encourage thinking: "What do you think will happen next?" "How could we do this?" • Consciously use new vocabulary in your day-to-day speech.
SCHOOL-AGED CHILDREN	
• Continue to ask questions that encourage thinking and creativity (e.g., "If dogs could talk, what would they say? What would your world be like if you were the size of a pencil?") • Read to them and encourage them to read. • Make up silly songs and rhymes together. • Continue to introduce new vocabulary as part of your natural speech.	

with the children on projects, who ensures that children have access to good quality books and art materials, who makes an attempt to learn phrases in a child's home language, and who consciously introduces new vocabulary is creating an environment where children learn to treasure language and are anxious to learn to read and write.

Table 12.1 offers some ways that we can stimulate language development for different age groups.

Emerging Literacy Skills

Literacy is the ability to read, write, listen, and speak in order to communicate effectively and make sense of the world. As we have seen, these are complex processes that begin early in life. In the stories earlier in this chapter, you see educators developing early literacy skills by talking, reading, singing, and providing opportunities for writing. In this section, we'll look at the specific skills that are a part of emerging literacy and ways that you, as an ECE, can help children build those skills.

Emerging literacy skills include the following:

- Motivation to read
- Sound awareness
- Print awareness
- Book awareness
- Alphabet knowledge
- Oral language skills

Motivation to Read

> Three-year-old Stefan approaches Jasmine, an ECE, bearing his favourite story about robots. Jasmine invites him to sit with her in the comfy reading corner, and they are soon joined by two other children. They talk about the pictures and the content and make predictions about what might happen next in the story. Jasmine points to the words as she reads them so the children can see that the print has meaning.

Jasmine is helping to build motivation to read; that is, interest in reading and learning to read. She makes reading a shared and special time. She lets Stefan choose the book he wants to read and is comfortable with other children wandering in and out according to their interest. She draws attention to the print in the book, as well as to other kinds of print in the room. She avoids mandatory, large-group story times, especially with younger children. She makes her reading interesting by using lots of expression and different voices for different characters. Often, she will use finger puppets or flannel board figures to illustrate the story and allow children to reenact it later. Reading becomes a very special activity for these children and they come to understand that reading opens a whole world to them.

Sound Awareness

> The children in the preschool room sing a rhyming song that incorporates their names.

Being aware of sounds is the first step to learning to sound out words. Songs and books that have rhyming patterns, tongue twisters, and games where children name words that begin with the same sound all help to encourage sound awareness.

Print Awareness

> Sofia is painting at an easel. When the ECE, Mateo, asks her about her work, Sofia tells a long story about what is happening in her picture. Mateo asks if she would like him to write the story for her. When she says she would, he asks if he should write it on the bottom of the page or on a separate sheet of paper.

Print awareness is the understanding that print is all around us and has meaning. Some ways to develop print awareness include pointing out letters, spaces, words, and lines of print in books and in the surrounding environment; labelling (or help children label) objects in the room that are important to them; and providing magnetic and other kinds of alphabet letters for children to manipulate. Samples of print in various languages show children not only that print has meaning but that different kinds of print can express the same meaning.

Book Awareness

> A number of board books are arranged on a low shelf. Gemma crawls over and takes out a book. She sits on the floor "reading" it, babbling as she flips the pages.

Gemma is beginning to develop book awareness—that is, an understanding of what a book is, how to hold it, and how to turn pages. Later, educators might begin to point out the parts of the book: the top and bottom of the page, where you begin reading, and the first word. They might also talk about different kinds of books, such as storybooks, poems, and information books.

Alphabet Knowledge

> Chelsea arranges magnetic alphabet letters on a board, naming them as she does so.

Alphabet knowledge refers to knowing the individual letter names, sounds, and shapes. Some ways educators can support alphabet knowledge are by having letter shapes available, pointing out letters in the environment, and singing the ABCs.

Oral Language Skills

> ECE Mya listens attentively as Charlie tells her the story of her weekend adventures.

Oral language skills include the ability to listen, share knowledge, describe things and events, and tell stories. Encouraging storytelling, engaging in conversations, modelling correct language use, and asking questions are some ways to encourage oral language skills.

Developing Writing Skills

> Three children have built a complex block structure. You notice that the two sides of the centre arch are symmetrical and that there is a ramp leading up to it. The children ask for your help to write a "Please don't touch" sign to put on the structure so they can continue work on it tomorrow. You write the words on a separate piece of paper and they copy it onto their sign.

? WHAT DO YOU THINK?

Children begin writing long before entering kindergarten. Try collecting writing samples from children of different ages and then compare them to see how writing skills progress. What do you think you'll find?

Writing is one of the most challenging tasks for children to learn because it requires visual and fine motor skills, as well as certain cognitive skills.

The strategies you use to build language and literacy skills will also support the development of writing skills. These include reading a variety of books, modelling writing, labelling items, and encouraging children to dictate stories to you. As well, you can ensure that children have ready access to writing materials: a variety of kinds and colours of paper and various writing instruments such as crayons, pencils, chalk, and markers.

Figure 12.1. Elena makes a sign

Encouraging Home Language

Steven is a 3-year-old boy in ECE Rita's playroom. Steven's family has just arrived recently to Canada. His family speaks Russian and Yiddish at home, so he does not yet know any English. Fortunately, one of the educators, Rita, comes from Uzbekistan and speaks Russian.

Steven is playing at the sand table and notices a toy scorpion figure. Let's take a closer look at Steven and educator Rita's interaction:

> Steven picks up the scorpion and exclaims, "*Pauk!*" which is the Russian word for spider. Rita responds by saying that it is a "*scorpion*," placing the accent on the last syllable, as that is how it is pronounced in Russian. She then explains in his home language that the word *scorpion* sounds almost the same in Russian as it does in English, but it is a bit different. "Scorpion," repeats Steven with a smile, using the English pronunciation.
>
> Rita notices that Steven is often drawn to the bug and animal figures when he plays. As he is putting them away one day, Rita identifies each in Russian and then adds the English translation. Each time, Steven proudly repeats the new word he has learned.
>
> Steven often asks Rita to read to him, and she does so in both English and Russian. It is not a surprise to her that he has chosen a book about animals today. As they read, he goes to the shelf and picks out a horse

figure, saying, "*U meny loshadka!*" Rita then translates, saying, "I have a horse!" and Steven proudly repeats the word horse.

Rita sees her communications with Steven as a reciprocal dance that is happening in both Russian and English. She knows that supporting his home language will help him as he acquires skills in speaking English.

It must be tremendously comforting to Steven and his parents to have an educator like Rita, who can ease Steven's transition to these new surroundings, new people, and new language. The fact that Rita speaks Steven's home language is a great advantage and points to the benefits of a multicultural workforce in child care.

While it's unlikely that every child and family will find a program where someone speaks their language, Rita's work with Steven still offers lessons that will help us work with children whose home language is different from the dominant language in the child care program.

Building a Relationship

First of all, we can see that Rita is building a relationship with Steven. Their relationship flourishes as Steven feels a sense of security in the child care centre with Rita supporting him; he knows that she is someone who he can count on for care and attention.

We have already seen that a "practice of relationships" is critically important to children's learning and development. The serve-and-return interactions Rita has with Steven strengthen his brain architecture and contribute to his later success in many ways: academic, interpersonal, and emotional.

In addition to building a close relationship, Rita is able to get to know Steven's interests. She builds on his interest in bugs and animals to extend his vocabulary and to provide play opportunities that help Steven form connections with other children. Rita invites other children into their play and translates back and forth so that Steven can begin to develop relationships with children in the playroom. Rita is teaching these children and her teammates some simple words and phrases in Russian so that they can also connect with Steven. Through his interactions with Rita and others, Steven is learning about the conventions of this new language—English—and is acquiring new vocabulary.

While Rita has the advantage of speaking one of Steven's home languages, we have seen that trusting relationships can be built even without the benefit of a shared language. Remember the story of Saroya in Chapter 5 (p. 65)? The educator, Sara, was able to build a bond with Saroya that helped her gradually overcome the trauma of her move to an unfamiliar environment, despite not speaking Saroya's home language.

In a situation where the educator does not speak the home language, they could ask parents or other community members to contribute key phrases to allow them to communicate with the child in their home language. Even better, perhaps the child might be able to teach them some words and phrases in that language. That would be a powerful affirmation of both the language and the child.

Steven's parents have made the decision to only speak Russian with him at home in the interest of giving him a solid foundation in his home language. In the sections that follow, we'll see why this is a wise decision.

Research on Maintaining Home Language

Steven's parents are committed to keeping and strengthening his home languages while he learns English at his child care centre and, later, in school. There are important reasons for this. As a multilingual person, he will be able to travel more easily and connect with new people. He will have an advantage in the job market. When his parents' Russian- and Yiddish-speaking friends come to visit, he can be part of the conversation. Perhaps most importantly, he will be able to stay in touch with his grandparents and other family members. His ability to speak his home languages connects him to his family's culture and contributes to his own cultural identity.

Obviously, there are many benefits to maintaining a child's home language. But are there drawbacks? There is sometimes concern that if children learn to speak their home language, it will stand in the way of their ability to do well in the majority language spoken outside the home. Research shows us that this is not the case; in fact, quite the opposite is true. There are academic, social, and emotional benefits to maintaining a strong foundation in the home language.

Brain research tells us that navigating between two or more languages strengthens parts of the brain that help us solve problems, plan, and multitask. This advantage lasts into our later years: people who are bilingual or multilingual are less likely to suffer from early dementia or Alzheimer disease because they have more cognitive reserves (Baumgart & Billick, 2018). Perhaps this research explains why children who initially learn and maintain their home language tend, in fact, to learn their second language more proficiently and be more successful academically than children who don't have a solid foundation in another language (August & Shanahan, 2010; Barak & Bialystok, 2011; Bialystok, 2006).

After reviewing studies from 25 years of research with about 14,500 participants, De Houwer (2015) concluded that children who do not acquire the language that their parents speak at home may feel embarrassment and shame; those who do acquire their home language have a sense of pride and increased self-esteem. Parents whose children do not, for whatever reason, learn their home language may feel incompetent, guilty, and rejected by their children. Other researchers affirm that maintaining a home language is connected to having a strong sense of identity (Bialystok, 2001). These individuals also derive various benefits being able to connect with their cultural heritage (Eisenchlas et al., 2013).

Finally, we know that programs that support home language acquisition and maintenance increase the status of the language (Baker, 2006) and boost the self-esteem of students who speak that language (Wright & Taylor, 1995). When we acknowledge someone else's language, we are acknowledging them as an individual.

As you can see, there is a great deal of evidence as to the value of a strong first-language foundation to the wellbeing of children and families. What can we do to support this learning?

Implications for Our Work with Children and Families

Many of us don't have the advantage of a second or third language. Still, there are plenty of things we can do to support children and families in the maintenance of their home languages. These include the following:

- Ensuring that parents understand why it is important for children to learn their home language
- Having a family meeting with activities that encourage sharing stories of culture and language (e.g., scrapbooking, puppet making)
- Encouraging family members to come to the program to sing or tell stories in their home language or make an audio or video recording to play for the children
- Asking family or community members if they will add text in their own language to popular children's books to expose children to many different kinds of script
- Asking children and families to teach educators words and phrases in their home language
- Making a collage for the door that has greetings in many different languages

- Learning greetings in different languages represented in the classroom and practising them with the children
- Providing books in more than one language, reading them with children, and teaching each other the words
- Singing songs and playing music from various cultures

You can also support the parents by speaking with them about the importance of maintaining their home language. In situations where each parent speaks a different language, let them know that it's a good idea for them each to speak their own home language with the child (and, if possible, with each other). This helps the child distinguish between the two languages and ensures that they have a good language model for each.

There are benefits for all children in these kinds of activities. For instance, when monolingual children (that is, children who speak one language) are exposed to a number of languages, they learn to be curious about languages and diverse ways of being. They come to understand that concepts can be expressed in more than one way, and they take pride in knowing words from other languages.

FRANCINE USES CREE IN THE PLAYROOM

Francine approaches the mat where Travis is napping and kneels beside the sleeping 3½ year old. All the other children are awake and playing. Travis grunts as she tries to gently rouse him. "*Waniskâ,*" she whispers as she touches his shoulder. "*Waniskâ,* Travis." He slowly opens his eyes and smiles at Francine; she notices that he responds much more positively when she speaks to him in Cree. Another child, Sarah, approaches and mimics Francine, saying, "*Waniskâ,* Travis. Time to wake up." They are creating a playroom community that values and supports differences.

Not only has Francine taught children some key phrases in Cree, but other educators in the room have also learned to greet Travis and his family each morning, saying, "*Tansi!*" and to invite him to lunch with "*Pe mitso,*" ("Come and eat"). Francine's teammates come from Eritrea and Ethiopia and realize how affirming it is to be spoken to in a familiar language; they speak in Tigrinya and Amharic with children who share the same home language as they do and translate what they have said for the other children.

Like Francine, who is Cree and has grown up in the city, Travis's family is also reconnecting with their Indigenous heritage. They have told Francine how much they appreciate that she is speaking Cree with him and that it has prompted them to begin using more Cree at home.

The opportunity to speak her Cree language and share Indigenous traditions in the playroom has been a powerful experience for Francine; she describes it as "opening a closed box" and something that has given her permission to be proud of her heritage. Beyond the impact on Francine, her actions have supported Travis's positive identity formation by validating his Cree roots and have had a positive impact on his language development.

Preserving Indigenous Languages

There are 70 Indigenous languages spoken in Canada, but unfortunately about 40 of these have fewer than 500 surviving speakers. These languages have been lost mainly because of colonial policies such as the Indian Act and residential schools, in which children were punished for speaking their mother tongue (Rice & Gallant, 2020).

Indigenous communities and educational institutions are now taking steps to preserve and revive Indigenous languages. These efforts are being supported by the Indigenous Languages Act tabled by the Government of Canada on February 5, 2019. These initiatives seem to be having some success, since there has recently been a slight increase in the number speakers of Indigenous languages (Rice et al., 2020).

The loss of a language is a sad thing. This is especially true because language is so closely intertwined with culture and identity. When a language is lost, so is much of the culture. Indeed, as philosopher George Steiner's often quoted saying goes, "When a language dies, a way of understanding the world dies with it." Recovering one's heritage language can not only reconnect people with their culture and give them a sense of pride in their history, but also restore diverse ways of seeing the world.

Supporting Language and Literacy Development

Hopefully the examples in this chapter show you many ways to help children build their language and literacy skills. You can see that your work is not about direct instruction—you won't be sitting young children down and having them write letters or match words. Instead, you will be providing a rich literacy environment while carefully observing and assessing children's individual skills and providing just the right prompts or experiences to help them progress.

The concepts of scaffolding and the zone of proximal development (ZPD) developed by Russian psychologist Lev Vygotsky (whom we met in Chapter 8, p. 102) are useful here. The ZPD distinguishes between what a child can do without help and what they can accomplish with competent assistance. Scaffolding occurs within the ZPD as the adult provides successive levels of temporary support so that the child can acquire skills that they couldn't reach without that support. In order to scaffold effectively, then, you need to know what the child is able to do on their own and what they can learn with your help. Let's have a look at how ECE Ellen applies scaffolding in the following situation:

> Ellen is writing a list of needed supplies when Camila brings a paper and pencil and sits beside her. Camila proceeds to fill her paper with wavy lines in a format that looks a lot like Ellen's list. Ellen knows that what Camila is doing is called "mark writing" and guesses that she might be interested in learning to print letters. She shows her how to make the letter *H*. Camila proceeds to fill her paper with *H*s. Later, when Camila's dad comes to pick her up, she runs proudly to show him what she has written.

Ellen noticed Camila's interest, recognized her readiness to learn, and scaffolded her to a next stage.

THE TRADITION AND ART OF STORYTELLING
Storytelling is the gift of the wind.
                          —*MONIQUE GRAY SMITH*

Long before there was writing, there was storytelling. Storytelling was used in every culture as a way to pass down historical and cultural knowledge, to build relationships, to share news, and to entertain. Stories might take the form of myths, fables, prayers, legends, proverbs, or the recounting of events. Often storytelling was used to teach lessons about how to live well as an individual and as a member of a community. For that reason, stories might play an important role in gently molding a child's understanding and behaviour.

Cultures might have traditions about when and how stories are told, and by whom. For example, some stories may be "owned" by certain groups and only told by a member of that group, while others can be told by anyone. There might also be restrictions as to who may listen to the stories; for example, in many Indigenous cultures, stories are considered to be gifts from the speaker to the listener, and some stories will only be shared when there is a relationship of trust and reciprocity (Strigley, 2016).

Certainly, storytelling plays an important role in supporting and transmitting Indigenous culture in Canada. Elders known as Knowledge Keepers are entrusted with responsibility for teaching the values, history, relationships, cultural beliefs, and sacred stories that are integral to Indigenous identity (First Nations Pedagogy, 2009). Stories, along with songs, dancing, drumming, pictographs, medicine wheels, and tipi rings, are valuable records of culture and history (Hanson, 2009).

Listening to a story being told is very different from listening to a story that is read. When children listen to an oral story, they use their imaginations to envision the actions they are hearing about. They have to remember the names of the characters and the action that has gone before. They hear how the plot builds and see how timing, intonation, gestures, and facial expressions can enhance a story.

Learning to tell a story well takes thought and practice but will be satisfying for both you and the children. Think about a story you love and work to make it into a compelling story to tell. Maybe you could use props like puppets, flannel board figures, stuffed animals, or appropriate household items to add interest.

Check out storytelling resources online or in your community. You might even take a storytelling course. Storytelling will build your confidence, enhance your relationships with children, and connect you to an ancient tradition that has had deep meaning throughout the ages.

TAKEAWAYS

Children develop their skills for speaking, reading, and writing in environments that are rich with language: where adults read and sing and talk with them, where they are listened to, where they are encouraged to be curious and think creatively, where their home languages are valued and supported, and where there are many opportunities to express themselves in many different ways.

Children develop their language and literacy skills at their own pace and in their own ways. Knowing the characteristics of emerging skills can help you to identify and support children's literacy interests and abilities.

REFLECTION AND DISCUSSION

- How might you respond to a parent who asks that you do literacy worksheets with their 4-year-old child for 20 minutes every day?

- Imagine you're observing a playroom at a child care centre. During the daily circle time, several of the toddlers show no interest and have to be strongly encouraged to sit and listen. What is wrong with this picture?

- How could you respond to a parent who asked you if they should speak their home language with their child? (Try role-playing this so you can be really comfortable if that discussion happens.)

13

Supporting Inquiry Skills

The important thing is not to stop questioning.
Curiosity has its own reason for existence.
—ALBERT EINSTEIN

||||||||||||||||||||||||||||||||||||||||||||||||||||||||||||||||||||||||||||||||||||||||||||||||||||||||||||||||||||||||||||||||

LEARNING OUTCOMES

When you have read this chapter, you will be able to answer these questions:
- What do we mean by inquiry skills?
- What part do inquiry skills play in science, social studies, and math?
- How can you, as an ECE, support children in developing inquiry skills?
- What do we mean by numeracy?
- What are some ways that you can help children develop numeracy skills?

Introduction

We learn by asking questions and being curious about the world. Young children are naturally curious and we, as educators, can support their learning by encouraging their curiosity and helping them find ways to explore their interests. Inquiry skills are the basis for learning in science, social studies, and math, among other subject areas.

Math learning plays an important role in the early years. This chapter explores the role of numeracy in our lives and the lives of children and the ways that we, as educators, can support children's numeracy skill development by nurturing inquiry skills.

"WHY DOES IT DO THAT?"

In the corner of the child care play yard, ECE Bejuna and several 4-year-olds are working on a small patch of earth, creating a garden. They have been digging up the dirt and are just about to begin planting. Jeremy finds an earthworm, and the other children gather around to examine it.

"What is it?"

"Where does it live?"

"What does it eat?"

"Will it hurt me?"

"Why is it that colour?"

Jeremy pokes at the worm gently with his finger, and it seems to shrink. "Look, it's getting smaller! Why does it do that?" he asks. Bejuna nods, adding, "I wonder how it does that!"

Bejuna asks the children if they have any ideas about how they can find some of the answers to their questions.

"We can look in a book," Henry suggests.

"We can Google it," says tech-savvy Tomas.

"My dad knows about worms," says Rahid.

"Let's look at it with the magnifying glass," Pria says, and proceeds to pull the magnifying glass from the bin of tools they've brought to the garden. "We can observe it."

Back in the playroom, Bejuna suggests that they might want to draw pictures of the worm showing what they observed. Several of the children embark enthusiastically on this task, while Henry searches through the book area to see if he can find any information on worms. When Henry runs out of books, Bejuna arranges for another educator to supervise while she and Henry go to the centre's library to find more.

When a child appears stuck, Bejuna asks questions, offers suggestions, and helps out only as needed. A few of the children maintain their strong interest throughout the project. Others pursue other interests or drop in from time to time.

Later on, the children discuss what they have found out. Those who have drawn pictures show them to the group and describe what they have drawn. Ema has even found a creative way to show the worm shrinking. Someone suggests that maybe they could measure the worm before and after it gets smaller. The book answers some of their questions, but they decide they should go back to the garden to observe the worm some more. "And we should take pictures of it!" exclaims Natalie. They will see if Rahid's dad might be willing to come and talk with them about worms.

Bejuna suggests they put together a display of their pictures along with some photos and stories they have dictated about their worm investigations. They decide to add to their display as they learn more.

Supporting Inquiry: The Importance of Asking Questions

Inquiry is about asking questions and is the basis for our learning. Children begin using inquiry skills from the moment they are born; they explore their environment in order to make sense of the world around them. When 4-month-old Evan is finally able to grab the shape on his mobile, he is able to explore the questions that have been in his mind, even if he doesn't yet have language for them: What is this? What does it feel like? Can I taste it? When he is older, he will be able to express his wonderings in words: Why are the rabbits changing colour? What would happen if we mixed all of the colours together?

Children take an active role in developing their understanding of the world and how things work. They learn best through physical and mental activity: when they work things out on their own and interact with others rather than receiving and carrying out explicit instruction. They explore, interact, and inquire.

As an ECE, you can support this process of inquiry in many ways:

- Providing an environment and experiences that provoke wonder
- Modelling curiosity and showing interest
- Resisting the urge to provide children with answers
- Asking questions that might encourage curiosity and exploration

In the story above, the children in Bejuna's playroom are learning quite a bit about worms. Bejuna supports, but doesn't dictate their inquiry. She is aware that creating a garden will provide valuable learning experiences for the children, though she knows that not all of the children will be interested. She lets those who are not interested or who lose interest go off to pursue their own activities. When they find the worm, she stays with them as they explore it, attempting to experience it through the children's eyes. She is curious about the questions they ask and has a few genuine questions of her own. She invites the children to suggest how they might find answers to their questions. Once they are back in the playroom, Bejuna is conscious of continuing to encourage the children to take ownership of their investigations. She does not lead but facilitates their investigations, for example, by taking Henry to the library. Later, she suggests that they document their work to show others what they have learned.

Of course, not all questions or experiences develop into a project. As well, the educator's level of involvement depends on the age of the child or children with whom they are working. When toddler Emily is playing in the water table with a boat and some small people figures, you might support her curiosity and imagination (and language skills) by asking more directed questions like, "I wonder if all those people could fit on the boat?" and "Where do you think they might be going?"

Figure 13.1. "What do you think is down there?"

Children use inquiry skills throughout their lives to answer questions about the world. In school, children use inquiry skills in every subject. Table 13.1 shows a list of inquiry skills, along with some ways that you, as an educator, can help children develop them.

Inquiry skills form the basis for learning in science, social studies, math, and other subject areas. Math and numeracy, in particular, are important to our day-to-day functioning. Let's take a closer look.

What Is Numeracy and Why Is It Important?

Simply defined, numeracy is the ability to confidently draw upon our math skills and knowledge in order to deal with the many different situations and contexts we encounter in our everyday lives. We express quantitative information by measuring and reporting amounts. We also use math skills to discover and talk about spatial information like location, area, direction, and shape (Liljedahl & Liu, 2013).

In the staff room, Saida has made a fresh pot of coffee and asks Anna if she'd like some. "Just half a cup," Anna replies. "I have to go back to work in 10 minutes."

Jessica is sewing a dress for her sister. The pattern tells her how much fabric she will need, but she believes she can figure out a way to lay the pieces out that uses less fabric.

Marc and Ellen have embarked on a fitness challenge. Today at lunch, Marc reports that he already has 8000 steps. Ellen is close behind with 7400.

Table 13.1. Inquiry Skills and Supporting Their Development in ECE

SKILL	THINGS YOU CAN DO TO SUPPORT INQUIRY	THINGS YOU CAN SAY TO SUPPORT INQUIRY
Explore objects, materials, and events.	• Provide opportunities for investigating materials, objects, and events.	• How do you think this happened?
Make careful observations.	• Provide time and opportunity for observations.	• Take some time to look carefully and think about what you are seeing.
Use a variety of simple tools to gather information.	• Provide tools such as magnifying glasses, containers of different sizes, and rulers.	• What can you see when you use the magnifying glass? • Which one of these do you think is longer? heavier? etc. • Were you expecting to see this?
Record observations using pictures, words, graphs, or charts.	• Provide the necessary tools and support.	• How can we show what we've found out?
Develop tentative explanations and ideas.	• Ask children to make predictions and speculate about explanations. • Allow time for thinking about and answering questions.	• Why do you think that happened? • What could we do to find out?
Ask open-ended questions.	• Show interest in the children's answers to their questions.	• What would you like to know about…? • What do you think will happen next?
Describe characteristics (including size, shape, pattern, and number), compare, sort, classify, and order.	• Model descriptive vocabulary for size, shape, and characteristics.	• How could we sort these into different piles? • Do you see any things here that are the same? different? • Would you like to tell me about the pattern you've made?

Table 13.1. *Continued*

SKILL	THINGS YOU CAN DO TO SUPPORT INQUIRY	THINGS YOU CAN SAY TO SUPPORT INQUIRY
Work collaboratively with others.	• Model cooperation and mutual respect in your interactions with children and colleagues.	• Can you tell us how you and…did that? • What happened when you and…did that together?
Share and discuss ideas; listen to new perspectives.	• Show interest when others are talking.	• How can you show people what you've discovered? • What do you think about what…is saying?

Adapted from *The Educational Assistant's Guide to Supporting Inclusion in a Diverse Society*, by C. Massing, B. Anderson, and C. Anderson, 2020, Brush Education, pp. 98–99. Copyright 2020 by C. Massing, B. Anderson, and C. Anderson.

We use numeracy skills all the time—at work, at home, and at play. In the scenarios above, you see people using numeracy skills to measure volume (half a cup), time (10 minutes), spatial relationships (how the pattern pieces can fit together), and distance (steps taken). We also need numeracy skills for budgeting and banking; playing games with children;

Figure 13.2. Using technology to support inquiry

making sense of charts, graphs, and statistics in the news; telling time; and participating in activities such as sewing, music, and dance. We use numeracy skills to weigh and measure; to use and understand spreadsheets, data, and diagrams; and to make change out of a till. We use them to make recipes, understand nutrition, calculate discounts and expenses, figure out tips, understand schedules, decide on routes... We could go on, but we think you get the point. Like literacy, numeracy is a skill we need to have in order to fully participate in society—and early childhood is an essential period for the development of numeracy skills.

How Do Numeracy Skills Develop?

Numeracy skills begin to develop in infancy, for example, when an infant is determining how far they have to reach for an object or putting pieces in a shape sorter. In the preschool years, children explore with concrete objects including blocks and other manipulatives. Children develop many of their foundational math skills before they reach school age or in the early years of formal education.

Neuropsychologists believe that humans are born with brain structures that are attuned to number sense (Dehaene, 1997). Because of this, infants who are just a few days old can tell the difference between a picture of two dots and a picture of three dots. By 5 to 6 months, they can tell that a container that is half full of juice is different from one that is full. Once they acquire language, children start to learn some number words and eventually learn to count. By the age of 5 or 6, children can use math concepts in many different ways: for example, they may be able to compare objects using words such as *larger, smaller, longer,* and *shorter.* These ages are approximate, of course, because children develop concepts at their own pace and in their own unique ways.

What Are Math Skills?

While numeracy is the ability to use math in everyday life, mathematics are the actual study of numbers, geometry, shapes, and quantities.

We often think of math as being about numbers and counting, but it is much more than that. Math has many dimensions, including the following:

- Number sense (e.g., the number 3 represents three objects; 3 is greater than 2 and less than 4)
- Geometry (e.g., patterns, shapes, and their unique features)
- Measurement (e.g., size, distance, amount, temperature, and time)

- The language of math (e.g., more than, less than, equal to)
- Spatial relations (e.g., in front of vs. behind; near vs. far)

Many of us have learned that "doing" math is about remembering and following various rules. As a result, a lot of us believe that we aren't good at math. Some people, however, love math and may even make careers as mathematicians. What is it that they see that others don't?

At its best, math is a source of wonder and curiosity. It encourages creativity and problem-solving. It can be fun. In fact, many games involve doing math—for instance, the games many of us play on our phones that involve finding or arranging objects in patterns. The question then, is not "How do we get children to do math?" but rather "How do we help children discover the playfulness and challenge in math?"

Supporting Children's Emerging Math Skills

Young children don't develop math skills through direct instruction, but rather through hands-on activities facilitated by skillful educators. Your observation skills allow you to see what math concepts children already have and then to build on those in your interactions and planning. Does Ema count out five beads, one for each of five friends? If so, she is demonstrating one-to-one correspondence. Can Rahid group objects that are the same? If so, he is showing that he understands the concepts "same" and "different." Can Pria describe the steps she will follow to build a spaceship? If so, she understands sequencing. These are all math skills.

Keeping math concepts at the top of your mind allows you to integrate them into your interactions and activities. Some of these concepts include the following:

- Light, heavy, heavier
- Small, medium, big, bigger
- Less, more, most
- Close, far, farther
- Before, after
- More, fewer/less, equal to
- Over, under, next to, around
- In front of, behind
- Top, middle, bottom
- First, second, third
- Higher, lower
- Inside, outside

- Numbers and fractions
- Shapes (e.g., round, square, triangle, circle, diamond)

To further children's math knowledge, you can integrate math concepts into your daily discussions wherever possible:

- If you are sitting with the children while they are using playdough, you can use concepts like small and big, lighter and heavier, less or more, shapes, and so on.
- When you are out on a walk, you can use concepts like higher and lower, bigger or smaller to describe trees, rocks, and other things you see. You could look for shapes as you walk down a street.
- If the children are lining up, you can use terms like *first, second, third* as well as *in front of* and *behind*.
- With little ones, count the stairs as you climb.
- When children are playing with blocks, mention the shapes of the blocks; for example, "I see that you've put the triangle on the top" or "You've put the biggest block at the bottom and the smaller ones on top."

You will find many, many opportunities to build math concepts into your daily conversations with children. Just be sure to incorporate them naturally into your speech rather than in a "teaching" or "testing" way. Math skills are "caught," not "taught."

Here are a few suggestions for other activities and experiences that will help children develop math skills:

- Ensure that there are lots of **loose parts** to manipulate. Include natural materials like rocks, sticks, and pine cones as well as recycled materials like spools, milk cartons, bread tags, and cardboard boxes that children can count and group in different ways.
- Include **finger plays, songs, and rhymes** that involve counting (e.g., "Five Little Monkeys").
- Go on a **math walk** and find groups of objects to count.
- Play games where children **roll dice** to move along a path (e.g., Snakes and Ladders).
- Construct a **grocery store** in the playroom. Children can price goods and pay with play money in different denominations.
- Make **matching games** to promote one-to-one correspondence (e.g., putting plastic eggs in an egg carton).
- Include children when **setting the table** to promote one-to-one correspondence (i.e., one plate for each child, one napkin for each plate).

- **Discuss math concepts** as they arise naturally (e.g., "Are there enough pencils for everyone at the table?" or "How can we share these cookies evenly between you and your friend?").
- A **bean bag toss** into a hula hoop shows how different combinations of numbers can add up to the same number (e.g., 10 bean bags might result in 5 inside the hoop and 5 outside, 7 inside and 3 outside, etc.).
- Read and discuss **counting books**.
- Point out **patterns** and encourage children to create patterns.
- Create **matching games** with dot cards.
- **Model counting** objects while pointing to them (e.g., "I see you have three blocks—one, two, three").

Figure 13.3. An invitation to sort buttons: a playful math experience

- Represent information visually using **graphs and tallies** (e.g., a tally about how children come to day care using the categories car, bus, walking, etc.).
- Engage children in **mathematical thinking** (e.g., "If we take one of these away, how many will be left?").
- Give **descriptive feedback** to reinforce children's use of math skills and teach math vocabulary (e.g., "I see you've used five plates. One glass per plate means you've also used five glasses. You've made sets of plates and glasses," or "That's an interesting pattern you've made with stones. I wonder what it would look like if you made it longer," or "You looked at the crayons and knew right away there are three of them").

As in everything else you do, your own enthusiasm will be contagious. You can inspire children to love math, and their interest will benefit them in their school years.

MATH AND CULTURE

Children's math learning is very much shaped by culture; in fact, the relationship between mathematics and culture is the focus of a field of study known as ethnomathematics (D'Ambrosio, 1985). Ethnomathematics covers a broad range of topics that include the kinds of number systems that are used in various areas of the world and how these have developed.

An important implication of ethnomathematics is that teaching math in culturally relevant ways will not only help students understand math but will also help them understand themselves and their community.

In Atlantic Canada, a program called *Show Me Your Math* encourages Indigenous students to explore the ways that math is connected to cultural practices in their communities. Dr. Lisa Lunney Borden and Dr. David Wagner began thinking about the program after speaking with the late Mi'kmaw Elder and quill box maker Dianne Toney about how she made the circular tops for her quill boxes. Toney explained that to make a ring, she first measured out lines that were three times the length of her wooden strips plus a thumb width—a concept that, in Euro-American terms, would be called *pi*. This inspired Lunney Borden and Wagner to look for other opportunities to make mathematics more culturally relevant for Mi'kmaw students.

 You can learn more about this ongoing work at http// showmeyourmath.ca/.

‖‖

TAKEAWAYS

Children learn by exploring and asking questions. As an ECE, you can support their learning by providing objects and environments for them to explore, showing genuine interest in their explorations, and providing opportunities for them to extend their learning. Inquiry skills form the basis for learning in science, social studies, math, and other subject areas.

To be numerate is to have the ability to apply mathematical skills and knowledge to situations in our everyday lives. Children begin to develop numeracy skills from an early age as they manipulate objects in their environment. It is important that they have many opportunities to explore with concrete objects and materials to help them build their knowledge and confidence.

ECEs can support and further their children's interest in and understanding of math concepts. Because all children develop in different ways, it's important to observe and document the understandings that children demonstrate so that you can build on these through the environment you provide and through your use of math concepts.

‖‖‖

REFLECTION AND DISCUSSION

- As a young child, what opportunities did you have for curiosity and imagination? What were some of the things you learned through your own discoveries? How did adults respond to your explorations?

- What are some questions you could ask now to facilitate your own learning?

- What are some of the ways in which you have used numeracy or math skills so far today?

- How do you feel about the math experiences you had in school? What did you enjoy? What was challenging?

- How do you feel about your ability to convey excitement about math concepts in your work with children?

- How might you learn about children's family experiences with math (e.g., whether children accompany their family to the grocery store) and the understandings they develop from those experiences?

PART V

The Intercultural ECE Professional: Skills, Responsibilities, and Challenges

14

Planning Curriculum

*It does not do to leave a live dragon out of
your calculations, if you live near one.*
—*J.R.R. TOLKIEN*

||||||||||||||||||||||||||||||||||||||||||||||||||||||||||||||||||||||||||||||||||||||||||||||||||||||||||||||||||||||||||||||||||||

LEARNING OUTCOMES

After you have read this chapter, you will be able to answer these questions:
- What is the purpose of curriculum guides for ECEC?
- Why is planning important?
- What is the role of observation in planning?
- What is emergent curriculum?
- How do planning webs support emergent curriculum?
- How is a planning web constructed?
- What is a provocation and why is it useful?
- How can we plan to meet the needs and interests of individual children?
- What is thematic planning and why is there movement away from it?

Introduction

Various provinces have developed curriculum frameworks to guide early childhood programming. Unlike the curriculum guides that we might be used to, these frameworks tend not to suggest specific activities; instead they outline overarching assumptions and goals for early childhood programs and programming. This is exciting because it allows us, as ECEs, to use our creativity to develop curriculum. In this chapter, we will discuss various approaches to planning experiences for children.

Regulations and Curriculum Documents

In Canada, education and child care are provincial responsibilities. Usually, early learning and child care falls under provincial child care legislation, while kindergarten or prekindergarten are the responsibility of the public education system. In each province, laws and acts provide the overall structure for the system, while regulations establish the minimal standards.

Each of the provinces and territories have established curriculum frameworks to guide programming and practice in early learning and child care. These documents don't prescribe content but do provide a holistic and flexible framework. Most take a sociocultural or social constructivist approach, reflecting the theories of Bronfenbrenner (see Chapter 2, p. 190) and Vygotsky (see Chapter 8, p. 102).

The frameworks differ in some respects, but there is overall agreement about three things:

1. That play is the way that children express themselves and learn
2. That programs need to provide quality environments and experiences
3. That it is important to engage parents as partners in children's learning

Assessment practices based on observation and documentation are recommended; these might include learning stories, portfolios, observational records, and/or documentation panels. Some provinces are focussed on developmental accomplishments, while others designate curriculum goals. New Brunswick and Alberta, for example, identify four holistic play-based goals:

1. Well-being
2. Play and playfulness
3. Communication and literacies
4. Diversity and social responsibility

British Columbia's goals are similar.

The Government of Canada has worked with Indigenous partners to develop the Indigenous Early Learning and Child Care Framework to support the development and implementation of Indigenous ECEC programs in Canada (Employment and Social Development Canada, 2018).

The framework outlines principles and goals that apply to all ECEC programs for Indigenous children and families, as well as frameworks that are geared to the specific needs and contexts of First Nations, Métis, and Inuit peoples.

Beyond recognizing that local context is important, neither the provincial frameworks nor the federal Indigenous framework provides a great deal of guidance for responding to the needs of Indigenous, immigrant, and refugee children who are part of diverse classrooms. Prochner et al. (2016) suggest that this lack of guidance may be a symptom of the tension that exists in child care settings between responding to the needs of diverse children and families and following governmentally regulated standards of care. As we have seen, these standards are largely developed based on the views and practices of the majority culture and may not be consistent with the beliefs and goals of some other cultures. Our work with interculturalism is an attempt to resolve some of those tensions.

You may find that there are situations where licensing regulations prevent you from meeting the needs of some children, in particular those coming from cultural backgrounds that differ from the majority culture. When this occurs, it's often because home practices differ from the practices required of child care programs in order to be licensed. For example, licensing might require that each child have a cot to themselves for sleeping. When two brothers are sobbing at nap time because they are used to sleeping together, this requirement creates an ethical dilemma. Fortunately, licensing officers are usually as committed to supporting children as you are. If you have a solid rationale for a practice that does not align with a licensing requirement, they might be able to accommodate it. Check with your licensing officer in advance before implementing a practice that might deviate from regulations, and be prepared to provide a sound rationale.

Regulations and curriculum guidelines, along with the particular philosophy behind each program, will serve as frameworks for your work with children in early child care settings. However, you will still need to fill this framework with plans for your day-to-day experiences with the children.

Why Plan?

Planning is essential for many reasons. If you are working as a member of a team, planning collaboratively allows you to exchange observations you have made about the children in your playroom with your teammates and work together to develop ideas about how to extend their play.

It lets you check your own perceptions against those of your teammates and solve problems together. Planning ensures that you pay attention to each child and support their individual strengths and abilities.

Planning also ensures you develop a wide range of stimulating and challenging experiences for children, both indoors and out. It gives you an opportunity to introduce new interests, including your own passions.

Planning helps keep you organized and working effectively with your team members. When you post your planning, you are making your work, and your professionalism, visible. If families or colleagues ask you about it, you will be able to discuss it clearly and confidently.

The Planning Cycle

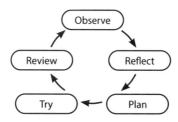

Figure 14.1. The planning cycle

As you can see in Figure 14.1, planning follows a cycle. Sometimes this cycle is shown as a spiral, because the children will often revisit their exploration and will rarely come back to exactly the same point in their exploration. Your planning will reflect that.

Let's look at the planning stages one by one:

1. Begin by observing a child to collect information about their abilities, knowledge, and interests.
2. Reflect on the information you've collected. What does it tell you?
3. Plan experiences to extend the child's learning.
4. Try the experiences with the child.
5. Review how the child responded and think about what that response told you.
6. Begin again with your new observation.

Planning Collaboratively

Let's take a look at an example. Team lead Indira and two other educators, Matt and Aisha, are sitting down in their playroom for their weekly planning meeting. They begin by discussing observations about the children's play.

> "Matija and Sofia spent a lot of time dressing up in 'dance clothes,'" Matt notes, "and Dakota joined them for a while. He was playing the drum for their dancing."
>
> "It's funny," said Aisha. "We put that drum out last week because Cassidy seemed to be so interested when Noah's dad brought his drum. But she didn't pay attention to it all week."
>
> "Chena, Joey, and Noah have started building in the block corner," Aisha observes. "I noticed that they were really interested in building a bridge."
>
> "Tomas has only been here for a couple of days," Indira mentions. "He still doesn't seem very comfortable. I wonder how we can help him settle in."
>
> Aisha responds, "He spent a lot of time playing in the water but not when other children were there."
>
> "I have an idea," says Matt. "It's warm now, so what if we move the bridge-building outside into the sand box. We can carry water over to make a river and the kids can build their bridge over it. Tomas likes waterplay, so this might draw him into the play. "And the other children will love it," Aisha adds. "Good messy fun. Let's remember to warn the parents."
>
> "I've been thinking about the dancing," Indira says. There's going to be a family round dance this week. The families have been invited, but let's mention to Dakota's, Sofia's, and Matija's parents that they've been especially interested in music and dancing lately and encourage them to attend." They go on to brainstorm other dance activities: adding more dance clothes to the dress-up collection, making drums and maracas, and so on.
>
> Indira shows them a learning story. "I wrote this learning story about Adam helping Isabelle with her 'baby.' He was so gentle. His mom will be happy. She worries that he won't grow up to be a caring dad because he doesn't have any close male influences."

The observation of Adam that prompted the learning story prompts them to find and read some books that show men caring for babies. Matt will be a good role model—he can make a point of spending time dressing the "babies" in the house area. They also look at the opportunities and possibilities that Indira included in the learning story she wrote to ensure that they are following through on supporting Adam's caring nature and his interest in babies.

Near the end of the meeting, the three educators summarize their plans and decide who will do what to prepare for the week.

It is also important to think about how individual interests can be extended and supported in different ways. The topic of bridges, for example, can be extended inside at the water table or the loose parts area as well as outdoors in the sand box. The educators might decide to support

this play   vehicles,
pictures, a   different
kinds of b   nd intro-
ducing rel: Since the
children in   e already
immersed   building
bridges, it v   o introduce any r   ely, let-
ting them t   er than
imposing ic   n their
level of inter   uld be
encouraged   ity and
learnings wi   oup.

Inevitably   veren't
initially part   iences
will be drav   ange-
ments. At tł   chil-
dren who ins   ; may
have comple   rests.
Educators need to be able to respond to these changes as they occur; a good supply of ideas, materials, books, and equipment makes it easy to do that. You can see that creativity plays a large part in supporting children's play and learning.

Planning in this way supports the interests and growth of each child because it is tailored to their needs and interests. It requires that we pay close attention to each child to determine what they are exploring in their play and what experiences might support further investigation.

When we're observing play, we have to watch and listen carefully to decide what a child's real interests are. If we see a child rolling a little car down a ramp, is the child interested in cars or in rolling things down an incline? Our planning might be quite different depending on our answer.

Our planning should include activities that reflect the abilities, interests, and family experiences of each child. If you have a child who is just learning English, is new to the group, or has a physical exceptionality or a developmental delay, your planning must consider how that child will be included as a member of the group.

? WHAT DO YOU THINK?

Can you identify all of the stages of planning cycle in this planning meeting?

The playroom in this example is quite small; it is important to note that, in most playrooms, you will have more children to consider in your planning, which means more interests to accommodate. Perhaps, for example, several children in the playroom are determined to learn to write their names. You could set up a writing area with magnetic letters as well as a sand tray to write in and a variety of paper, pencils, and crayons. Maybe a group of children are particularly interested in nature, and a field trip is planned to go to the park and look for signs of autumn. Perhaps, too, parents can be involved in planning—for instance, a mom can be invited to teach the children a song in her native language.

Emergent Curriculum

Indira, Matt, and Aisha's planning session illustrates an *emergent curriculum* approach—that is, curriculum that is developed according to what the children in the playroom find engaging, interesting, and important.

Echo also uses an emergent curriculum approach to planning in her playroom. Since she can never quite be sure how and when children's interests are going to show themselves, she knows that it helps to be flexible and able think on her feet:

> Echo is about to take the children outside on a leaf walk when Rayan spots a large beetle on the playroom floor. He shouts, "Look, I found a bug!" and the other children quickly gather around. "Let's get our magnifying glasses," Rayan says. With Echo's help, the children carefully capture the beetle in a jar and make a habitat of sticks and grasses for it.
>
> "What does it need to eat?" Rayan asks. "What's it called?" another child asks. Some children make suggestions. The walk is forgotten as the beetle becomes a focus of study.
>
> Some children use the magnifying glass to study the beetle more closely. "Can you see how many legs it has?" Echo asks. Two of the children draw careful diagrams of the beetle. One child checks for books on insects on the playroom bookshelf but finds little. Echo takes this child and two others to the library beside the director's office. "We're researching a bug," a child tells the director as they pass by.
>
> This topic holds interest for some of the children for several days, long after the beetle has been released outdoors. They find "their" beetle in a book about insects and share their discovery with the other children. They make a model of the beetle with playdough, give it a name, and create a story about it. Other children lose interest much sooner and move on to other activities.

Figure 14.2. Checking out the bug

As a skilled and experienced educator, Echo quickly recognizes an opportunity to build upon the children's spontaneous interest in the beetle, and she has some ideas about how to do that. This takes both practice and planning. As we'll discuss in the next section, *planning webs* can be used to help educators be ready to capitalize on children's spur-of-the-moment interests.

Planning Webs

If children show interest in a topic, you can construct a planning web that builds on it. This is, for example, something that Indira, Aisha, and Matt could do as they think about ways to expand the children's exploration of bridges. *Webbing* is a method of brainstorming; it helps you think about many different aspects of a topic and the experiences that might grow from it. Then, as the children engage with the topic, you are ready to follow their interest in whatever directions it might take. The more complete your planning web is, the better prepared you will be.

When Indira's team creates a planning web, they begin with a big sheet of paper and write the central interest—in this case, "Bridges"—in the middle of it. Then they brainstorm questions about this central interest. They might even involve the children in this phase. Then, they choose three to five questions that will allow for interesting exploration. Usually, the questions they choose will begin with words like *what, when, who,* and *how.* At this point, the web might look something like Figure 14.3.

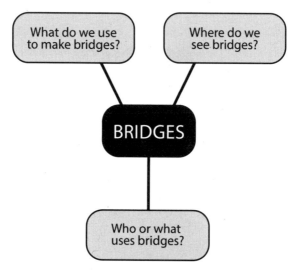

Figure 14.3. Beginning a planning web by asking questions

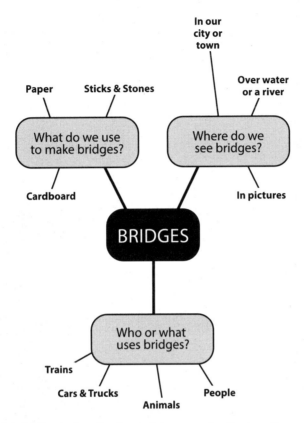

Figure 14.4. Adding to the planning web by answering the questions

Each one of these questions sparks yet another layer of brainstorming to answer the questions (Figure 14.4). Then, you might begin to think of experiences to do with the children based on those answers (Figure 14.5).

The point in webbing is not to carry out each and every activity you've come up with. The web is a brainstorming tool that equips you with a lot of ideas so that you can build on whatever interests the children show and respond spontaneously depending on where children take this play.

Some programs create several simple webs to reflect the interests of various children. This would be a possibility in the planning session with Indira, Matt, and Aisha; they might construct webs for two or three topics that are currently important to the children in the playroom—perhaps bridges, water, and music. This would certainly ensure that they would have lots of ideas to draw from as the play progressed.

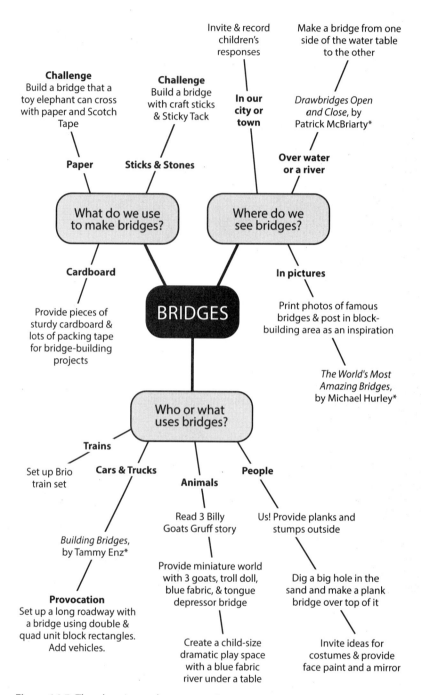

Figure 14.5. The planning web grows again

*Enz, T.L. (2017). *Building bridges*. Chicago, IL: Heinemann-Raintree.

Hurley, M. (2011). *The world's most amazing bridges*. Chicago, IL: Raintree.

McBriarty, P. (2014). *Drawbridges open and close*. Carlisle, MA: Curly Q Press, an imprint of Applewood Press.

Careful observations of the children's play will tell you whether you should continue drawing from the experiences in the flowcharts you've created or move on to explore other interests.

Provocations

One way to assess the nature and level of children's interest about a particular topic is to set up a *provocation*—an inviting or intriguing display of materials related to the topic—to see if it provokes children's curiosity and involvement. If it does, you will want to find ways to further develop and support their interest. If your provocation doesn't engage children's interest at all in the way you anticipated, don't force it. This is likely a signal to move on, continue observing, adapt, and offer new provocations.

Planning that begins with observations based on a child's or children's interests are likely to encourage that child or those children to become deeply involved in the planned experiences. Planning based on your own enthusiasm about a certain topic can also be effective when done in combination with observation-based planning. Children are likely to pick up on your enthusiasm and develop an interest that might be new to them. If you have a particular hobby or skill, don't hesitate to share it with the children in age-appropriate ways and then wait to see if they are interested and how they respond.

Figure 14.6. A provocation using natural materials

Figure 14.7. A musical provocation

Emergent Curriculum Planning as Pedagogical Documentation

As we have mentioned, emergent curriculum begins with observation. Planning that emerges from observed interests of children—individuals and small groups alike—is not linear in nature. It is also not time-specific, meaning it does not begin and end within a designated time frame. Several interests might be pursued at one time depending on children's engagement. An emergent approach to planning accommodates support for spontaneous interests as well as more in-depth investigations when children's engagement in a particular topic is sustained. As one educator commented, "This type of planning is true. It shows what we are really doing."

Because the emergent curriculum approach is nonlinear, however, the parts of the planning cycle may, at a glance, be less obvious. If your planning includes photos and observations and articulates the significance of what children are showing through their play, your planning document might be considered a piece of *pedagogical documentation* (discussed further in Chapter 15). Planning cycles can be transformed into pieces of pedagogical documentation by including, along with observations of children and the resulting planned activities, analyses of the significance of what is happening in the playroom that makes children's learning visible.

And remember: just because emergent curriculum planning is nonlinear doesn't mean it shouldn't be organized. Take a look at the planning cycle document in Figure 14.8. Consider colour-coding or using different shapes of bubbles in your planning document to organize the information. For instance, you could highlight educator observations in one colour or shape, educator analysis of children's learning in another colour or shape, and strategies to support further learning in yet another. This helps educators see at a glance if they are engaged in all the aspects of planning—observation, analysis, and the adults' responses, which

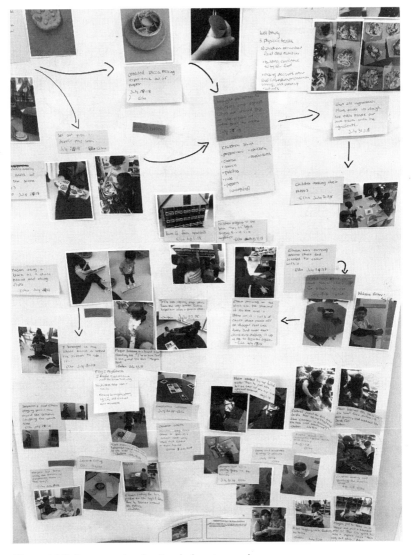

Figure 14.8. An example of a visual planning cycle

may include play experiences, books, materials, organization of time, and educator participation with children. Another strategy to clearly make parts of the planning cycle visible is to identify and label these items on the planning cycle.

Figure 14.9. Educators collaborate on planning

LIYA'S MEAL

Walking into the preschool room one morning, I noticed that Liya had lined up bowls on a piece of cloth that was on the floor. She then placed a piece of play food in each bowl and stood proudly pointing to it. "Oh, you put a piece in each bowl! Liya, you have garlic, peppers, and chilies," I commented, describing what I saw.

Later, I spoke with Aatifa, one of the playroom educators, about what I noticed. From my lens as a former university lecturer, I saw Liya engaging with a math concept—one-to-one correspondence—when she put a piece of food in each bowl. Aatifa smiled, saying, "We eat like this at home." Seeing my confusion, Aatifa explained that Liya was setting up a traditional Eritrean meal.

A colleague once told me, "We only see what we already know." Our cultures and our previous experiences influence the lenses through which we see the world. The lens I was looking through was one that knew about early math concepts. Aatifa saw what Liya was doing through the lens of their shared Eritrean heritage. Aatifa was able to recognize the cultural script that Liya was recreating in her play. As a result of Aatifa's interpretation and insights, she responded by preparing a lunch of injera and lentils for the children later that week. They ate this in the traditional manner, seated around a communal bowl on the floor.

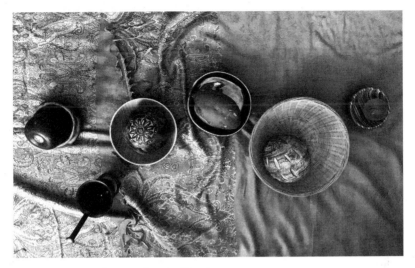

Figure 14.10. Liya lines up bowls of food

Recognizing Cultural Scripts in Play

The story above shows how easy it is to misinterpret a child's play, especially in intercultural situations. Such misinterpretations may also mean that we miss out on a wonderful opportunity to affirm children's interests and play. In the case of Liya's play, Aatifa had an opportunity not only to affirm Liya's culture through her play, but also to invite her to share her cultural practice with her playmates and educators.

When we don't share the same cultural background, we may not see the ways in which children are expressing their cultural scripts through play. Inviting the perspectives of other educators, and of families, may help us see other possibilities.

? WHAT DO YOU THINK?

If you were one of Liya's educators and observed her lining up bowls and putting a piece of food in each, what might you have concluded? How might you have approached the situation to find out more about the meaning of her play?

A NOTE ABOUT THEME PLANNING

For many years, early childhood programs planned around themes. Often, these were broad themes such as *Families* or *Farm Animals,* and all of the activities for that week or month would be built around the theme. Sometimes themes were based on observation of the children and other times themes were decided upon by educators. Proponents of this type of planning argued that a theme approach allowed children to gain an in-depth knowledge of one topic.

As ECEs have changed their image of children and how they learn, they have moved away from themes. Why? Themes are imposed by the educator, with no recognition of children's interests or prior knowledge. When themes are explored for a limited period of time, they don't in fact support the in-depth involvement they intend to provide, nor do they respond to multiple interests in a playroom at the same time. They can encourage educators to prolong a theme past the point where children are interested or engaged. Finally, educators may have difficulty finding a week's or month's worth of meaningful activities related to a single theme. As a result, planning may seem forced, with activities added just to fill all the boxes on a planning sheet.

Still, themed planning resources can be useful if you use them wisely—that is, if you pick and choose open-ended activities from these resources that respond to the interests and needs of a child or group of children based on your observations.

Making Time for Planning

One of the biggest barriers to effective planning is lack of time. Ideally, ECEC centres set time aside each week for educators from each playroom to get together and plan. When that isn't possible, you and your teammates will need to find creative ways to carve out time for sharing your observations of the children and for planning. For example, you could do some planning in the playroom during nap time once the children are resting quietly. When all educators in a playroom team are involved in planning, it becomes a mutual responsibility to contribute observations, analysis, and ideas for play to the playroom planning cycle, even when the whole team may not have designated time to meet together.

If you work with older children, you can involve them in planning. These children can identify an interest, brainstorm questions they would like to research about that topic, and suggest ways to find answers. This is often motivating for them and gives them some ownership over their learning.

Making time for planning is also important for you, as an educator. It can be an excellent opportunity for checking in with your teammates

Figure 14.11. Inviting children's input in planning

beyond what each of you have observed and for building team relationships. Brainstorming is a way to not only share ideas, but to also build on interests and to have fun. Planning a squishy mud experience, for example, is a chance to bring out your inner child. When you're planning, it's fine to take some risks and see what happens!

‖‖

TAKEAWAYS

Provincial regulations, curriculum guides, and your program's philosophy together provide an overall framework for your approach to early learning and child care. However, they don't stipulate particular activities. As an ECE, you are responsible for planning experiences that respond to the abilities and interests of each child in your group.

Planning that responds to children's interests is called *emergent curriculum*. Emergent curriculum begins with your observations of children and the relationships you have with them.

Provocations are a way to check whether your guesses about children's interests are correct; planning webs are tools to help better prepare you to respond to children's interests with relevant, meaningful activities. Planning meetings can be an excellent opportunity to check in with teammates and to share observations and ideas.

Finally, remember that your planning should reflect the needs and interests of all of the children in your playroom. Planning for and with children can be a great deal of fun—a chance to be creative and playful!

REFLECTION AND DISCUSSION

- Check out the licensing regulations and curriculum frameworks for your province or territory. What do they tell you about how to plan for children?

- Try constructing a planning web around a topic that interests you. If possible, brainstorm with a colleague or friend. Is this an approach you would find comfortable when you are planning for children? Why or why not?

- Think about an interest or skill you have that you could bring to your work with children. Is there a way that you could make it interesting and appropriate for a group of preschoolers? What kind of provocation could you try to see if children are interested in the topic?

- Let's look again at the J.R.R. Tolkien quotation that began this chapter: "It does not do to leave a live dragon out of your calculations, if you live near one." Now that you've thought a bit more about planning, how would you say this quote speaks to the process and purpose of planning for children?

15

Observation, Documentation, and Assessment

LEARNING OUTCOMES

When you have read this chapter, you will be able to answer these questions:

- What is assessment?
- Why is observation an important skill for ECEs?
- What are some kinds of observation and how might each be used?
- Why might it be important to be as objective as possible when doing observations?
- What is the value and purpose of documentation?
- What makes documentation pedagogical?
- What are learning stories and why are they useful?

Introduction

In previous chapters, we've talked a lot about the importance of observing children. Our careful attention to children tells us about their interests, their personalities, their abilities, and their understandings. Knowing these things tells us how to interact with and plan for children in ways that support their wellbeing and learning.

This chapter situates observation as part of a larger plan for assessment. It discusses various kinds of observation: anecdotal, running, checklists, and event and time sampling. Observations may become part of a portfolio that documents children's growth and activities. Children's experiences may be documented in a number of ways, but the documentation is only considered "pedagogical" if it is accompanied by an explanation as to the significance of the experience for the child and their learning.

We will also discuss *learning stories*. The idea of learning stories as assessment originated in New Zealand but has become more widespread in recent years. Learning stories are narratives that make children's learning visible and identify possibilities to support them further; they are formative—that is, they inform and influence our planning. They are "subjective" in the sense that the educator is a part of the story; as such, they help to foster the relationship between the educator and child and between the educator and the family. But this subjectivity does not mean learning stories are not based in close observation and fact. To be effective, learning stories must be solidly based in the educators' recognition and understanding of children's dispositions for learning and learning outcomes or goals.

What Is Assessment?

> Three-year-old Stella has just moved into Matt's playroom. Matt wants to learn more about her and find out how he can help her feel comfortable in her new setting.
>
> Matt and his teammates are meeting for planning, and Matt wants to know what experiences to plan in order to extend the children's interests. He also notes that there seem to be a lot of conflicts when the children are getting ready to go outdoors. Matt wonders if changing the transition process might help to decrease the difficulties.
>
> At the end of the day, Adam's parents ask if they can meet with Matt to discuss Adam's progress and behaviour.

Assessment is process of observing, recording, and documenting what children do and how they do it in order to do the following:

- Identify children's needs, interests, and development
- Make decisions about how best to support children
- Improve your program to make the environment more peaceful, happy, and stimulating
- Be able to communicate effectively to families, colleagues, consultants, and others about children's growth and activities

Assessment will help Matt get to know more about Stella, contribute meaningfully to the planning meeting, discover how he can make the transition process operate more smoothly, and respond knowledgeably to Adam's parents.

Principles that Underlie Assessment

There are various tools and strategies that are useful in assessment. Underlying these are certain principles (Victoria State Government, 2021):

- Assessment should be based on children's strengths. All children have strengths and abilities, and their growth and development arise from these. Educators who appreciate and understand children's strengths can more effectively support their development and learning.
- A strength-based approach to assessment is fair and equitable because it focuses on what children can do, rather than what they can't do. It values the life knowledge that children bring.
- Assessment acknowledges that some children have challenges and need support but focuses on the problem, rather than the child.
- Assessment is part of reflective practice: the continuous process of questioning and examining our practice in order to increase our knowledge and effectiveness.

Assessment involves collecting information through various methods and in a variety of circumstances. We might, for example, use informal and formal observations, checklists, and portfolios. Learning stories are a particularly effective strength-based form of documenting or assessing children's learning, as we will see later in this chapter.

Observations

We observe informally all the time. When we notice that Jeffrey and Caitlin have invented a game, or that Lucas hasn't eaten his soup, or that Eva has spent a long time at the paint easel, we are observing. We can also observe in more formal ways, using various approaches. Formal or informal, observations are an important tool for ECEs. The act of focusing closely on a child connects us with that child and guides our interactions with them. By telling us what a child knows and can do and what their interests are, observations form the basis for our planning. They help us to communicate with families and colleagues about a child's activities and learning. They are also tools for our own professional learning: as we observe children, we learn more about patterns of development and learning.

Formal Observation

Formal observations may be anecdotal or running. Each will give you different kinds of information.

Anecdotal observations. Anecdotal observations will likely be your most often used type of observation, as they fit most easily into a busy day. Anecdotal observations are written after an event has occurred, so you might find yourself writing them while you are on a break or during a quiet moment in the playroom. You might jot down one or two words while you are in the midst of playroom activities just to help you remember to write about an incident later. (Sticky notes and a pen on top of a file cabinet or high shelf can be both a reminder and a useful tool to make these observations.) Sometimes, taking a photograph can help us remember what occurred.

An anecdotal observation need not be long, but it should give as complete a picture as possible of an event that seems significant. It should include all important details in the order in which they occurred. If possible, you should include what the child (or children) said and did, their body language, and other relevant details. You should note approximately when and where the observation occurred, as well as the age of the child.

> Nov. 13, 2020
>
> 10:45 a.m.
>
> Anisa (age 4.2) sat alone in the reading corner while the other children played. She had a book about families on her lap and appeared to be studying it closely. She turned the pages one at a time and followed the print with her finger as if she were reading. After about 5 minutes, Aryn joined her. She looked up at Aryn, smiled, and pointed, saying, "Look— here's my family, and here's yours."

Running observations. Running observations are recorded while an action or activity is occurring. They provide a more detailed account of a child's behaviour.

> Nov. 13, 2020.
>
> 9:30–9:35 a.m.
>
> Theo (age 3.5) is sitting at a table with Ahmed and Jared. There are two containers of playdough on the table with them, one pink and one green. Theo has a ball of pink playdough in his right hand. He says, "Watch this." He pats his playdough ball flat with his right hand, making a circle. "I'm making pizza," he says. He looks at Ahmed who is on his

left and smiles. "Put some cheese on it," Ahmed says. Theo
takes a piece of green playdough from the larger ball in the
container. He holds it in his left hand while pinching off small
pieces with his right. As he pinches each piece, he sprinkles it
on the "pizza." "There," he says, "Now it's got cheese. I like
cheese pizza best."

"Can I have a piece?" Ahmed asks. "Sure," Theo responds. He
reaches to the centre of the table and picks up a plastic
knife, then carefully cuts a triangular piece. "There's your
piece," he says to Ahmed.

When you are reading a good running observation, you should be able
to visualize quite clearly what is happening. This kind of detail can be difficult to capture as it is happening, so
skilled observers use their own short-
hand, including stick figures to show
body positions, then rewrite these
notes as a final copy. Video recording can assist educators to accurately
complete a running observation as
long as it is done discreetly and does
not significantly impact children's
behaviour.

WHAT DO YOU THINK?

What can you learn about Theo's development by reading this running observation? Think, in particular, about what the running observation tells you about his

- Fine motor skills
- Cognitive develop-ment (what he knows and understands)
- Social skills
- Language development

Other Observation Tools

Checklists and rating scales. Checklists and rating scales are
intended to show whether or not children have mastered a certain skill
and can be useful for some purposes; for example, as part of a developmental assessment that might support a referral to other services.
However, checklists focus on a narrow set of abilities and tend to focus
on what a child can't do rather than what they can do. For example,
2-year-old Ana may not be able to stack three blocks on top of each
other, but she is extraordinarily warm and empathic with other children.
This positive trait may not show up in a developmental checklist—we
would only see that she can't perform the particular motor activity.

Unfortunately, checklists can also be subject to cultural bias. Children
who, because of their family experience, are unfamiliar with the language or activities specified in the checklist will be disadvantaged by the

lens of the checklist. For example, children who are accustomed to eating with their hands may appear clumsy when asked to use utensils, but this doesn't necessarily mean that they lag in their development. Similarly, children who speak a home language other than English may appear to have a language delay when, in fact, they are busy becoming proficient in two (or more) languages.

If you are interpreting the results of a checklist, be aware that children follow different patterns in their development: they may be very strong in some areas and not in others. They can also reach developmental milestones at quite different ages. This is why it is important to use various types of assessment in order to build a wholistic picture of the child.

The bottom line is this: when you interpret the results of a checklist, keep in mind that children might score badly on items on the checklist that don't reflect their own experience.

Time and event samples. You might use time or event samples to give you specific kinds of information about a particular child's activities or behaviour or about patterns in the room. Maybe Grace's parents are concerned that she doesn't seem to have friends in the program. You could make a plan to do a time sample to create a map of her interactions throughout the day. You could carry a notepad and pencil with you through the morning and record every 5 minutes who Grace is with (or whether she is alone). This would give you concrete information to report to her parents and also help you know whether, and how, to support her in building some relationships with other children. This is time sampling.

Event sampling could also help you learn about Grace's social interactions. While time sampling involves recording actions at set intervals, event sampling means recording them when they occur. This would mean making a note whenever Grace interacted with another child. Event samples are often used to track changes in behaviour—for example, the number of times that Jared hits another child (a behaviour that you are working to help him decrease).

The A-B-C approach to understanding behaviour is built around event sampling. It is focussed on gathering information on a child's specific behaviour, often one that is challenging. In this approach, you would record what comes before the behaviour (A: antecedent), the child's response to the antecedent (B: behaviour) and what happens after the behaviour (C: consequence). This helps you determine what triggered the behaviour, the specifics of the behaviour, and what happens as a result of the behaviour. An A-B-C analysis of Jared's hitting behaviour might tell you that he is most likely to hit when he is tired or hungry, that he often targets the same child, but that he seems concerned when that child cries. This can help you understand what is happening.

? WHAT DO YOU THINK?

Based on the A-B-C analysis of Jared's behaviour, what might be some ways to decrease his hitting?

Objectivity in Observations

To be an objective observer means to only write what we see and hear without making any judgments. This can be harder than it sounds. Many of the descriptive words that we use to communicate an observation may also convey a bias or personal interpretation of a situation that may not actually be present in the situation itself.

Table 15.1. Objective Versus Subjective Observations

SUBJECTIVE OBSERVATION	OBJECTIVE OBSERVATION
Ethan is happy that he can finally reach the mobile.	Ethan reaches for the mobile with his right hand. He grabs the star and smiles.
Anisa doesn't want to play with the other children.	While the other children are playing, Anisa is sitting alone in the reading area with a book in her lap.

Compare the observations in Table 15.1. When you read these examples, you can see that adding opinions can lead to conclusions that are inaccurate. Anisa, for example, might indeed want to play with the other children but be too shy to join in.

It's important to be as descriptive and detailed as possible but to avoid any judgments. This is where it's important to recognize your own *unconscious biases* (see Chapter 4) to ensure that they don't enter into your observations or your interpretations of your observations. It's also important to recognize that your presence, whether or not the child seems aware of you, will influence what is happening. Try to be as unobtrusive as possible when you are observing.

We need to be aware that any kind of observation gives a picture of a child's behaviour at a particular time and in a particular circumstance; individual observations cannot be generalized into an overall picture of the child. Perhaps you made your observation at a time when the child isn't at their best. Maybe they are ill or distracted. As well, observations may focus on only one aspect of the child's behaviour, rather than giving us a holistic picture of the child. Finally, we have to be aware that some forms of observational assessment, such as standardized checklists, may lead us to focus on a child's deficits rather than on their strengths.

As you will see in the next section, pedagogical documentation can provide a holistic assessment that focuses on a child's strengths.

Pedagogical Documentation

Pedagogical documentation tells the story of children's learning, whether of one child or of a group of children. Documentation becomes "pedagogical" when we do the work of analyzing and interpreting in ways that showcase children's learning and their dispositions to learn—that is, the characteristics and/or inclinations that support them as powerful learners. This interpretation is essential to pedagogical documentation; without it, our photographs and children's quotes would simply be considered display. While children and families certainly enjoy seeing displays of photographs of play, celebrations, and field trips, the element of interpretation or analysis of children's learning takes display to a different professional level.

Figure 15.1. Picture-rich documentation mounted at children's level

Why Document?

Pedagogical documentation has many purposes and uses for our work with children and families and for us as educators.

Table 15.2. Benefits of Documentation for Children, Families, and Educators

BENEFITS FOR CHILDREN	BENEFITS FOR FAMILIES
• Documentation gives children the opportunity to revisit their learning and experiences. • If children are involved in creating the documentation and see themselves in the documentation, they derive new insights about their experience and may be inspired to build on what they have done. • Children's comments as they create or review the documentation will tell you about their understanding and thought processes, and may show you how to extend their learning even further. • Documentation of an individual child's experience, as with a learning story, can create an intimate connection and trusting relationship with the child.	• Documentation makes children's learning visible to families. • Documentation makes the educator's practice and professionalism visible to families. • Families are able to see what their children have been doing and understand the significance and value of their play. • When educators document a child's learning, it builds relationships between the educator and families. • Documentation can provide evidence to support concerns about a child's development.

BENEFITS FOR EDUCATORS
• Documentation provides an opportunity for educator research to inform practice and planning to support learning further. • It provides the opportunity to recall and reflect on what has occurred in the playroom. • It deepens educators' understanding of individual children. • It provides a platform for engaging in dialogue with families about their children.

Types of Documentation

Children's experiences can be documented in many ways: on documentation panels or bulletin boards, in children's portfolios, and in learning stories. In this section, we'll discuss documentation panels as a way of highlighting group experiences and the use of children's portfolios to document the experiences of individual children. Learning stories will be addressed in more detail in the next section.

Documentation panels and bulletin boards. Documentation panels can highlight the significance of children's play and their dispositions to learn. Individual experiences and group projects can be presented on a bulletin board, on a tri-fold display board, or on playroom walls at children's level so they can revisit their experiences. These panels might capture learning moments, playful events, and projects; they include photos, observations, and an analysis of the significance of what has occurred. Outcomes or holistic goals from your province's curriculum framework can be useful for determining the significance of children's play. Remember that pedagogical documentation goes beyond simply displaying photos of children and playroom events; it includes interpretation that explains what children are learning and what characteristics for learning they are exhibiting. In other words, it articulates why the experiences are important.

Children's portfolios. Individual portfolios may include samples of a child's artwork, photographs, observations, and artifacts, all dated and annotated or described to show the child's growth over time. They are a useful way to reflect on a child's growth and to share with families.

What might go into a child's portfolio? Here are a few suggestions:

- A "Welcome to Your Playroom" letter from educators
- "Educators' stories" that introduce each educator (and centre administration staff), complete with photos
- A copy of the child's learning stories
- A child's artwork, dated and documented with a description of what was happening and why it is important (perhaps identifying the child's stage of art development or the child's process or effort that went into creating it), sometimes accompanied by a photo of the child in the process of creating it
- A child's significant learning moments, complete with a photo, description of what happened, and its importance
- "Family stories" in which families are invited to create a page for their child's portfolio with their own photos

In the past, children's portfolios or folders were often kept in locked filing cabinets out of the reach of everyone but the playroom educators and shared on occasion with families. But what if children's portfolios were created *for* children? On a recent study tour to New Zealand, we were introduced to a different kind of children's portfolio—one that celebrated children's accomplishments and was readily available for children to look at on a daily basis. This inspired our centre to store portfolio binders on a low shelf in each playroom with children's names and pictures easily visible on the binder spine. Below, Mary Lynne tells a story about what happened when the centre where she was working shared their children's portfolios with parents for the first time at a family meeting.

Figure 15.2. Zoe enjoys a learning story in her portfolio

RETHINKING CHILDREN'S PORTFOLIOS

After our centre introduced a new kind of children's portfolio (binders with stories about playroom educators, the child's annotated artwork, and copies of the child's learning stories), we invited families to an evening session to introduce them to the new portfolio binders and learning stories. We brought each child's portfolio to the meeting and handed them out to families to look at as we explained their purpose and what was in them. Initially, we had included just the child's play-room educators' introduction stories in their portfolio binder; however, that evening families asked us for the stories of all the centre educators and administrative team members. Of course, we immediately responded by adding everyone's story.

That evening we also invited families to add their own story and photos to their child's portfolio. We explained how important it was for children to see their families in the playroom and that including their photos in their child's portfolio was another way to do this. We supplied a variety of paper and writing implements to take home and received back several family pages, some using the materials we supplied and others creating them electronically. Not only did children benefit from having their families present in their portfolios, but we learned more about extended family, pets, pastimes, and family cultural backgrounds and traditions.

Learning Stories

Learning stories are a philosophy of assessment and teaching. They give the child a chance to revisit their learning, they contribute to the child's identity formation, and they build connections with family and *whānau* [Māori: extended family]. (Wendy Lee, personal communication, November 16, 2016)

Learning stories come to us from New Zealand, where they were developed in 1996 by Margaret Carr as a form of documentation and assessment that fit with that country's new bicultural curriculum, Te Whariki (Carr & Lee, 2019). The Intercultural Children and Family Centres, which use learning stories, have also drawn on the work of New Zealand educator and learning story expert Wendy Lee.

Learning stories are a particular form of pedagogical documentation that has the potential to foster even closer bonds with both children and families and to avoid possible cultural bias in traditional assessment methods. Much like some other forms of documentation, learning stories notice and focus on what a child is doing, recognize the significance of their actions, and respond in ways that further support the child's learning. What makes learning stories different and particularly significant is that they are personal and evocative, written subjectively from the educator to the child, in ways that solicit an emotional response. Learning stories always focus on children's strengths and are written in a way that makes the relationship between the educators and child visible.

Learning stories recognize and support *learning dispositions*: the characteristics and tendencies that contribute to a child's success as a learner. Educators who recognize and understand these dispositions will be more likely to understand the significance of the behaviours they see and know how to support further growth. New Zealand has identified five critical learning dispositions: taking an interest, pursuing an interest, persisting under difficulty, communicating, and taking responsibility. Similar dispositions are recognized in some provincial ECEC curriculum frameworks in Canada, and educators are encouraged to notice, recognize, and nurture dispositions to learn in order to support children as mighty learners (Makovichuk et al., 2014, p. 61; see also Chapter 14 in this volume).

The Parts of a Learning Story

The story. The story describes the occurrence or series of observations that you are focusing on; this might focus on change over time or a significant incident that tells us about the child and what the child is learning and discovering. The story is written *to* the child rather than *about* the child. Unlike running observations, anecdotal records, and other forms of observation, learning stories include the educator's subjective responses: thoughts and feelings related to what has occurred.

The analysis. The analysis section of a learning story highlights the child's learning, thinking, and/or disposition to learn. The analysis is the educator's interpretation of the importance of what has occurred or is occurring. When writing an analysis, you can use your local curriculum framework for goals, outcomes, indicators, and dispositions as a guide for describing the significance of the story. You can also use your understanding of schemas and development to explain the importance of what the child is doing.

Opportunities and possibilities. This part of a learning story details the ways in which educators propose to further support the child's learning and nurture their dispositions to learn. When we intentionally integrate these opportunities and possibilities into our planning, the learning story is truly formative—that is, it guides what we plan and do in the playroom. In addition to identifying materials and spaces to further support the child, we can also identify if any changes need to be made with regard to time (e.g., giving the child more time to complete what they are doing, saving their creation to work on later) or to our conscious participation with the child (e.g., being engaged in role-playing, inviting their ideas, describing what they are doing). Some centres include the opportunities and possibilities from children's learning stories right on their planning documents to serve as a reminder to implement the supports they have identified. This provides a structure for accountability.

Family's response. When we invite families into the discussion of their child's learning, we benefit from their perspectives and input. Wendy Lee (personal communication, 2019) suggests asking the family a specific, open-ended question related to the story to encourage their engagement (e.g., "Angelica seems to know a lot about caring for babies. How do you think she knows so much?"). Other strategies to invite and support family engagement include the following:

- Reading the story to the child before sending a copy home
- Gifting the story directly to the family by the educator who has written it

- If a family is not comfortable with writing a family response, asking if you can write down how they have responded
- Inviting families to respond in their home language and then translating it for educators who do not share that language with the family
- Giving families time to respond
- Following up with families who have not submitted a response

When to Write a Learning Story

Now that you know what a learning story looks like, you might be wondering: When should I actually *write* a learning story?

You could write a learning story when children

- Surprise you with their understanding, what they know, or what they are trying to do or figure out
- Inspire you to write about what is happening
- Are trying to master something new
- Are excited about their discoveries
- Are exhibiting dispositions for learning
- Are exhibiting curriculum framework goals

Steven's Learning Story

In Chapter 12, we read about ECE Rita's interactions with Steven, a child who had just arrived in Rita's playroom at the Intercultural Child and Family Centre and who was learning to speak English. This is the learning story that Rita wrote to Steven about their experience together.

STEVEN BUILDS HIS ENGLISH VOCABULARY THROUGH PLAY WITH HIS FAVOURITE TOYS

Written by: Rita

Steven, from the very first day that you joined us at the centre, I have noticed that animals, bugs, and dinosaurs are your favourite toys. You play with them joyfully. You even change the tone of your voice as you imagine the different animals talking to each other. Every time you and I play together and you pick a toy, I name it in both Russian and English. Then you repeat the words in English.

Today you found a scorpion and exclaimed, "*Pauk!*" (in Russian, it means a spider). I said that it was a scorpion. I pronounced the word with the stress on the last syllable, as that is how it sounds in Russian. You repeated, "Scorpion!" and I added, "In English, it sounds almost the same." Together, we practised saying the word, repeating it in Russian and in English.

I notice that you always choose books about animals. I think they are your favourite! You point at the pictures and name the animals, birds, and insects. The other day you said, "*U menya loshadka!*" as you were putting away a toy. "I have a horse!" I translated. And you smiled and repeated, "Horse!"

Before nap time the other day, you picked a book and asked me to read. I read in English and translated some sentences and words to Russian, the home language we share. Steven, you always repeat the new words with a smile. You are so eager to learn and very persistent with asking me to translate. I know that you will be speaking English in no time!

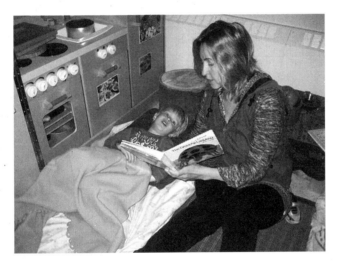

Figure 15.3. Rita reads to Steven and translates words into Russian

WHY THIS IS IMPORTANT

As he plays and we interact, Steven is learning new vocabulary as well as how English sounds. He is developing a sense of trust in others through knowing that I am a person he can depend on for help and care in his new environment. Steven's growing English vocabulary is also helping him form relationships with other children, and he seems so eager to learn. He is very persistent as he practises repeating words with me and this will help him be successful. Steven also knows that his family's language is being used and respected here, and this supports him as he gets used to being in a new country.

OPPORTUNITIES AND POSSIBILITIES

- I will invite other children to be involved in manipulative play with animal toys to further help Steven build relationships with new playmates.

- All of us will work to enhance Steven's English vocabulary by repeating simple words and phrases in English with actions, gestures, and pointing to objects.
- I can teach other educators and children key words and simple phrases in Russian to help them connect with Steven.
- I will continue to read books about animals to Steven and translate words into Russian. I will also bring in some of my children's storybooks written in Russian and read them to Steven and the other children, translating as I read.

Rita recalls that Steven's parents responded positively to the story. Later, Rita asked Steven's mother if she would share her thoughts again. This was her response:

FAMILY'S RESPONSE

When we were newcomers in Canada, we chose Intercultural Child and Family Centre on purpose. We are so grateful to all staff and teachers there. Especially, we are grateful to Rita, who was the first person in Canada who helped Steven improve his English. Rita explained and translated to Steven all unknown words and phrases from English to Russian. He was 3 years old and he didn't stress out at all when we sent him to day care because he could understand everything with Rita's help and felt himself in a familiar environment. Thus, he improved his English and kept his native language. It was a great support for us as parents too as we are trying to keep the Russian language for our children by speaking and reading in Russian at home.

Figure 15.4. Learning story booklets

The Intercultural Child and Family Centre prints children's learning stories as booklets that are rich in pictures. A photo on each page corresponds with the text. This was an intentional decision to support early literacy since many of our children and families are English language learners. We hoped that having a paper copy of the child's learning story at home would support home reading. An electronic copy was sent to families who requested it to send to relatives back home, and a copy of their learning story was placed in the child's portfolio so they could revisit it during the day.

 Learn more about learning stories by watching Wendy Lee's conversations with Dr. Anna Kirova and Dr. Larry Prochner:

Part One: *Learning Stories Are More than Just a Form of Assessment, They Are a Philosophical Approach*[1]

Part Two: *What Are the Key Components of a Learning Story?*[2]

Part Three: *A Child's Culture Cannot Enter a Classroom Before It First Enters a Teacher's Conscience*[3]

1 Educational Leadership Project Ltd. (2019a, February 19). *Part one: Learning stories – A philosophical approach* [Video]. YouTube. https://youtu.be/jpor4bXCf44
2 Educational Leadership Project Ltd. (2019b, March 3). *Part two: Learning stories – The key components* [Video]. YouTube. https://youtu.be/GU2ZIlfsR7s
3 Educational Leadership Project Ltd. (2019c, March 11). *Part three: Learning stories – Culture in the classroom* [Video]. YouTube. https://youtu.be/LrdP9EztPGA

TAKEAWAYS

Assessment is a process of observing, recording, and documenting what children do and how. This helps us identify children's needs, interests, and development; plan for experiences to facilitate their growth and learning; improve the program as a whole; and communicate effectively with families and others about children's growth and activities.

Assessment must be strength-based so as to value the life knowledge that children bring. It may acknowledge that some children have extra challenges and need support in certain areas, but when this happens the goal is to assess the challenge, not label the child. Reflective practice is an important piece of assessment; educators must be open to questioning and learning.

Observation has long been a critical skill for ECEs. Observations guide our interactions with children and the planning that we do. They help us communicate with colleagues and learn more about patterns of development. There are various kinds of observations, and the one(s) you choose to use will depend on your reason for observing. Observations give a picture of a child's behaviour in a particular place and time but can also be part of a more holistic picture of a child's development and learning.

Individual portfolios of artwork, observations, and developmental checklists allow us to track children's abilities and growth. They are an important source of information for communicating with families and can help to support requests for additional supports for a child. While children's files with screening tools and checklists have traditionally been confidential and not shared with the child, there is a trend towards making a portfolio focusing on children's strengths available to children as a way of further involving them in their own learning process.

Recently, and consistent with a view of a child as a competent and capable learner, we have moved to methods of documentation that include the child in the documentation process. For example, we might post documentation that shows the steps of a project that the children have completed. This may invite the children to consider what they have done. There might be things that they would do differently another time, or ideas for extending the project. In this way, children contribute to the planning process and give us valuable information about what they already know and what they want to explore further. When their families come to pick them up, the children can use the documentation to share their activities and learnings. The educators use the panel to explain the significance of the children's process, which helps families understand what their children are learning and conveys the professionality of the educators.

Learning stories take the power of storytelling to assessment. They bring the child and family into the assessment process, celebrate the child's strengths, and point to directions to support future learnings.

REFLECTION AND DISCUSSION

- What images of the child do you see reflected in the various approaches to documentation and assessment that are described in this chapter?

- What do you see as the significance of writing *to* the child rather than *about* the child in a learning story?

- How might you use pedagogical documentation to communicate the value of play to a parent who wants their child to focus on academics?

16

Understanding and Connecting with Families

When you talk, you are only repeating
what you already know. But if you listen,
you might learn something new.
—*DALAI LAMA*

||||||||||||||||||||||||||||||||||||||||||||||||||||||||||||||||||||||||||||||||||||||||||||||||||||||||||||||||||||||||||||||||||||||

LEARNING OUTCOMES

After reading this chapter, you will be able to answer these questions:

- Why it is important to form close connections with the families of children with whom you work?
- Why it is important not to generalize about families and their experiences?
- What are some significant experiences in the lives and histories of families who identify as part of the following groups?
  - › Indigenous families
  - › Immigrant and refugee families
  - › Gender-diverse or sexually diverse families
  - › Families with children who have special needs
  - › Families with socioeconomic challenges
- What is intergenerational trauma, and how might it affect the lives of Indigenous families? of refugee families?
- What are some ways to connect with families and to build community among the families in your program?

225

Introduction

You've likely noticed by now that effective early childhood practice, and especially effective intercultural practice, depends on forming close connections with families. We have to recognize that families are the experts on their children. This applies regardless of their familiarity with the mainstream culture, their ability to speak English, their socioeconomic or educational status, or the age of their child. Our challenge is to find ways to build trusting, reciprocal relationships with them so we can work together in the interests of their children.

Every family is unique; it cannot be defined by culture. In fact, there is as much variation within cultures as there is between them. It is important, then, to get to know the individual children and families with whom you work—their experiences, home practices, and traditions. Still, it can be helpful to have a starting point. For this reason, we begin this chapter with a discussion of some experiences that families who belong to certain groups are more likely to have had. We hope this brief information will help you to make some informed guesses when it comes to puzzling situations that you encounter with families—but it will be important not to generalize. We cannot assume that we know a particular family because we have information about a group to which they might belong.

Finally, this chapter will share some ideas about how to connect with families. It will revisit the idea of an intercultural dialogue (first introduced in Chapter 1) to address differences in perspective between educators and families.

Why Build Relationships with Families?

As Sabah, one of our advisory group members, told us, "The parent knows most about the child and can give the most guidance about how to deal with the child. Parents have a lot to give us. They know best about this child." Tsedale, another advisory group member, added, "When parents are leaving their child, they have a trust with the staff. There are things they can communicate to them...Open communication is very important." In short, our relationships with families are key to our ability to provide responsive care to their children.

While supporting children is our first priority as educators, it is useful to keep in mind that well-managed early childhood programs and friendly educators can build community, bringing together diverse families around a common interest in the wellbeing of children.

Family Experiences

Again, it is vital to get to know the individual families with whom you work. Nonetheless, understanding some of the challenges that families who belong to certain groups have historically faced or may currently face can be a useful starting point in this process. We'll begin the chapter by looking at some of these experiences in the context of Indigenous families, immigrant and refugee families, gender-diverse or sexually diverse families, as well as families of children with exceptionalities, those experiencing socioeconomic challenges, and those with diverse religious practices. These descriptions will not tell you about the circumstances and challenges of a particular family, but they may help you to be more sensitive to the possibilities of their experience.

Indigenous Families

Let's take a look at an experience ECE Tanisha had in one of her playrooms:

> Aiyana, 3 years old, had been attending the centre for a month when her mother approached Tanisha with tears in her eyes. "Thank you for teaching Aiyana some Cree words," she said. "I want to learn to speak Cree, but my grandmother doesn't remember much. She was taken off to residential school when she was young and they didn't let her speak her language."

This brief story can alert us to many issues, both historical and contemporary, faced by Indigenous people in Canada. The term *Indigenous* is used to refer to First Nations, Inuit, and Métis people. Indigenous Peoples have inhabited the land we now call Canada for thousands of years beginning, by some estimates, approximately 11,000 years before the arrival of European settlers (Stonechild, 2006). Contrary to the beliefs of early explorers, governors, missionaries, fur traders, and settlers—and even many people today—Indigenous Peoples were far from "primitive." They lived in highly organized, collectively oriented communities supported by hunting, fishing, gathering, and agriculture; systems of government and spirituality; and a family life that cherished Elders and children. They had a deep and respectful relationship with land and nature. Early civilizations also experienced the hardships of starvation and disease, and sometimes conflict between rival nations (Belshaw, 2015).

Here, we offer a very brief account of some of the challenges and injustices faced by Indigenous people since the arrival of European settlers; we encourage you to seek out more complete information elsewhere.

By some accounts, the earliest relationships between Indigenous people and the European newcomers were often amicable and mutually helpful. That changed rather drastically over time as the English and French arrived in Canada in increasing numbers, imposing colonial attitudes, policies, and activities intended to extinguish Indigenous cultures, languages, and spiritualities. The colonial government aimed to "clear them from the land" (Daschuk, 2013/2019). It sought to convince the colonized peoples of their inferiority and the superiority of European civilization and religion, and to make them dependent on the meagre resources and will of the colonizers.

Daschuk (2013/2019) documents policies of deliberate starvation by Prime Minister John A. McDonald's government. For example, the bison, which had long provided food and other resources to Indigenous groups on the plains, were hunted to near extinction. The result of the loss of the bison was widespread famine and increased susceptibility to epidemics of tuberculosis, measles, and smallpox (the latter of which many believe was deliberately introduced). First Nations populations were decimated.

The federal government signed treaties with many First Nations that gave the government title to traditional lands to make way for settlement, agriculture, industry, and the railroad. In return (though it was far from a fair trade), reserves were established for First Nations, often in undesirable areas. The treaties may have been mistranslated to those who signed them (meaning they thought they were signing different documents). The courts today have largely upheld the view that treaties, even in the language of the time, prescribed to the Canadian government enduring obligations in many areas (e.g., the provision of a "medicine chest" is taken to mean comprehensive medical care in modern terms). Much of the relationship between First Nations and the federal government was governed by the Indian Act. Whether the government has held up their side of the treaty bargain by properly funding support services and infrastructure can be and is debated today. Today's crises in housing and drinkable water on many reserves are particularly serious issues. It is also important to note that some First Nations groups, particularly on the west coast, have never signed treaties with the Canadian government, but that they have nonetheless been pushed out of traditional territories.

Métis peoples have a very different history from First Nations people. The Métis Nation traces its roots to the seventeenth-century fur trade. Liaisons and "country marriages" between European fur traders and First Nation women gave fur trading companies valuable contacts and language skills to negotiate with First Nations communities, as well as a market for goods that could be exchanged for furs. Their offspring became known as Métis, a word derived from the French *métissage*, meaning the mixing of people considered to be of different races. The women offered valuable knowledge and domestic and survival skills, not to mention care for the children. "The development of a unique Métis culture began to unfold" (Vizina, 2008, para. 4).

Vizina (2008) and Teillet (2019) each present accounts of a lively and vibrant Métis culture, past and present. The versatility and ability of Métis men and women to overcome incredible tests of intellect, strength, and endurance during the fur trade contributed to a growing sense of consciousness of what it was to be Métis. That sense of character, combined with a shared history and language, created a sense of Métis nationhood that would have a significant impact on the development of Canada itself (Vizina, 2008). The Canadian government's moves in the late nineteenth century to take away land traditionally settled by Métis families in the Red River Settlement (among other factors) led to the rebellions of 1870 and 1885 (commonly known as the Red River Resistance and the Riel Resistance). After both these events, many Métis families settled farther west across the prairies. Because of the corruption and failure of the government's scrip system for land allocation, many families were not given access to quality land allotments and had to settle on road allowances, which are strips of public land reserved for future roads. Politically speaking, the Métis Nation has always had a fraught relationship with the Canadian government, especially concerning issues of land and self-determination. Life was undoubtedly very hard in the face of poverty and racism. This was compounded by the fact that Métis were considered to be neither White nor First Nations in the eyes of the Canadian government. This changed in 1982, when the Métis were included as an Aboriginal People in section 35 of the Constitution Act. However, prior to the Supreme Court decision of Daniels v. Canada on April 14, 2016, Métis people did not have any of the benefits of treaty rights that First Nations people had, problematic though those benefits might be.

Inuit in Canada also have a unique culture and history. Their traditional territory is called Inuit Nunangat (which includes the Canadian territory of Nunavut and the Arctic coasts of Quebec, the Northwest Territories, and Labrador). There are also Inuit Peoples in Greenland and Alaska. In Canada, they are recognized under section 35 of the Constitution Act of 1982 as an Aboriginal group separate from First Nations and Métis. Before this recognition, however, a 1939 court decision that mandated federal government "responsibility" over Inuit people led to a series of policy decisions that seem to have been aimed at

cultural assimilation and control. For example, in the 1950s, the federal government used their powers over Inuit people to move them to
extremely remote northern areas without adequate support in an effort
to assert sovereignty in the North, prompted by concerns emerging from
the Cold War (Madwan, 2018).

This was also the era of the disk law mandating numbered identification disks to enable government officials to identify individuals without
having to learn to pronounce traditional names. In the same era, the
government started to persuade and even force Inuit families to relocate
from small camps and settlements to bigger centres to facilitate more
efficient administration of services. The effect was to extinguish traditional lifestyles and food sources and to create dependency on scarce
housing and expensive and less healthy foods from the south (Qikiqtani
Truth Commission, 2014). Having said that, many Inuit families today
hunt for wild game as part of their diet.

Nunavat is self-governing today, though it is still heavily reliant on
federal funding. With support of the territorial government, schools and
other institutions have been and are being built (or, rather, rebuilt) on
cultural principles (Qikiqtani Inuit Association, 2014). Increasing cultural influence and pressures of cultural conformity in the digital age
are an added challenge in these endeavours. Challenges today include
pressing issues related to pollution and climate change, which are much
more dramatic than climate issues in the South. There are also serious
shortages of appropriate housing and economic problems with the high
cost of food and other goods in northern communities.

The 2015 Truth and Reconciliation Commission Report showed
the devastating effects of Canada's residential school system, which
was designed to erase Indigenous languages and cultures and destroy
children's connections to their families—with a particular focus on
First Nations and Inuit Peoples (TRC, 2015; see also Fine, 2015). Since
then, the National Inquiry into Missing and Murdered Indigenous
Women and Girls (2019) has shed light on high rates of violence against
Indigenous women, and low rates of investigation and offender appre-
hension. Compared to other segments of the population, Indigenous
children have long been apprehended in disproportionate numbers by
the child welfare system and Indigenous people are overrepresented in
the correctional system (Monkman, 2019).

These examples point to anti-Indigenous systemic racism in
Canada—that is, racism that is built into the structures of our society
(Woods, 2020)—which has been built up over many generations. The
longstanding, unjust treatment of Indigenous Peoples in Canada has

led to experiences of intergenerational trauma (discussed in Chapter 5). High levels of suicide, substance abuse, and mental health issues in many Indigenous communities may be linked to past and present experiences of colonialism (Hackett et al., 2016; Poole et al., 2017).

In the face of this history of oppression, Indigenous Peoples of Canada are resourceful and are working to reclaim and strengthen their cultural identities and languages. This work is well underway at individual, family, community, and political levels. However, given the experiences of violence, racism, and cultural destruction Indigenous people have experienced, and continue to experience, in connection with Canadian educational, health, legal, and justice institutions, we should not be surprised if many distrust these institutions today, particularly those that continue to demonstrate that they do not recognize the challenges and aspirations of Indigenous people.

Contrary to what many people believe, historical issues do not tend to "go away." As Canadians, we all have a responsibility for reconciliation, whether we are working directly with Indigenous people or not. For most, it is painful to hear about the history of unjust treatment of Indigenous Peoples in Canada. However, it is essential to educate ourselves about Canada's relationships with Indigenous Peoples. Reconciliation, however, is about more than just recognition and understanding. It is about making tangible and lasting changes to our practice and to the institutions we represent. It is a commonplace but true observation that people of all cultures must be able to "see themselves" in social institutions such as schools, child care centres, and health care systems. And it is crucially important to work toward institutions free of racism.

What does all of this mean for you as an ECE professional?

- To create an ECE environment that welcomes and serves Indigenous families, it is important to begin with a recognition of their histories, their challenges, and their aspirations. It is critically important to acknowledge and honour their cultural traditions and practices.
- Cultural traditions and practices will vary widely by individual and family preferences and experiences, and by political affiliation, Nation membership, or geographic location. Effective practice with children and parents is all about relationships, conversation, and the sharing of experiences and viewpoints.
- It is important to challenge stereotypes, assumptions, and caricatures that we see in the media and in our schools and that have become embedded in our own memories about Indigenous people.

- It is important to recognize Indigenous colleagues and acquaintances (or yourself, if you are Indigenous!) as important resources because they may more immediately understand the life circumstances and experiences of Indigenous families (Kemble, 2019) and because they may be able to suggest culturally meaningful and authentic practices and activities for children.

Immigrant and Refugee Families

Raising a child in Canada is the most important and difficult task of immigrants.
—SABAH (ADVISORY GROUP MEMBER)

Immigrants and refugees form a sizable and ever-increasing proportion of Canada's population. Morency et al. (2017) estimate that, by 2036, nearly half of Canada's population will be comprised of first- or second-generation immigrants. Understanding the experiences of newcomers to Canada helps us to better support them and their children.

Newcomers are inevitably faced with challenges: culture shock, language barriers, loss of extended family support, loneliness, unfamiliar systems, discrimination, and a new climate, to name a few. Lack of recognition of credentials from their home countries often results in unemployment or underemployment. Families may also experience role reversals. In some families, the children may become the "experts" of the new culture more quickly than their parents, leading parents to depend on their children to navigate their new home. In other families, husbands may have to adjust to losing their traditional role as the breadwinners of their families. The stress associated with these challenges may influence family members' emotional and physical wellbeing.

These are issues that many newcomers face, even if they have moved voluntarily and have had an opportunity to plan for their move. Refugees, however, have been forced to leave their home country because of war, persecution, or natural disasters. They may have ongoing challenges arising from their premigration, migration, and settlement experiences. Many, including children and young people, have witnessed violence or have been direct victims of violence and/or abuse. Usually, refugees come to Canada by way of one or more other asylum countries. The conditions in those countries, not to mention being constantly on the move, may have been very difficult experiences as well. Once settled in Canada, they face all of the challenges of finding their way in a new environment, along with the effects of the trauma they have experienced prior to and on their journey to Canada.

Families who arrive as refugees may not know, as they leave their home country, what their final destination will be, and have had little time to prepare for life in their new country. Their children arrive with varying educational backgrounds and often without the language of their new school. The trauma they have suffered may manifest itself in symptoms that will affect them in school, such as disturbed sleep, difficulty concentrating, anxiety, anger, or hopelessness (Jesuit Social Services, 2009). At the same time, it is important to remember that they are survivors, with strengths and resilience.

Our MCHB advisory group described the extent of the culture shock that children and families experience when they come to an early childhood program in Canada. "Everything is different," Ying Ying maintained. She continued as follows:

> There is a language barrier, and the music, songs, stories, and the overall teaching environment are different. Even the expectations for cleanliness are different. That's why many parents look for programs where there is someone from their own culture, someone who speaks their own language.

The MCHB advisory group also pointed out that Western programs tend to be rooted in individualistic values that conflict with the communal approaches of many other cultures. As Tsedale explained from her own cultural perspective,

> When grandparents come, they aren't comfortable with their grandchildren because everything is "mine." "My clothes, my plate." At home, we share everything. We even share food together from a big plate. The grandparents say, "You are taking that away from the children."

Western culture promotes independence: children are expected to learn to feed and dress themselves. This value of independence is not shared by all cultures, however; some cultures value the opportunity to show caring for the children by doing these things for them. Children who are accustomed to sleeping with their parents or siblings are expected, in Western child care programs, to sleep alone.

"Western programs are cold," one advisory group member said. "Ours is a trusting and warm culture. There are lots of hugs and kisses...It's not okay to say, 'Oh, it will be fine' to a crying child" (a practice she had seen in Western programs in which she had worked). This is partly a cultural difference, but it may also be related to the constraints of caring for children in larger groups. As advisory group member Yvonne Chiu summarized, "There is a family way of loving and caring for children and an institutional way of loving and caring for the children."

What are the implications for early childhood programs? We can see that immigrant families value programs where there is someone who speaks their language and understands their culture. Where this is not possible, it is important for educators to find ways to make connections across language and cultural differences. As the MCHB advisory group emphasized, "The parent knows most about the child and can give the most guidance about how to deal with the child."

> ### ? WHAT DO
> ### ▪ YOU THINK?
>
> The term *intergenerational trauma* is defined as the transmission of historical oppression, abuse, or violation and its negative consequences across generations. The incidence of intergenerational trauma certainly isn't restricted to Indigenous and refugee populations but, knowing about their histories, why might people from these groups be particularly at risk for this kind of trauma?

Gender-Diverse and Sexually Diverse Families

> Tara's family consists of herself, her wife, Sharon, and their daughter, Annika. As Tara says, "People soon realize we're just a pretty average family."

Our society is becoming more open with respect to matters of gender diversity and sexual orientation. Same-sex couples are increasingly visible, and it is very possible that you will encounter parents with various sexual orientations and gender identities.

In 2005, Canada became the fourth country in the world to legalize same-sex marriage. By 2016, there were 72,880 same-sex couples in Canada, one-third of whom were married. In 2016, about 12% of same-sex couples had children living with them, compared with about half of opposite-sex couples (Statistics Canada, 2017b).

Knowing some of the terms associated with sexual orientation and gender identity can help you be more comfortable in dealing with gender and sexual diversity. The term *LGBTQ2* is the acronym used by the Government of Canada to refer to gender-diverse and sexually diverse individuals in Canada (Canadian Heritage LGBTQ2 Secretariat, 2020). The letters of the acronym stand for the words *lesbian, gay, bisexual, transgender, queer,* and *two-spirit.* You may see other, similar acronyms that include other identities, as well. The term *queer,* though at one time a derogatory word, has been reclaimed by the LGBTQ2 community and is sometimes used to describe gender-diverse and sexually diverse individuals in general.

An individual's *gender identity* refers to the way in which they define themselves in relation to the masculine and feminine norms of their culture. Many people identify as male or female. If this gender matches the gender they were assigned at birth, they may describe themselves with the term *cisgender*. If it does not correspond with the gender they were assigned at birth, they may use the term *transgender*—a term that may also, along with *nonbinary* and *gender-fluid*, describe gender identities that fall somewhere between male and female, may change from day to day, or may be outside of this binary all together. The term *two-spirit* is an umbrella term that refers to traditional gender identities in Indigenous communities that comprise both male and female spirits. *Sexual orientation*, on the other hand, has to do with the people to whom a person is romantically attracted, whether this be to people of the same sex or gender, a different sex or gender, both males and females, or people of all genders. Some of the words to describe these diverse sexual orientations include *heterosexual, lesbian, gay, bisexual,* and *pansexual*. Some people are *asexual* or *aromantic* and do not experience sexual or romantic attraction at all (Canadian Heritage LGBTQ2 Secretariat, 2020).

Though increasingly common, gender-diverse and sexually diverse families are still sometimes met with curiosity or suspicion in the larger society. Programs that encourage families to get to know one another can help to allay misconceptions. It is, of course, critically important to the wellbeing of families and their children to convey acceptance and appreciation of all families. Family events that encourage families to get to know one another can help break down barriers.

Families of Children with Exceptionalities

When you have a child with special needs, it's important to have more than one person involved with the child. Daycare is a relief, but it's more than that. You feel so alone when you have a child who's different, and the day care lets you be part of a community.
—DESTINY (ADVISORY GROUP MEMBER)

The terms *exceptionalities* and *special needs* are broad. Children with exceptionalities may be gifted or talented, or they may have mild or severe intellectual disabilities. They may have autism spectrum disorders, attention deficit disorder (ADD) or attention deficit hyperactivity disorder (ADHD), learning disabilities, or socioemotional or behavioural needs. They may have communication, speech, and language needs (including those related to learning English as an additional language). They may have sensory needs (e.g., related to vision, hearing) or chronic health or medical needs (Hutchinson & Specht, 2020).

Different cultures view exceptionalities differently; families may see their exceptional child as a source of shame or one of pride. Definitions of exceptionality may depend on cultural norms; for example, in cultures (such as mainstream Canadian culture) where direct eye contact is expected when communicating with others, children who fail to make eye contact because of different cultural norms may be falsely labelled as having exceptionalities.

Generally speaking, Canadian society has moved from segregating children who have exceptionalities to including them in mainstream environments and activities. Parents and inclusion advocates argue for this approach, maintaining that it gives children with special needs chances to learn from peers, to build relationships with other children and adults, and to practise social skills. They also believe that inclusion can foster attitudes of respect and belonging amongst children.

Families of children with exceptionalities have challenges associated with learning about their child or children's exceptionalities, finding effective treatments and resources, getting to appointments with the many people involved with their child, advocating for appropriate care, and possibly paying for treatment not covered by health insurance. They may be exhausted from the demands of caring for their exceptional child (Boston University, n.d.).

The emotional impact on families is high. They may worry about their child's pain and suffering and about the child's future. They might feel guilty about focusing so much attention on one particular child at the expense of others in the family. They may also feel isolated from or resentful of families of "normally" developing children. They might grieve for the loss of the hopes they had for their child and for themselves as parents (Boston University, n.d.).

Families of children with exceptionalities benefit hugely from the respite and support they receive from early childhood programs. Understanding the stresses these families may be experiencing will help you, as an ECE, to respond appropriately to them.

Families Experiencing Poverty

> Poverty drains the spirit and leads to low hope. That's not a great place to be when you're trying to raise children. (Ford-Jones, cited in Delisle, 2019, "What effects does poverty have," para. 2)

Statistics Canada (2020) found that, in 2018, 3.2 million Canadians, including over 560,000 children, were living in poverty. This was actually a decrease in child poverty from 2012. At the time of writing, it is difficult to say exactly what impact the COVID-19 pandemic will have on these rates. However, we can say that the impact of this crisis, and the impacts of crises we will experience in the future, are likely to be significant.

Children living in lone-parent families are more likely to experience poverty. The Statistics Canada survey found that the rate of child poverty in lone-parent families was 26.2% compared with a rate of 5.8% in families with two parents.

Parents experiencing poverty, and even those who don't officially live below the poverty line, can be struggling to survive. They may be in precarious work and living situations. They may not know how they will provide food and other necessities of life for their children. These stresses can impact on their ability to be the parents they would like to be. They live in a state of uncertainty and anxiety, which their children will perceive as well.

Living in poverty may mean that children experience health problems due to factors such as poorly maintained housing, poor nutrition, and lack of dental care. They may compare themselves with other children who have new clothes, expensive toys, birthday parties, and interesting holidays. They may be bullied by other children for their lack of such privileges.

Early childhood programs help to alleviate negative effects of poverty by providing a stable day-to-day environment as well as nutritious meals and snacks. Children may be particularly hungry on Mondays, so provisions could be made for larger meals that day. Some programs are able to solicit donations from bakeries and grocery stores for their own use and for distribution to families. Sending a bit of food home on Fridays can be particularly helpful.

Sometimes ECEs use food as a craft material or fill sensory bins with rice or noodles. This seems not only wasteful, but disrespectful of families for whom that food would be valuable. There are many non-food alternatives that can give children equally beneficial play experiences, such as using aquarium stones, pea gravel, all natural paper pet bedding, and wood pellets. Always check the list of ingredients to ensure safety

Programs must also respond sensitively to, and make accommodations for, the fact that some families will be unable to afford extra charges such as field trip fees or won't be able to wear a particular colour of shirt for a special day. Neither the children nor the family should ever feel humiliated by being set apart in these situations.

Religious Diversity

Let us put our minds together and see
what life we can make for our children
                            —*SITTING BULL*

Canada has no official religion, and the Charter of Rights and Freedoms supports freedom of religion.

The 2011 Canadian census found that Christianity had the greatest number of adherents (67.3%). People who reported having no religion represented 23.9% of the population. The remainder of the population was split among Islam (3.2%), Hinduism (1.5%), Sikhism (1.4%), Buddhism (1.1%), and Judaism (1.0%) (Statistics Canada, 2016).

Controversy has arisen around the celebration of religious holidays, particularly Christmas (Friesen & Bascaramurty, 2011; Taylor, 2014). Some programs continue to focus on Christmas and other dominant holidays. Others have changed traditional Christmas programs to a more general holiday theme. A few acknowledge the whole range of holidays celebrated by all the children in the program.

In our view, when ECE programs respect and affirm children's home culture, it sends a powerful message of inclusion to children, families, and educators. They see that their perspectives have value and can contribute to new understandings about child care practice.

An Intercultural Approach to Celebration

Our centre was founded by members of the Ethiopian and Eritrean communities and in the early years at the centre, all our families came from these communities; as a result, deciding what to celebrate with the children was a relatively simple decision. As our children and families became more diverse, we realized that we needed to revisit our practices and make some conscious decisions about what we celebrate now. We realized that celebrating every holiday and occasion would be too overwhelming for children and educators and might lead us down the path of too many adult-directed experiences. On the other hand, if we celebrated nothing, we would lose the richness of who we are as a centre.

What to celebrate? It would have been quick and easy to make this decision ourselves and then explain our rationale to families, but instead we decided to invite their input. With a certain amount of hesitation and a lot of risk-taking, we engaged with them at a family gathering, explaining our conundrum and inviting them to take part in an exercise created by Anna Kirova, a professor of early childhood education from the

Our Families Reflect on Celebration

Celebrations: Birthdays, Christmas, Eid, Easter, Ramadan, Thanksgiving, Good Friday

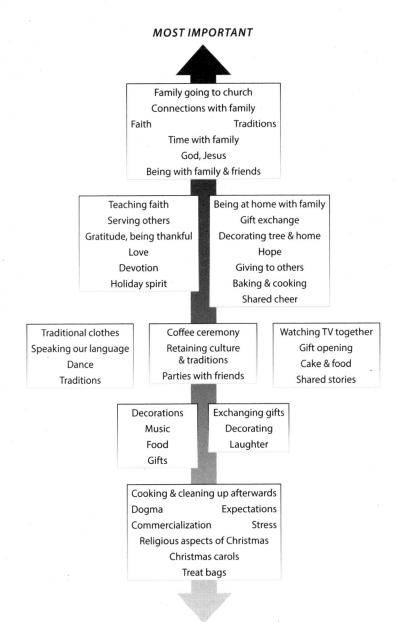

Figure 16.1. Compilation of family responses

University of Alberta. In it, each family picks a celebration that is important to them as their focus. They rate the aspects of that celebration from what is most important to them to what they could do without. In our discussion afterward, the most valued parts of the celebration turned out to involve being together as a family, faith, and going to church, while the least valuable aspects included stress, expectations, commercialization, and all the cooking, shopping, and cleaning up afterward.

At a workshop we attended in 2016, Kirova explained, "In child care, we cannot do justice to the deep, meaningful aspects of all cultural celebrations." This is especially true when we may not have a personal connection to the celebration and the culture itself. In discussion with our families, we expressed our concern about cultural appropriation—when a person from one cultural group adopts the fashion, practices, or styles from another culture—and our desire to offer authentic cultural experiences. We also talked about our fear of engaging children in activities that may not be appropriate for them developmentally, such as making toddlers sit quietly for a prolonged period while an adult explains a tradition or shows them artifacts that they cannot touch.

In the end, we have proposed a partnership in which we work with families in each playroom to identify what is important for them and what they want to share with the children and us. The families' role is to bring their cultural expertise; our role is to find ways to celebrate with children that are hands-on and meaningful for them. For example, knowing that our youngest children are in the sensorimotor stage of cognitive development, we want to provide experiences that invite them to experience through their senses, their movement, and the manipulation of objects. Rather than focus specifically on a series of specific celebrations, our goal is now to find ways to honour the cultural practices of families and educators in an authentic and meaningful way in our everyday practice.

Finding Ways to Connect with Families

Throughout this book, we've mentioned various approaches and conditions that can strengthen the connections between families and child care programs. Here is a short list of suggestions, including both ideas that we have already suggested and some new ones:

- Employ educators from diverse cultures, with particular attention to cultures represented in the population of families.
- Ensure regular conversations with all families to inform them of their children's activities in the program. Invite family input on

their child's strengths, the family's home routines, their guidance practices, and so on. (Note that when there is a significant language barrier, it may be important to have a translator available.)

- Maintain environments and programming that reflect the cultural mix of the families in your centre (see Chapter 10).
- Provide regular newsletters that include information about the children's activities as well as community resources that families can access. If possible, these should be translated into the home languages of the families in the program.
- Hold family events that invite families to get to know one another. Sometimes, this requires creativity. For example, in the midst of the COVID-19 lockdown, one centre sent packages home with each child that included tree cookies and painting materials. The families were asked to work with their children to paint the tree cookies in ways that showed their feelings about the pandemic. The painted cookies were sent back to the centre and assembled in a composition in the shape of a heart in the centre's waiting area (Figure 16.2).

Figure 16.2. Family composition: messages of hope

NAMING OUR PLAYROOMS

At one point, we began to notice an inconsistency between being a centre that embraces intercultural practice and the names of our playrooms: the yellow room, the purple room, the blue room, and the green room. How, we wondered, might we name our playrooms in a way that would capture the culturally responsive nature of the care we aspire to provide and demonstrate two of our centre's values: engagement and collaboration?

We talked a long time about renaming the rooms. Finally, we realized that this conversation needed to begin with our educators. We asked them: Who are the children in your playrooms? What do you want for these children while they are in your care? Their responses led us to ask one more question: What if we engaged families in discussions, shared educators' visions for each room, and invited families to contribute words and phrases in their home languages that might speak to the essence of what they and educators imagined?

We did this at several family evenings where we shared supper with children and families. We then met separately with parents over coffee and dessert while their children were cared for in one of our playrooms, and the discussions were rich with possibilities. We were patient with our process, introducing the naming discussion over time at several meetings with different families. It took more than a year to come to a place where we felt we could complete this project and introduce the new names.

One evening, as we were sitting around a table, a father of a child from northern Spain offered us the Spanish words *El Nido* to capture the essence of the room for our youngest children. It just felt right.

El Nido Playroom

In Spanish El Nido means "The Nest".

This name was chosen for our youngest children, ages 12 – 24 months, to reflect the warm, nurturing environment in which children will begin their time with us at ICFC.

Salaam Playroom
سلام

Parents and staff chose the name Salaam for the room for our children ages 24-36 months. Salaam means "Peace" or "Welcome" in Arabic, Tigrinya, and Amharic.

We named this room Salaam to honour the initiative and vision of ICFC's founding members.

Natonam Playroom
ᐊᑕᐠ

Our staff see children ages 3-5 years old as explorers who continually make sense of the world around them through their play.
In Cree, Natonam means "one who seeks or searches" and we think this describes these children well.

Kapatiran Playroom

In Tagalog, Kapatiran means fraternity or a feeling of community.

The concept of brotherhood or sisterhood captures the essence of what we envision for our oldest children in Kapatiran.

Figure 16.3. It was worth taking the time to come to these meaningful names

> While it would have been expedient to have just renamed the rooms ourselves, we would have missed out on the opportunity to engage in collaboration with educators and families alike. To this day, this project is one that fills us with great pride!
> The results of our journey with educators and families are these beautiful room names, which reflect some of the diversity and intercultural collaboration in our centre.

Connecting through Learning Stories

Learning stories have the potential to create and maintain a connection with both children and families. These stories communicate that you have noticed their child and let families know what their child is learning. In the family response section of a learning story, educators invite the family's input, valuing their knowledge as the primary caregivers to their child (see Chapter 15).

Soon after 15-month-old Athena began in ECE Tiffany's playroom, Tiffany wrote a learning story about using Cantonese words and phrases while the two of them engaged in play and ate lunch. At the end of the story, Tiffany invited Athena's family to respond to the story. She wrote:

> Athena seems to show some understanding when I speak to her in Cantonese. What are some of your goals related to Athena in terms of learning Cantonese and English at home and at the centre?

This is what Athena's mother and father wrote in response:

> Thank you so much for speaking to Athena in Cantonese. We are so happy that she is being exposed to her mother's language at the centre. She does understand quite a bit of Cantonese as I speak it with her almost exclusively. My goals are aligned with what you have done so far: colours and foods. I have already taught her colours, but she does need more practice.
> Try asking her to count her toes! She will gesture 1 to 5 by pointing to each toe ☺. She also knows hygiene routines: Try asking her in Cantonese to wash hands, wash face, brush teeth, and brush/comb her hair.
> Keep up the awesome work with Athena! Thank you, Tiffany! ☺

This partnership between the centre and home was nurtured through Tiffany's intentional interactions with Athena, which she shared with the family in daily conversations and in the learning story she wrote. By inviting the family to respond to her efforts, Tiffany gained an opportunity to learn what the family valued as well as strategies they were using to help Athena learn Cantonese. This way, both the centre and home could collaborate to support Athena.

Connecting through Intercultural Dialogue

An intercultural dialogue involves two individuals or groups with differing perspectives who, by dialoguing with one another, are able to find a middle ground that is agreeable to each of them (see Chapter 1). An intercultural dialogue is like a bridge: individuals who begin at either end are able to meet in the middle. This is a mutually respectful process that results in new learning for each individual.

Let's look at an example of an intercultural dialogue and see how it can deepen connections between families and child care centres. Jacinda's parents have recently moved to Canada from a tropical country. Jacinda's parents approach Mel, Jacinda's educator, to request that Jacinda be excused from outside play in the winter. Their dialogue with Jacinda's educator, Mel, might take shape as follows:

Parents: *It's very cold outside. Can you please keep Jacinda inside on days like this?*

Mel: *[paraphrasing what she understood] You're worried about her being outside on cold days?*

Parents: *Yes. She's never experienced cold like this and we're worried that she will get ill.*

Mel: *This winter weather must be new to all of you. It can be kind of scary, can't it?*

Parents: *Yes! I'm afraid we're going to freeze when we go outside!*

Mel has been listening attentively and is now at the point where she feels she can understand and empathize with their fears. Now Mel can introduce her own perspective:

Mel: *I can see why you'd hesitate to have Jacinda go outside. The snow and cold was new to me when I came here, and I only moved from Vancouver! I enjoy it now, though, because I've discovered all of the outdoor sports that you can do in the winter. You know, we have so many months of winter each year that we really try to help the children be comfortable outdoors and find lots of ways to enjoy the snow.*

Parents: *But don't they get cold?*

Mel: *We don't go out when it's colder than –20°C. Even when it's warmer than that, we bring the children inside when they get uncomfortable. We also make sure that they are dressed warmly. I wonder if you've noticed the poster in the hallway that describes how to dress children warmly for winter play.*

Parents: *We did see it, but we really don't have a lot of warm clothes yet.*

Mel: *You know, children outgrow their clothes so quickly that we have a clothing exchange at each parent night. There's one this Thursday, and I know there are a lot of warm winter clothes. Why don't you come by then and see what you can find for Jacinda?*

Parents: *I guess we could try having her go outside, but will you promise to bring her inside right away if she cries that she's cold?*

Mel: *Yes, I can promise that. We want her to have a good experience when she's outdoors and not to feel like it's a punishment!*

You'll notice in this dialogue that Mel listens attentively until she feels she fully understands the family's concerns. She empathizes with their concerns by sharing her own experience of moving from a warmer city to a colder one. She explains the program's policy about outdoor temperatures and why it is in place—to give children a good experience of the outdoors. She offers resources to the family—the clothing exchange—and they reach an agreement that is satisfactory to both of them. The result of this dialogue is a closer relationship: Mel understands the family better, and they know that Mel shares their concern for their child.

The *RAISED Between Cultures* model was developed to assist early learning and child care educators to understand the realities of immigrant and refugee families in order to provide an intercultural environment that honours them and benefits all children. We encourage you to access the 14 minute video and reflective guidebook at https://www.ualberta.ca/community-university-partnership/resources/reference-materials.html.

TAKEAWAYS

Close relationships with families are an essential component of intercultural care. Parents are the experts when it comes to their children and we must respect and benefit from their expertise. While we must not generalize about any family, it can be useful to know the possibilities of their experiences. This can help us to be more sensitive to them and to understand their children better. This chapter suggests a number of ways to connect and engage with families to create a strong child care community. Learning stories are a powerful way to include families in their children's lives in the program, while intercultural dialogue can help to resolve differences in a respectful and mutually satisfying manner.

ll

REFLECTION AND DISCUSSION

Consider the following situation in Nasima's playroom:

> Nasima has set out a foot painting experience for the children. Many participate enthusiastically. Nasima notices that Chloe looks interested, but when she invites her to join in, Chloe shakes her head. "My mommy doesn't like me to get dirty," Chloe reveals.

Nasima is concerned that Chloe is missing out on experiences, but she wants to respect her mother's viewpoint. Imagine an intercultural dialogue that might take place between Nasima and Chloe's mom to find a shared solution.

17

Caring for Yourself and Others

When we truly care for ourselves, it becomes possible to care far more profoundly about other people.

—*EDA LASHAN*

LEARNING OUTCOMES

When you have read this chapter, you will be able to do the following:

- List some important characteristics of quality early child care environments
- Identify organizations that you could access for support and professional development opportunities
- Develop a plan that will enable you to bring your best self to your work with children and families

Introduction

Early childhood educators can make a profound difference in the lives of young children and their families. ECEC programs ensure that families can go comfortably about their lives at work or school knowing that their children are in a safe, nurturing, and stimulating environment. At their best, ECEC programs can be much like an extended family, where adults other than the parents or guardians know and care about the children and can share in the joys and the challenges of their growing years.

We hope this book has excited you about the possibilities of an intercultural approach to an early childhood education career. This chapter is devoted to information that will support your success as an ECE. It summarizes things to look for when you are considering an ECEC position and suggests ways of looking after yourself and your wellbeing in a career that can be both hugely satisfying and highly demanding. Among the supports that can be useful to you as an ECEC educator are professional organizations at the local, provincial, and national levels. The specific organizations and resources available to you will depend on where you work and live, but we have included some examples in Appendix E to give you an idea of what is available.

We begin this chapter with a section intended to help you with your job hunt by considering characteristics of quality care in ECEC settings.

Identifying Quality in Child Care

If you have been working in early childhood settings already, you probably have a good idea as to the kinds of environments that are good for children, families, and yourself as an educator. However, if you are fairly new to the field or looking for a change, here are some ideas about questions to ask to identify quality child care environments:

- How big are the group sizes? Are they small enough to provide for meaningful one-on-one time with children?
- Are there dividers or walls to keep noise at a minimum?
- What opportunities are there for educator professional development?
- What qualifications do the educators who work here have?
- How much staff turnover is there? (A low staff turnover probably means that staff are happy with their situation.)
- Do the relationships between the educators and children seem to be positive?
- Does the programming respond to the interests and needs of the children?
- Are there enough materials and equipment for the number of children in each playroom?
- Do the children seem engaged and purposeful?
- Is the environment in the playrooms comfortable, well organized, interesting, and culturally responsive?
- Does the program meet licensing and (if applicable) accreditation standards? Are you able to review recent licensing reports?

- Does the centre maintain good health and safety practices? Is it clean and well organized? Do all educators know what to do in case of an emergency?
- How does the program support and reflect the cultures of the families it serves?
- What is the relationship of the program with its families? Are families welcome in the playrooms? Can they be involved with the program? Are there regular family events? What kinds of communication does the program have with families?

 The Canadian Child Care Federation provides information about certification requirements, employment conditions, and training opportunities in each province and territory in Canada. Visit https://ccf-fcsge.ca for more details.[1]

1 Canadian Child Care Federation. (2021). ECE guide by province or territory. https://cccf-fcsge.ca/ece-resources/professional-development/journey-early-childhood-education/provincial-data-child-care-certification/

Caring for Yourself

As an ECE, your own days will be busy and demanding, but also fun and satisfying. You'll need to be alert to children's activities and moods, and respond quickly as new learning interests arise. The work is both physically and emotionally demanding. Physically, you'll spend time running in the park, lifting children, and squatting to talk with them at eye level. You'll be frequently exposed to illness. The noise level may be stressful at times. Emotionally, the children will trust you with their triumphs, their fears and tears, and their questions. You'll need to be your best self in order to give them your fullest and deepest attention. All of these factors mean that you'll need to find ways to look after yourself.

The intensity of caring for children can be stressful, and being overly stressed can have serious physical and emotional effects. Signs of stress include the following:

- Decreased energy
- Not sleeping well
- Feeling overwhelmed or constantly worried
- Often feeling tired
- Losing interest in activities you used to enjoy
- Having frequent headaches, body pain, or other physical problems
- Gaining or losing weight
- Feeling irritable or worried

- Having difficulty concentrating
- Using tobacco, alcohol, or other drugs to relieve stress

It is impossible to avoid stress completely, but you can find ways to reduce unnecessary stress and deal with the stresses you do have in healthy ways.

Sleep. Scientists have discovered that sleep plays a critical role in boosting our immune system, regulating our metabolism, repairing damaged tissues, and supporting memory and learning. It reduces stress hormones and adjusts the hormones that control appetite. To get the recommended seven to eight hours of sleep, it is recommended that your give yourself time to unwind and relax before you go to bed, and that you not bring screens with you to bed—that includes your phone!

Eat Healthily. Eating a wide variety of foods in healthy, balanced meals helps you have the energy and alertness you need for a day spent with children. Healthy eating helps to prevent disease and illnesses such as diabetes and heart disease. Substitute fruit and vegetables for sugary or salty snacks. Avoid too much caffeine, and make sure you drink lots of water. Check Canada's Food Guide for recommendations. Remember, too, that you are modelling healthy eating for children.

> Canada's Food Guide was updated in 2019 to reflect recent findings in medicine and dietetics. Find the food guide here: https://food-guide.canada.ca/.

Laugh. Laughter has been found to have a positive effect on many organs, including your heart, lungs, and muscles. It has also been shown to release endorphins, chemicals that increase feelings of wellbeing. Laughter relieves your stress response, decreasing your heart rate and blood pressure. It can relax your muscles and stimulate circulation. The Mayo Clinic (2019) adds that, over the long term, laughter can improve your immune system, relieve pain, help you cope with difficult situations, connect with people, and fight depression and anxiety.

Life with children can be filled with humorous incidents if we take the time to enjoy them. Carole offers a favourite example:

> When I was the director of a child care centre, a couple of 5-year-old boys came rushing into my office to tell me that they had thrown a ball up into the air and it hadn't come down. "What do you think happened to it?" I asked. One of the boys shrugged, "I don't know. Maybe God grabbed it."

Of course, there are many other ways to add humour to our lives. Television comedies and videos of baby goats were some of our favourite escapes during the COVID-19 pandemic.

Exercise. Research shows that exercise reduces stress hormones such as cortisol and helps to release endorphins. Regular exercise can improve sleep quality and can help you feel more physically and emotionally confident, which can in turn enhance your mental wellbeing.

Exercising might feel like the last thing you want to do at the end of a busy day with children. However, you don't have to go to the gym or train for a marathon in order to gain the benefits of exercise (though you can if you want to!). Think about ways you can build walking and stretching into your day, perhaps in activities you do with colleagues during your lunch break or with the children. Doing this will also model healthy exercise habits.

Cultivate spirituality. Spirituality has been shown to provide stress relief and improve mental health. It can give you a sense of purpose and help you connect with what is meaningful in your life. Spirituality can take many forms. It may or may not be associated with religious adherence.

Listen to music. Listening to calming music or nature sounds can be soothing, but any music you enjoy can help to relieve your stress. In child care, the gentle music that you play during nap time will benefit both you and the children, while energetic dancing at other times, as a form of exercise, can relieve both their stress and yours.

Learn to say no. Take control over the parts of your life that you can change by not taking on more than you can handle. Consider that for every new thing you take on, there may be one or more things that you have to let go; choose wisely.

Avoid procrastinating. Leaving things to the last minute adds to stress. Make a to-do list organized by priorities, and give yourself realistic deadlines to work through that list. Be sure to add enough time for the unexpected demands that may well arise.

Touch. Positive touch, whether cuddling with your child, your partner, or your puppy, has been found to foster the release of oxytocin—a hormone associated with love and bonding—and lower blood pressure.

Breathe. Deep breathing activates a relaxation response. There are various methods for learning to breathe deeply. Practices that focus on body and breath awareness such as yoga, Pilates, and meditation have been found to be effective ways to relieve stress.

You can practice deep breathing by sitting in a chair with your feet flat on the floor and your hands on your knees. Breathe slowly in and out for 3 to 5 minutes, fully expanding your lungs on your breath in. Children might be interested in joining you in this exercise.

Journal. Keeping a journal can help relieve stress and anxiety. You can write down what you are stressed about or use the journal to record and remind you of things you are grateful for in your life and work.

Volunteer. Volunteering connects you with other people and contributes to the community. It also helps to combat stress, anger, depression, and anxiety. Researchers have discovered that being helpful to others contributes to our own happiness.

Build a social network. Having strong social ties outside of work can help you gain perspective, weather stressful times, and lower your anxiety levels. Belonging to a club, singing in a choir, or being part of a sports team all have the benefit of connecting you to other people. Confidentiality considerations mean that you can't take your work situations to your social supports; this can be a good reminder that your work is just one part of your life.

Become an advocate. Advocating for causes you believe in can give you a sense of purpose and reinforce your feeling of being part of a community that has a common focus. Advocating for the needs and rights of children in your care can be tremendously empowering. The same is true of advocating for your own profession and its public perception, or for changes in your professional community or working conditions.

Build a professional support network. Your professional connections can help you solve problems or gain new perspectives on work situations. As an early childhood professional, you are part of a large community of people who share a common concern for children and child care. They understand the value of good quality child care and cooperate in various ways to solve problems, generate new knowledge, and improve conditions for children and educators. Professional organizations give you the opportunity to be involved with individuals throughout Canada who share your commitment to child care. We encourage you to get involved; see Appendix E for a list of professional organizations.

Intercultural Perspectives on Self-Care

Individuals vary in their experiences of stress and in the self-care practices that are helpful to them. Family circumstances and history, cultural background, gender, religious beliefs, and age are just some of the factors that may affect the kinds of self-care that are the most available and helpful to someone.

Nicholson et al. (2019) point out that in the Western world, self-care therapies and strategies tend to focus on the individual. These approaches, however, may seem less authentic to persons whose focus is more on community and relationships (Nicholson et al., 2019, p. 189). One implication of this is that where cultural norms discourage discussing negative feelings or expressing emotions, self-care strategies based on self-reflection may be less helpful than other, more relationship-oriented approaches.

For this reason, Nicholson et al. (2019) characterize self-care strategies in two categories: those that involve turning inward (e.g., journalling, mindfulness, and other forms of self-reflection) and those that turn outward (connecting with others).

Differences in the ways that individuals respond to stress make it important to be particularly sensitive and supportive with colleagues and families. They may not show their stress in ways that you would expect, so you will need to be alert to subtle signs that they may be feeling overwhelmed. Similarly, the self-care strategies that you find useful may not be as helpful to them.

WHO AM I?

Take a moment to consider your own self-care practices:

- What are ways that you already take care of your mental and physical health? What areas of personal wellness could use more attention?
- What is one action you could take to look after yourself better? (Think small— changing habits takes time.) How could you plan to make this change?
- Looking at the self-care strategies in this chapter, which would you categorize as "turning inward" and which as "turning outward"? Which ones resonate the most with you?

A Final Thought

In this book, we've tried to cover basic theory as well as some alternative ways of looking at ECEC practice. Sometimes the two are contradictory. This can be confusing, especially if you are a beginning educator and just want some answers. However, your ability to look beyond taken-for-granted assumptions is what will help to make you a great educator. Because you understand that there are many different ways of being in the world, you will be able to respond more sensitively to children, families, and co-workers.

Although it may appear that there are no givens when we are working with diversity (and we are always working with diversity), there is one thing we can rely on: in any situation, the bottom line is the wellbeing of the child. An intercultural approach tells us that truly understanding the child and what is best for them means taking into account their family, their community, and their culture as well. We hope you come away from this book feeling that you have some tools to begin to do that.

TAKEAWAYS

If you are a new early childhood professional, it's important that you find employment in programs that offer good quality care for children and provide support for families and staff. Know what to look for and what questions to ask. Look after your physical and mental health so you can enjoy your time with children and set a good example for them.

Unfortunately, work in ECE doesn't pay nearly as well as it should given its importance. We can only hope and advocate for better recognition in the future. In the meantime, it's encouraging to remember that, as ECEs, we have a lasting impact on the children in our care and, through them, the future of our society. Children who are nurtured and stimulated will move confidently into the world and live productive lives. Intercultural child care helps us create the Canada we hope for in the future because we are building communities where people can develop close relationships and learn from one another. In a society in which there are concerns about racism and inequality, we are modelling and teaching respect and justice for all.

REFLECTION AND DISCUSSION

- Take some time to check out the professional organizations available to you nationally and in the province where you live.
  › What advocacy activities are they involved with?
  › What resources do they offer?
  › Are there opportunities for professional development?

  › Is there an organization you'd like to join?
- How do you feel now about your ability to navigate between and among cultures in an ECEC context? What questions do you still have, and how can you answer them?

Canadian Child Care
Federation Code of Ethics*

Child care practitioners[1] work with one of society's most vulnerable groups—young children. The quality of the interactions between young children and the adults who care for them has a significant, enduring impact on children's lives. The intimacy of the relationship and the potential to do harm call for a commitment on the part of child care practitioners to the highest standards of ethical practice.

Child care practitioners accept the ethical obligation to understand and work effectively with children in the context of family, culture, and community. Child care practitioners care for and educate young children. However, ethical practice extends beyond the child/practitioner relationship. Child care practitioners also support parents[2] as primary caregivers of their children and liaise with other professionals and community resources on behalf of children and families.

The Canadian Child Care Federation and its affiliate organizations recognize their responsibility to promote ethical practices and attitudes on the part of child care practitioners. The following principles, explanations, and standards of practice are designed to help child care practitioners monitor their professional practice and guide their

---

* Reprinted with minor edits with permission from "Our Code of Ethics," by the Canadian Child Care Federation, 2020 (https://cccf-fcsge.ca/about-canadian-child-care-federation/values/code-ethics/). Copyright 2021 by the Canadian Child Care Federation.

1 This code uses the term *child care practitioner* to refer to adults who work in the field of child care including: early childhood educators; family child care providers; family resource program personnel; resource and referral program personnel; and instructors in early childhood care and education programs in postsecondary institutions.

2 This code uses the term *parent* to refer to the parent or legal guardian or the adult who assumes the parental role in the care of the child.

decision-making. These ethical principles are based on the *Code of Ethics* of the Early Childhood Educators of BC (2008). They have been adapted for use by adults who work with children and families in a variety of child care and related settings. They are intended both to guide practitioners and to protect the children and families with whom they work. Professionalism creates additional ethical obligations to colleagues and to the profession.

Eight ethical principles of practice are presented. These principles are intended to guide child care practitioners in deciding what conduct is most appropriate when they encounter ethical problems in the course of their work. Each principle is followed by an explanation and a list of standards of practice that represent an application of the principle in a child care or related setting.

The ethical practice of child care practitioners reflects the eight principles. However, the resolution of ethical dilemmas can be difficult and there will be circumstances in which the ethical principles will conflict. In these difficult situations, it is recommended that child care practitioners carefully think through the likely consequences of giving priority to particular principles. By evaluating the consequences, it may become clear which principle ought to be given more weight. The preferred action should be the one that produces the least amount of avoidable harm. Child care practitioners are also encouraged to consult with colleagues to obtain different perspectives on the problem, always being mindful of confidentiality issues. However, the final decision will be made by the individual practitioner facing the ethical dilemma.

The Principles of the Code

1. Child care practitioners promote the health and wellbeing of all children.

2. Child care practitioners enable children to participate to their full potential in environments carefully planned to serve individual needs and to facilitate the child's progress in the social, emotional, physical, and cognitive areas of development.

3. Child care practitioners demonstrate caring for all children in all aspects of their practice.

4. Child care practitioners work in partnership with parents, recognizing that parents have primary responsibility for the care of their children, valuing their commitment to the children, and supporting them in meeting their responsibilities to their children.

5. Child care practitioners work in partnership with colleagues and other service providers in the community to support the wellbeing of children and their families.

6. Child care practitioners work in ways that enhance human dignity in trusting, caring, and cooperative relationships that respect the worth and uniqueness of the individual.

7. Child care practitioners pursue, on an ongoing basis, the knowledge, skills, and self-awareness needed to be professionally competent.

8. Child care practitioners demonstrate integrity in all of their professional relationships.

1. Child care practitioners promote the health and wellbeing of all children. Child care practitioners are responsible for the children in their care. They create environments for children that are safe, secure, and supportive of good health in the broadest sense. They design programs that provide children with opportunities to develop physically, socially, emotionally, morally, spiritually, cognitively, and creatively. A healthy environment for children is one in which each child's self-esteem is enhanced, play is encouraged, and a warm, loving atmosphere is maintained.

In following this principle, a child care practitioner:

- Promotes each child's health and wellbeing
- Creates and maintains safe and healthy environments for children
- Fosters all facets of children's development in the context of the child, their family, and their community
- Enhances each child's feelings of competence, independence, and self-esteem
- Refrains from in any way degrading, endangering, frightening, or harming children
- Acts as an advocate on behalf of all children for public policies, programs, and services that enhance their health and wellbeing
- Acts promptly in situations where the wellbeing of the child is compromised

2. Child care practitioners enable children to participate to their full potential in environments that are carefully planned to serve individual needs and to facilitate the child's progress in the social, emotional, physical, and cognitive areas of development. Child care practitioners understand the sequences and patterns of child development and cultural influences on those patterns. They use this knowledge to create environments and plan programs that are responsive to the children in their care. Child care practitioners implement programs and use guidance techniques that take into account the ages of the children and individual variations in their development.

In following this principle, a child care practitioner:

- Considers cross-cultural variations in child-rearing approaches when assessing child development
- Applies the knowledge that the stages of physical, social, emotional, moral, and cognitive development of each child may be different
- Determines where each child is on the various developmental continua and uses that knowledge to create programs that allow for individual differences and preferences
- Uses developmentally appropriate methods and materials in working with children

3. Child care practitioners demonstrate caring for all children in all aspects of their practice. Caring involves both love and labour. Caring is at the core of early childhood education and is reflected in the mental, emotional, and physical efforts of child care practitioners in their interactions with all children. Being cared for and cared about is consistently communicated to all children.

In following this principle, a child care practitioner:

- Responds appropriately to each child's expressions of need
- Provides children with experiences that build trust
- Expresses warmth, appropriate affection, consideration, and acceptance for children both verbally and nonverbally
- Communicates to children a genuine interest in their activities, ideas, opinions, and concerns
- Supports children as they experience different emotions and models acceptable ways of expressing emotions

4. Child care practitioners work in partnership with parents, recognizing that the parents have primary responsibility for the care of their children, valuing their commitment to their children and supporting them in meeting their responsibilities to their children. Child care practitioners share joint interest in the children in their care while recognizing that parents have primary responsibility for child-rearing and decision-making on behalf of their children. Child care practitioners complement and support parents as they carry out these responsibilities. Through positive, respectful, and supportive relationships with parents, child care practitioners advance the wellbeing of children.

In following this principle, a child care practitioner:
- Promotes considerate relationships with the parents of the children in care
- Respects the rights of parents to transmit their values, beliefs, and cultural heritage to their children
- Supports parents with knowledge, skills, and resources that will enhance their ability to nurture their children
- Encourages and provides opportunities for parents to participate actively in all aspects of planning and decision-making affecting their children
- Builds upon strengths and competencies in supporting parents in their task of nurturing children

5. Child care practitioners work in partnership with colleagues and other service providers in the community to support the wellbeing of children and their families. Child care practitioners recognize that nurturing family environments benefit children. Child care practitioners work with other helping professionals to provide a network of support for families.

In following this principle, a child care practitioner:
- Supports and encourages families by developing programs that meet the needs of those families being serviced
- Assists families in obtaining needed specialized services provided by other professionals
- Advocates for public policies and community services that are supportive of families

6. Child care practitioners work in ways that enhance human dignity in trusting, caring, and cooperative relationships that respect the worth and uniqueness of the individual. Child care practitioners welcome and cherish children unconditionally. They respect the dignity of children, parents, colleagues, and others with whom they interact. They demonstrate respect for diversity by valuing individuality and appreciating diverse characteristics, including ideas and perspectives.

In following this principle, a child care practitioner:
- Communicates respect by practising and promoting anti-bias interactions
- Supports and promotes the dignity of self and others by engaging in mutually enhancing relationships
- Plans inclusive programs that communicate respect for diversity regarding ability, culture, gender, socioeconomic status, sexual orientation, and family composition

- Provides opportunities for all children to participate in childhood activities.

7. Child care practitioners pursue, on an ongoing basis, the knowledge, skills, and self-awareness needed to be professionally competent. Early childhood professional practice is based on an expanding body of literature and research. Continuing education is essential. In-service skills training and self-awareness work prepare child care practitioners to fulfil their responsibilities more effectively.

In following this principle, a child care practitioner:

- Recognizes the need for continuous learning
- Pursues professional development opportunities
- Incorporates into practice current knowledge in the field of early childhood care and education and related disciplines
- Assesses personal and professional strengths and limitations and undertakes self-improvement
- Articulates a personal philosophy of practice and justifies practices on the basis of theoretical perspectives
- Shares knowledge to support the development of the field

8. Child care practitioners demonstrate integrity in all of their professional relationships. Child care practitioners are truthful and trustworthy. They communicate honestly and openly and endeavour to be accurate and objective. Child care practitioners treat as confidential information about the children, families, and colleagues with whom they work. Information may be shared with colleagues and other helping professionals as required for the care and support of the children or as required by law. Child care practitioners acknowledge real or potential conflicts of interest and act in accordance with the principles of this code of ethics.

In following this principle, a child care practitioner:

- Communicates with children, parents, colleagues, and other professionals in an honest, straightforward manner
- Conscientiously carries out professional responsibilities and duties
- Identifies personal values and beliefs and strives to be objective
- Treats as confidential information concerning children, families, and colleagues unless failure to disclose would put children at risk
- Recognizes the potential for real or perceived conflicts of interest and acts in accordance with the principles of the code where dual relationships with colleagues or families exist and/or develop

Children's Books

Children's books are a wonderful way to introduce issues of caring and equality. This section includes a few that you could explore. They are grouped roughly by topic, although many of the themes overlap. The books on the list are intended mainly for preschoolers, but the age suggestions are very approximate. Children should be read to from the day they are born, and their preferences often surprise us.

Beyond this list, there are many excellent Canadian picture books that have received such awards as the Amelia Francis Howard-Gibbon Illustrator's Award and the Elizabeth Mrazik-Cleaver Canadian Picture Book Award. You can find these lists online.

Books with Characters of Colour

Age 2+
The Snowy Day, by Ezra Jack Keats (Puffin Books, 1962)
- A classic book capturing a child's delight in freshly fallen snow.

Age 3+
The Airport Book, by Lisa Brown (Roaring Brook Press, 2016)
- An account of a family's travel day tells all about airports.

Hands Up! by Breanna J. McDaniel (Dial Books, 2019)
- A triumphant picture book showing phases of a Black girl's everyday life—hands up for a hug, hands up in class, hands up

for a high five—before culminating in a moment of resistance at a protest march.

I Am Perfectly Designed, by Karamo Brown and Jason "Rachel" Brown (Henry Hold, 2019)
- A story of a gentle, loving and affirming father–son relationship.

Last Stop on Market Street, by Matt de la Pena (Putnam, 2015)
- Nana shows her grandson beauty from a bus.

When's My Birthday, by Julie Fogliano (Roaring Book Press, 2017)
- A story of giddy excitement about an upcoming birthday.

Whistle for Willie, by Ezra Jack Keats (Viking Books, 1964)
- A boy learns to whistle for his pup.

Age 4+

Carmela Full of Wishes, by Matt de la Pena (Putnam, 2018)
- A poignant tale of a young girl from an immigrant family.

I Am Enough, by Grace Byers (Balzer & Bray, 2019)
- A girl celebrates her identity in a poetic picture book.

In Plain Sight, by Richard Jackson (Roaring Brook Press, 2017)
- A sweet tale of a playful and loving relationship with a grandpa.

Mixed Me! by Taye Diggs (Feiwel & Friends, 2015)
- A boy embraces his uniqueness.

Parker Looks Up: An Extraordinary Moment, by Parker Curry and Jessica Curry (Aladdin, 2020)
- A girl finds a role model who looks like her.

Princess Cupcake Jones and the Missing Tutu, by Ylleya Fields (Bell Publishing, 2016)
- A tale of responsibility that avoids princess stereotypes.

Sulwe, by Lupita Nyong'o (Simon & Schuster, 2019)
- A girl learns to embrace her dark skin.

Under My Hijab, by Hena Khan (Lee & Low, 2019)
- A story about a headscarf with positive messages and beautiful art.

You Matter, by Christian Robinson (Atheneum Books, 2020)
- A message of self-worth with gorgeous illustrations.

Books with Indigenous Characters and Stories

A comprehensive list of Indigenous legends and folktales can be found on the Strong Nations website (https://www.strongnations.com/).

Age 0

I Was Born Precious and Sacred, by Debora Abood (Peppermint Toast Publishing, 2014)

- A tale that tells, in simple language and with poignant photographs, the ancestral teachings about the sanctity of each and every Little Person born into Indigenous communities.

Little You, by Richard Van Camp (Orca Books, 2013)

- A poem telling a child they are unique and special.

Sweetest Kulu, by Celina Kalluk (Inhabit Media, 2014)

- A bedtime poem about all the gifts given to a newborn from the animals of the Arctic.

Age 3+

My Heart Fills with Happiness, by Monique Gray Smith (Orca Books, 2016)

- A beautifully illustrated board book drawing attention to deep joys that can be found in everyday life.

Age 4+

Blackflies (2017), by Robert Munsch (Scholastic Canada, 2021)

- A story shared with the author by a First Nations family he met in Fort McMurray.

The Elders Are Watching, by David Bouchard (Raincoast Books, 2003)

- A story that teaches the importance of the environment and respect for the wisdom and knowledge passed on from Elders. Gorgeous artwork and lyrical storytelling.

Gifts from Raven, by Kung Jaadee (Medicine Wheel Education, 2019)

- The idea that we have each received a special gift from Raven that is our special talent or passion to share with the world.

Rabbit and Bear Paws: Sacred Seven, by Chad Solomon (Little Spirit Bear Productions, 2006–2011)

- A set of seven humorous books on the Seven Grandfather teachings: courage, humility, love, respect, truth, and wisdom.

Two brother and their friend learn the meaning of the values by copying the actions of a featured animal.

Sometimes I Feel Like a Fox, by Danielle Daniel (Groundwood Books, 2015)

- A series of portraits of children as animals, each with their own set of feelings and characteristics grounded in the Anishinaabe tradition of totem animals.

What's the Most Beautiful Thing You Know About Horses? by Richard Van Camp (Children's Book Press, 2013)

- A tale that captures the dark humour of being a mixed-heritage Indigenous child.

When We Are Kind, by Monique Gray Smith (Orca Books, 2020)

- A book that celebrates simple acts of kindness and encourages children to explore how they feel when they initiate and receive acts of kindness in their lives.

When We Were Alone, by David Alexander Robertson (Highwater Press, 2016)

- A story about empowerment and strength during a residential school experience.

All Ages

Owls See Clearly at Night: A Michif Alphabet, by Julie Flett (Simply Read Books, 2010)

- A stunning alphabet book that takes you through the language of the Métis, Michif.

Books about Identity

Age 2+

Shades of People, by Shelley Rotner and Sheila M. Kelly (Holiday House, 2009)

- People come in all shades, even in the same family. Available as a board book and a paperback.

Skin Like Mine, by LaTashia M. Perry (G Publishing, 2016)

- Part of the *Kids Like Mine* series, which also includes *Hair Like Mine* (2015) and *Imaginations Like Mine* (2017). Carry the message that we are special and unique in our own way. Rhyming and repetition make the books attractive to young listeners and readers.

Age 3+

All the Colors We Are: The Story of How We Got Our Skin Color (20th anniversary edition), by Katie Kissinger (Redleaf Press, 2014)
- English/Spanish text that showcases the beautiful diversity of skin colour.

Shades of Black: A Celebration of Our Children, by Sandra L. Pinkney (Scholastic, 2000)
- Photographs and poetic text celebrate the beauty and diversity of African American children.

Intersection Allies, by Chelsea Johnson, LaToya Council, and Carolyn Choi (Dottir Press, 2019)
- Children of many genders, races, sexualities, abilities, cultures, and origins can see their whole selves reflected, respected, and celebrated.

Stories about Being the Same and Being Different

Age 1+

Everywhere Babies, by Susan Meyers (HMH Books, 2004)
- A story showing babies being loved and cared for in their different families.

Age 3+

The Colors of Us, by Karen Katz (Henry Holt, 1999)
- A little girl is painting a self-portrait and wants to use brown paint for her skin. But when she and her mother take a walk through the neighbourhood, she learns that brown comes in many different shades.

The Skin You Live In, by Michael Tyler (Chicago Children's Museum, 2005)
- A story of social acceptance with illustrations of activities enjoyed by children of all cultures.

Age 4+

Everybody Bakes Bread, by Norah Dooley (First Avenue Editions, 1996)

- Carrie is sent on a mission by her mother: to search the neighbourhood for a "three-handled rolling pin." While on her quest, Carrie discovers that although her neighbours hail from several different countries, they all enjoy the tastes and smells of home-baked bread.

Everybody Cooks Rice, by Norah Dooley (First Avenue Editions, 1992)

- Carrie goes from one neighbour's house to the next looking for her brother, who is late for dinner. She discovers that although each family is from a different country, everyone makes a rice dish at dinnertime. A multicultural picture book with recipes.

It's Okay to Be Different, by Todd Parr (Little, Brown Books for Young Readers, 2004)

- A story with messages of acceptance, understanding, and confidence in an accessible, child-friendly format featuring bold, bright colours and silly scenes.

Same, Same But Different, by Jenny Sue Kostecki-Shaw (Henry Holt, 2011)

- Elliot lives in America and Kailash lives in India. By exchanging letters and pictures, they learn that they have many interests in common.

Books about Gender

Age 3+

The Boy & the Bindi, by Vivek Shraya (Arsenal Pulp Press, 2016)

- A 5-year-old South Asian boy becomes fascinated with his mother's bindi, the red dot commonly worn by Hindu women. He wishes to have one of his own. Rather than chastise her son, she agrees, giving him permission to be more fully himself.

Bunnybear, by Andrea J. Loney (Albert Whitman, 2017)

- Although Bunnybear was born a bear, he feels more like a bunny. The other bears don't understand him, and neither do the bunnies. Will Bunnybear ever find a friend who likes him just the way he is?

Introducing Teddy: A Gentle Story about Gender and Friendship, by Jess Walton (Bloomsbury, 2016)

- An accessible and heartwarming story about being true to yourself and being a good friend.

It Feels Good to Be Yourself, by Theresa Thorn (Henry Holt, 2019)
- Some people are boys. Some people are girls. Some people are both, neither, or somewhere in between. This story is a straightforward exploration of gender identity, providing young readers and adults with the vocabulary to discuss the topic with sensitivity.

The Paper Bag Princess, by Robert Munsch (Annick Press, 1980)
- This classic book reverses the princess stereotype.

Pink Is for Boys, by Robb Pearlman (Running Press, 2018)
- An empowering and educational picture book that proves colours are for everyone, regardless of gender.

Age 4+

Annie's Plaid Shirt, by Stacy B. Davids (Upswing Press, 2015)
- Annie's mom tells her that she must wear a dress to her uncle's wedding. Annie protests, but her mom buys her a fancy new dress anyway. Annie is miserable. Why can't her mom understand? Then, Annie has an idea. But will her mom agree?

Jacob's New Dress, by Sarah Hoffman and Ian Hoffman (Albert Whitman, 2014)
- Jacob loves playing dress-up because he can be anything he wants to be. Some kids at school say he can't wear "girl" clothes, but Jacob wants to wear a dress. Can he convince his parents to let him wear what he wants?

Julián Is a Mermaid, by Jessica Love (Candlewick, 2018)
- A glimpse of costumed mermaids leaves one boy flooded with wonder and ready to dazzle the world.

When Aidan Became a Big Brother, by Kyle Lukoff (Lee & Low, 2019)
- When Aidan was born, everyone thought he was a girl, but as he grew older, he realized he was a trans boy. When he finds out he is going to be a big brother, he learns the most important thing about being an older sibling: how to love with his whole self.

Books about Nontraditional Families

Age 0–2+

I'm Adopted, by Shelley Rotner and Sheila M. Kelly (Holiday House, 2012)

- With a perceptive text and dynamic photographs, the creators of this book demystify adoption for young children and celebrate the joy that comes with adding to a family.

Love Makes a Family, by Sophie Beer (Little Hare Publishing, 2018)

- In this exuberant board book, many different families are shown in happy activity, from an early-morning wake-up to a kiss before bed. Whether a child has two moms, two dads, one parent, or one of each, this simple preschool read-aloud demonstrates that what's most important is the love the family members share.

Mommy, Mama, and Me and *Daddy, Papa and Me,* by Leslea Newman (Tricycle Press, 2009)

- Both books shows a toddler going about the day with their family.

Age 3+

And Tango Makes Three, by Justin Richardson and Peter Parnell (Simon & Schuster, 2005)

- The heartwarming true story of two penguins who create a nontraditional family.

The Family Book, by Todd Parr (Little, Brown Books for Young Readers, 2003)

- A story that assures children that no matter what kind of family they have, every family is special in its own unique way.

Heather Has Two Mommies, by Leslzéa Newman (Alyson Books, 1989)

- When Heather goes to school for the first time, someone asks her about her daddy, but Heather doesn't have a daddy. Then something interesting happens. When Heather and her classmates all draw pictures of their families, not one drawing is the same.

Keesha & Her Two Moms Go Swimming, by Monica Bey-Clarke and Cheril N. Clarke (Dodi Press, 2011)

- Keesha and her two moms go for a fun day of swimming at the pool, where she meets up with her best friend, Trevor, and his two dads. The books shows different kinds of families, but is really about Keesha being kind and making new friends.

My Mommy, My Mama, My Brother, and Me, by Natalie Meisner (Nimbus Publishing, 2019)

- Inspired by the author's adventures with her wife and two sons in Nova Scotia, this beautifully illustrated book captures the warmth and magic of time spent with family by the sea.

Age 4+

ABC: A Family Alphabet Book, by Bobbie Combs (Two Lives Publishing, 2012)

- An alphabet book showing everyday things from children's lives but in the context of same-sex parents doing everyday things like baking cookies and going to the aquarium.

The Flower Girl Wore Celery, by Meryl G. Gordon (Kar-Ben Publishing, 2016)

- Emma has been asked to be a flower girl at her cousin's wedding. But nothing turns out to be quite what she's expecting: the "ring bear" she's heard about is just a boy, her dress isn't celery, and Hannah's new spouse turns out to be another bride!

Jalapeno Bagels, by Natasha Wing (Atheneum, 1996)

- While trying to decide what to take for his school's International Day, Pablo helps his Mexican mother and Jewish father at their bakery and discovers a food that represents both his parents' backgrounds.

Love Is What Makes Us a Family, by Julia E. Morrison (Archway Publishing, 2016)

- Eliza is a 6-year-old girl whose mom and dad are divorced. As Eliza adjusts to the changes in her family, she also realizes her mom is dating a woman. Eliza has many questions about this new situation, and through conversations with both of her parents, she begins to understand that families can take many forms. The love they have for one another is what is most important.

Books that Challenge Stereotypes

Age 3+

Drum Dream Girl: How One Girl's Dream Changed Music, by Margarita Engle (Houghton Mifflin Harcourt, 2015)

- A lively, true story inspired by the childhood of Millo Castro Zaldarriaga, a Chinese-African-Cuban girl who broke Cuba's traditional taboo against female drummers.

The Knight Who Was Afraid of the Dark, by Barbara Shook Hazen (Puffin, 1989)

- A brave knight named Sir Fred is not afraid of anything...well, except maybe the dark.

Age 4+

The Different Dragon, by Jennifer Bryan; illustrated by Danamarie Hosler (Two Lives Publishing, 2011)

- An imaginative boy and one of his moms weave a bedtime story about a dragon who is sad about having to act fierce all the time.

Books about Religious Customs

Age 4+

The Proudest Blue: A Story of Hijab and Family, by Ibtihaj Muhammad and S.K. Ali (Little, Brown Books for Young Readers, 2019)

- An uplifting, universal story of new experiences, the unbreakable bond between siblings, and of being proud of who you are.

The Purim Superhero, by Elisabeth Kushner (Kar-Ben Publishing, 2013)

- All his friends want to dress as superheroes for the Jewish holiday Purim, but Nate has a different idea. His dads talk to him about the meaning of the day and help him figure out his own costume. Nate learns about the power he has when he does something that is important to him and that reflects his own individuality.

Mommy's Khimar, by Jamilah Thompkins-Bigelow (Salaam Reads / Simon & Schuster, 2018)

- A young Muslim girl spends a busy day wrapped up in her mother's colourful headscarf in this sweet and fanciful picture book. Her playful joy with the scarves celebrates her family's culture and beliefs.

Under My Hijab, by Hena Khan (Lee & Low, 2019)

- The significant women in this girl's life sometimes wear hijabs and sometimes don't. They inspire her with all that they do and who they are. It's an important slice-of-life story featuring strong, inspiring Muslim women.

Books that Celebrate Being Different

Age 3+

Just a Little Different, by Gina Mayer and Mercer Mayer (Golden Books, 2001)

- Part of the Little Critter world, this book tells the story of a new kid who has just moved in next door. He's a nice kid but he's just a little bit different: his mother is a rabbit and his father is a turtle.

Age 4+

Frederick, by Leo Lionni (Dragonfly Books, 1973)

- A classic story about a field mouse who is different. Frederick, an apparently lazy mouse, becomes a hero. Instead of gathering food for the winter, Frederick gathers rays from the sun, a rainbow of colours, and marvelous words.

Red, a Crayon's Story, by Michael Hall Red (Greenwillow Books, 2015)

- Red has a bright red label, but he is, in fact, blue. This is a story is about being true to your inner self and following your own path despite obstacles that may come your way.

Understanding Exceptionalities

Age 3+

We Can Do It! by Laura Dwight (Star Bright Books, 2005)

- A book showing five preschool children, each with a disability, leading full, productive, and happy lives.

A Very Special Critter, by Gina Mayer and Mercer Mayer (Golden Books, 1993)

- Little Critter discovers that the new boy in class is really not so different from anyone else, even though he is in a wheelchair.

Age 4+

I Talk Like a River, by Jordan Scott (Neal Porter Books, 2020)

- A boy's stuttering feels devastating, but his father shows him that the river mirrors how he talks—bubbling, churning, crashing, and whirling—and that metaphor becomes a lifeline for him.

My Brother Charlie, by Holly Robinson Peete (Scholastic, 2010)

- A realistic fiction picture book about a set of twins, one of whom has autism.

Age 5+

All My Stripes, A Story for Children with Autism, by Shania Rudolph and Danielle Royer (Magination Press, 2015)

- Zane the zebra feels different from the rest of his classmates. He worries that all they notice about him is his "autism stripe." With the help of his Mama, Zane comes to appreciate all his stripes— the unique strengths that make him who he is.

A Boy Called Bat, by Elana Arnold (Walden Pond Press, 2017)
- A boy with autism strives to raise a baby skunk. Bat's mom is a veterinarian who helped rescue the skunk kit after its mother and siblings died in an accident.

Don't Feed the WorryBug, by Andi Green (Monsters in My Head, 2011)
- Wince worries about everything. And when Wince starts to worry, his WorryBug appears. At first the WorryBug is small and non-threatening, but the more Wince worries, the more his WorryBug grows. This book can help start a conversation about anxiety.

My Sister, Alicia May, by Nancy Tupper Ling (Pleasant Street Press, 2009)
- A story written from the perspective of Rachel, whose younger sister has Down syndrome.

Poverty and Homelessness

Age 3+

The One with the Scraggly Beard, by Elizabeth Withey (Orca Books, 2020)
- A compassionate book inspired by the author's son's experience meeting his uncle, who lives on the street.

Age 5+

Four Feet, Two Sandals, by Karen Lynn Williams and Khadra Mohammed (Eerdmans Books, 2007)
- When relief workers bring used clothing to a refugee camp in Pakistan, 10-year-old Lina is thrilled when she finds a sandal that fits her foot perfectly—until she sees that another girl has the matching shoe. But soon, Lina and Feroza meet and decide that it is better to share the sandals than for each to wear only one.

The Magic Beads, by Susin Nielsen (Simply Read Books, 2007)
- Lillian and her mother have just moved away from Lillian's abusive father and into a family shelter, leaving behind all of their possessions. She is anxious about what to bring for her show-and-tell day at her new school but finally realizes that imagination can make anything magical, even an ordinary string of beads.

Nice Try, Charlie, by Matt James (Groundwood Books, 2020)
- Charlie finds things, and when he finds a pie, he wants to make sure it doesn't belong to anyone else. As he wends his ways

through his neighbourhood looking for the owner, he alerts the reader to how they might see the people in their neighbourhoods, particularly street people and people who are homeless.

A Shelter in Our Car, by Monica Gunning (Children's Book Press, 2004)
- Since she left Jamaica for America after her father died, Zettie has lived in a car with her mother while they both go to school and plan for a real home.

Appreciating Nature

Age 2+

Tree: A Peek-Through Picture Book, by Britta Teckentrup (Doubleday Books, 2016)
- Children can watch the tree change as each page is turned.

Age 3+

The Curious Garden, by Peter Brown (Little, Brown Books for Young Readers, 2009)
- While out exploring one day, a little boy named Liam discovers a struggling garden and decides to take care of it. As time passes, the garden spreads throughout the dark, gray city, transforming it into a lush, green world.

Outside Your Window: A First Book of Nature, by Nicola Davies (Candlewick, 2012)
- A gorgeously illustrated book of poetry that will inspire children to explore nature.

Age 4+

The Big Book of Bugs, by Yuval Zommer (Thames & Hudson, 2016)
- A well-illustrated book of facts about bugs to interest children in the vast array of bugs that share their world.

The Old Woman, by Joanne Schwartz (Groundwood Books, 2020)
- An old woman and her scruffy dog wander in the woods on a fall day.

When Green Becomes Tomatoes: Poems for All Seasons, by Julie Fogliano (Roaring Book Press, 2016)
- Poems for all seasons to charm children with the beauty of words.

Recognizing Child Abuse, Neglect, and Sexual Exploitation*

WHAT IT IS	SIGNS AND SYMPTOMS
NEGLECT	
A child is considered to be neglected when a parent or guardian does not provide them with basic, age-appropriate care such as: • Food • Clothing • Shelter • Love and affection • Protection from harm	• Being hungry often • Stealing or hoarding food • Being underweight or dehydrated • Having poor hygiene • Wearing clothes that are torn, dirty, do not fit, or are not right for the season • Trying to take on age-inappropriate responsibilities (such as caring for siblings and doing household tasks when very young, or looking after a parent) • Saying that parents are rarely home or that they don't want to go home • Having medical or dental problems that will not go away, such as infected sores, decayed teeth, or vision difficulties that are not being addressed

---

* Information in this appendix is adapted from Government of Alberta (2021) *What Is Child Abuse, Neglect, and Exploitation?* (https://www.alberta.ca/what-is-child-abuse-neglect-and-sexual-exploitation.aspx). Copyright 2021 by Government of Alberta.

WHAT IT IS	SIGNS AND SYMPTOMS
EMOTIONAL ABUSE	
A parent or guardian is emotionally abusive when they behave in ways that are actively detrimental to a child's emotional wellbeing. This may include: • Humiliating the child by blaming or belittling them • Refusing to comfort the child when the child is upset or frightened • Criticizing the child by calling them names like stupid, bad, useless, or troublemaker • Setting unrealistic expectations that the child cannot meet • Threatening or accusing the child • Exposing the child to violence or chronic drug or alcohol use in the home • Punishing the child in cruel and unusual ways	• Constant apologizing • Try excessively hard to please others • Showing signs of anxiety, fears, or depression • Having trouble concentrating, learning, or sleeping • Having episodes of aggressive, angry, and demanding behaviour • Crying for no apparent reason • Having problems with bed-wetting or lack of bowel control
PHYSICAL ABUSE	
Physical child abuse is an action or behaviour by a parent or guardian that causes injury or trauma to any part of the child's body. Physical abuse can happen only once or many times. It may involve behaviours including, but not limited to: • Hitting, choking, and kicking • Biting, scratching, and pulling hair • Throwing objects at a child or hitting them with objects • Breaking bones	Physical abuse may cause external injuries that leave bruises and marks that can be seen, such as: • Bruises, cuts, scrapes, welts, fractures, sprains, dislocations, or head injuries • Injuries that could not have happened by accident, like a bruised earlobe or cut behind the knee • Visible handprints, fingerprints, or other marks • Burns on various parts of their body It may also cause internal and/ or emotional injuries that are harder to spot, such as: • Unusual behaviour or appearance • Prior injuries that are visible in X-ray results

WHAT IT IS	SIGNS AND SYMPTOMS
SEXUAL ABUSE	

Sexual abuse happens when a parent, guardian, or other caretaker exposes a child to or fails to protect a child from inappropriate sexual contact, activity, or behaviour. This may include:
 	
• Activities that do not involve sexual touch, such as:
  › Having inappropriately sexual phone calls or conversations
  › Making the child watch someone expose themselves
  › Showing the child pornographic material
• Activities that do involve sexual touch, such as:
  › Fondling
  › Making the child touch an adult's or other child's genital area
  › Sexual intercourse with the child or youth
• Sexual exploitation activities
	• Having more knowledge about sex than others their age
	• Behaving in sexually explicit or aggressive ways with peers, educators, or other adults
	• Using sexual language or making drawings with sexual content
	• Wetting or soiling their pants, wetting the bed, or thumb-sucking
	• Being afraid to go to sleep, having nightmares, or sleeping long hours
	• Becoming withdrawn, anxious, fearful, or depressed
	• Having physical trauma or irritations in the anal and genital areas

SEXUAL EXPLOITATION	
Sexual exploitation is a form of sexual abuse that can be committed by anyone who seeks out a child for sexual purposes. It may involve: • Luring a child over the Internet, social media, or other means for sexual purposes • Coercing a child into sexual activity in exchange for basic needs or anything of value to a child (e.g., toys, electronics, or money) • Using a child to create child pornography • Selling or distributing child pornography	• Withdrawing from friends and family • Keeping secrets about who they see and what they do • Being unusually protective about new relationships or friendships • Hanging around with older people • Having possessions, including clothing, jewelry, and electronics, that are not age appropriate • Carrying condoms or sexual aids • Being secretive or reactive about browser history, websites they visit, or contacts on their phone

Culturally Responsive Practice at the Intercultural Child and Family Centre*

Jasvinder Heran and Mary Lynne Matheson

"Tell me what makes your centre intercultural," our visitor asked. As director of the Intercultural Child and Family Centre (ICFC), I proudly described all the supports we have in place for our families: assistance with subsidy application and registration, help with accessing resources such as the Food Bank, translation and counselling services right in our building, referrals, support for families pertaining to settlement issues, and monthly parent events with meals and child-minding. Our staff are good at singing and speaking in their own and children's home languages; cooking ethnic food with children; and celebrating culture through clothing, rituals, music, and dance.

On our tour of the centre, we visited the toddler room. Our visitor gently provoked us by saying, "It's interesting that aside from the educators and children themselves, you could be in any day care in the city." I looked around the toddler room as if for the first time and took in the row of Fisher Price high chairs along one wall, six cribs lined up along another wall, and two change tables in the centre of the room. To my dismay, I realized that this was a room that screamed "custodial care" and it did not speak to the cultural diversity of our centre's families and

* Reprinted with permission and minor edits from "Culturally Responsive Practice at the Intercultural Child and Family Centre," by J. Heran and M.L. Matheson, 2016, *Interaction*, 30(2) (https://cccf-fcsge.ca/ece-resources/browse/interaction-magazine-archive/). Copyright 2016 by the Canadian Child Care Federation.

staff. Any artifacts that represented culture were hanging from the ceiling or up high on a bulletin board where children couldn't see them. We realized right then that we had some work to do on our playroom environments. But how might we begin with such a huge task?

A little while later, when ICFC became a participant in the pilot for *Play, Participation, and Possibilities: An Early Learning and Child Care Curriculum Framework for Alberta* (PPP) (Makovichuk et al., 2014), we visited other participating programs and became further inspired by the framework's goal of Diversity and Social Responsibility and, in particular, an indicator for Inclusiveness and Equity:

> Children appreciate their own distinctiveness and that of others learning about their cultural heritage and those of other families within the centre and broader society. (Makovichuk et al., 2014, p. 111)

In order to help children appreciate their distinctiveness and that of others, we knew that we had to respect their backgrounds and reflect those in the playroom itself. Staff became excited when they realized that reflecting culture in the playroom environments was as valuable as the food, dance, and songs that they were already sharing. Our mentor from the PPP pilot project from MacEwan University suggested that if we were feeling overwhelmed, we might want to start with the housekeeping centre and ask ourselves, "How can this space look like children's homes?" This is where our focus began; however, inspired by this project, our educators were keen to expand to the entire room.

The initial transformation of the preschool house area included adding a homemade low table, ethnic fabrics, pictures depicting spices and dishes from Ethiopia and Eritrea, wooden bowls, babies of all colours, and cultural clothing and footwear. We soon noticed that the hominess and location of the couch in this area invited families past the doorway and into the room.

We looked at the children, families, and staff in each of our three playrooms and thought about how those spaces could better reflect the communities in each. Our educators participated in a shopping trip to a local charity store in search of culturally relevant dress-up clothes and other artifacts; they also brought in items from home that spoke to their own cultural backgrounds. Seeing this happening, some families reciprocated by contributing personal items for the rooms. As we collected these, we realized that we had to be aware of adding genuine artifacts and respecting the cultural integrity of precious items; this continues to be a challenge as we try to make conscious decisions about what to have in our room environments.

At the same time as we began adding to rooms, we began removing the plastic and commercial toys while incorporating more natural materials and loose parts. Decluttering was a big part of our transformation as we sorted through years of accumulations on shelves and window sills— something we have to be aware of even now. With these new changes to our room environments, we soon realized that we could take down the "multicultural bulletin boards" that had been created for our first accreditation visit because our whole room spoke of the intercultural nature of our children, families, and educators.

While transforming the environments in each room, we needed to be consciously aware of who the educators and children were in each and resist the urge to duplicate generic cultural artifacts in all rooms. For example, we suspended a piece of lattice from the ceiling in two of the playrooms above the housekeeping areas and from each hung kitchen items, something we had seen in a centre we had visited as part of the PPP pilot project. In the toddler room we hung miniature Ethiopian bread baskets, and in out-of-school care we hung chopsticks and lanterns to reflect the backgrounds of children and staff in each of the rooms at that time. We got rid of the cribs in the toddler room except for one, which was placed on its side with a mattress and pillows to create a cozy "alone" spot for reading or cuddling. The whole toddler room was transformed from a space that had previously depicted custodial care to a place that invited our youngest children to play and discover.

Shortly after our initial room transformations, we invited families into the playrooms and asked them, "What in the playroom feels like your home?" "What represents your culture?" and "What could be added or changed to better represent your family and culture?"

Parents indicated that the natural elements reminded them of their home countries. Many recognized artifacts such as the *sungka* (a game that an educator brought back from a trip to the Philippines), the Ethiopian bread baskets, and the sealed bottles with small amounts of lentils and beans. We needed to make a conscious decision about using these real food items in our play kitchen since many of our families experience food scarcity issues; a dialogue with some parents in the preschool room led to their consent and contribution of special ingredients they use at home.

Our staff have been hired, as much as possible, to reflect the cultural diversity of the families in the centre. This means that there is usually someone in the room who is able to talk with parents and children in their home language. It also means that educators have a diverse repertoire and knowledge of cultural practices. As a result of our involvement in the PPP pilot and guidance from our pedagogical mentor, staff have been encouraged to document these experiences and write learning stories to recognize cultural practices they observe in children's play. Some of our most memorable learning stories have been titled "My mom's bread is thin," a comment from children's conversations while making an Ethiopian bread called *himbasha*; "We eat like this at home," a comment upon seeing a lunch of *mesir wat, tikel gomen*, and *injera* served on a communal plate on the floor; and "Safwan understands Somali," an insight by an educator when she realized a toddler who seemed nonresponsive and nonverbal responded to instructions spoken in Somali.

Another PPP indicator for Inclusiveness and Equity—"Children appreciate their own distinctiveness and that of others becoming knowledgeable and confident in their various identities, including cultural, racial, physical, spiritual, linguistic, gender, and socioeconomic" (Makovichuk et al., 2014, p. 111)—prompted an educator to write a learning story entitled "The Blessing." This story recognized a child's knowledge of religious traditions as he blessed play food before sharing it with other children and prayed before "eating" it. Because spiritual identity was identified in PPP, it was validated as an important aspect of identity for this educator and was recognized and named in this learning story.

We would like to say that our centre has become pretty good at integrating the more visible aspects of culture, such as music, clothing, food, dance, and the physical spaces in our playrooms. However, at a recent staff meeting, we looked further at culture and realized that we knew less about the more invisible, deeper aspects of culture, such as values and beliefs, child-rearing practices, roles within families, and gender roles. This has led us on a new path with the realization that these are things that we will be privileged to when we build deeper relationships with parents, genuinely wanting to find out more and engaging in more intimate dialogues with families. This was highlighted in the toddler room when a child who was new to the centre was having a hard time settling at naptime despite staff's efforts using traditional early childhood practices such as back rubbing and singing. When we created an opportunity to connect more closely with her parents, we learned that baby-wearing, co-sleeping, and continued breastfeeding were practiced at home—little wonder that this child had a hard time falling asleep on a cot by herself, even with a caring educator by her side attempting to soothe her. This experience taught us that child-rearing practices are an integral part of the culture of our families and that our future direction needs to move beyond our playroom environments and artifacts.

We humbly acknowledge that we have much to do and much to learn in our quest to be more culturally responsive in meaningful and deeper ways. Our hope is to be more aware of and responsive to the hidden or invisible aspects of culture and respond with wise practice by integrating the best of early childhood practice and the best of cultural practice into our work with children, families, and our room teams.

Reference

Makovichuk, L., Hewes, J., Lirette, P. & Thomas, N. (2014). *Play, participation, and possibilities: An early learning and child care curriculum framework for Alberta*. www.childcareframework.com

Professional Resources

Provincial ECE Organizations[1]

British Columbia
- Early Childhood Educators of BC (ECEBC; http://www.ecebc.ca/)
- British Columbia Family Child Care Association (BCFCCA; https://bcfcca.ca)

Alberta
- Association of Early Childhood Educators of Alberta (AECEA; https://aecea.ca/)
- Alberta Family Child Care Association (AFCCA; https://afcca.ca)

Saskatchewan
- Saskatchewan Early Childhood Association (SECA; http://seca-sk.ca/)

Manitoba
- Manitoba Child Care Association (MCCA; http://mccahouse.org/)

---

1 Please note that this is not an exhaustive list of provincial resources.

Ontario

- L'Association francophone à l'éducation des services à l'enfance de l'Ontario (AFESEO; https://www.afeseo.ca/)
- Association of Early Childhood Educators Ontario (AECEO; https://www.aeceo.ca/)
- Home Child Care Association of Ontario (HCCAO; https://hccao.com/)
- Ontario Coalition for Better Child Care (https://www.childcareontario.org/)

Quebec

- The Quebec Association for Preschool Professional Development (QAPPD; https://qappd.com/)
- L'Association québéciose des CPE (AQCPE; https://aqcpe.com/)

Nova Scotia

- Association of Early Childhood Educators of Nova Scotia (AECENS; https://aecens.ca/)

New Brunswick

- Early Childhood Care & Education New Brunswick / Soins et éducation à la petite enfance Nouveau-Brunswick (ECCENB-SEPENB; https://eccenb-sepenb.ca/en/

Prince Edward Island

- Early Childhood Development Association of PEI (ECDA; http://www.ecdaofpei.ca/)

Newfoundland and Labrador

- Association of Early Childhood Educators of Newfoundland and Labrador (AECENL; https://aecenl.ca/)
- Family and Child Care Connections (https://www.familyandchildcareconnections.ca/)

Yukon

- Yukon Child Care Association (https://www.facebook.com/YukonCCA/)

Canada-wide Resources[2]

Canadian Child Care Federation

(CCCF; https://www.cccf-fcsge.ca)

- The CCCF provides Canadians with the very best in early learning and child care knowledge and ECE best practices through research and knowledge dissemination and the creation and nurturing of active networks.

Child Care Advocacy Association of Canada

(CCAAC; http://childcareadvocacy.ca/about-ccaac/)

- The CCAAC advocates for a framework that provides entitlement for all children in Canada to publicly funded, quality child care within a comprehensive range of early childhood services and family policies. Projects, provincial reports, consultation papers, and events are available online. Some content is available in French.

Child Care Human Resources Sector Council

(http://www.ccsc-cssge.ca/)

- The Child Care Human Resources Sector Council is a pan-Canadian, nonprofit organization dedicated to moving forward on the human resource issues in child care. It brings together national partners and other sector representatives to develop a confident, skilled, and respected workforce valued for its contribution to early childhood care and education. The website includes council publications, press releases, and projects and is also available in French.

Child Care Now

(https://timeforchildcare.ca/)

- Child Care Now is dedicated to advocating for a publicly funded, inclusive, quality, nonprofit child care system. This is a not-for-profit, membership-based, and regionally representative organization.

Childcare Resource and Research Unit

(CRRU; https://www.childcarecanada.org/)

---

2 Please note that this is not an exhaustive list of Canadian resources. The descriptions of these organizations are derived from their websites.

- The CRRU is a policy research institute with a goal of early childhood education and child care for all—fundamental for women's equality and a right for all children. It includes current news and research, a database of online documents, guides for families looking for quality child care, and listings of child care organizations.

SpeciaLink

(https://specialinkcanada.org/)

- SpeciaLink's goal is to expand the quality and quantity of opportunities for inclusion in child care, recreation, education, and other community settings to young children with special needs and their families. It provides referrals to other organizations as well as information and technical assistance. SpeciaLink also provides newsletters, fact sheets, books, videos, and a speakers bureau.

Glossary

active listening. A skill for responding to others when they are having problems that reflects what they might be experiencing: their feelings, thoughts, and desires. Active listening sends the message not only that we are listening but also that we want to understand what is happening for the person to whom we are listening.

bias. A tendency to prefer one person, group, or thing over another, often in a way that is considered to be unfair.

biophobia. Fear of the natural world.

cognitive development. The process of learning to use thought processes such as remembering, problem-solving, and decision-making.

community of practice. A group of people who share a common interest or concern who come together on a regular basis to share knowledge and improve practice.

cultural humility. Hook et al. (2015) define this term as "having an interpersonal stance that is other-oriented rather than self-focussed, characterized by respect and lack of superiority toward an individual's cultural background and experience" (p. 361).

culturally responsive practice. In the context of early child care, responding respectfully to the nuances of culture as experienced by each family, child, and staff member.

culture. Culture can be defined broadly as the characteristics and knowledge of a particular group of people. We use the term in this way to include all of the diversities that we find in our society: ethnicities, races, languages, family configurations, socioeconomic circumstances, abilities, religions, and gender and sexuality identifications.

developmental milestones. Guideposts intended to show what an average child can do at a given age.

discrimination. The unfair treatment of a group of people, especially based on characteristics such as gender, age, or race/ethnicity.

emergent curriculum. A philosophy of teaching and way of planning curriculum that builds on children's interests in order to create meaningful learning experiences.

emotional development. The process of learning to recognize, express, and manage feelings and to have empathy for the feelings of others; closely tied to social development.

ethnocentrism. Ethnocentrism refers to the practice of evaluating other cultures according to the standards and customs of one's own.

ethnomathematics. The study of the relationship between mathematics and culture (D'Ambrosio, 1985).

fine motor skills. The coordination of small muscles of the fingers, hands, wrists, feet, or toes with the eyes to give the ability to grasp and manipulate objects.

gender identity. The way in which a person defines themselves in relation to the masculine and feminine norms of their culture and in relation to the gender they were assigned at birth.

gross motor skills. The coordinated use of large muscle groups of the torso, arms, and legs.

intercultural practice. In the context of early child care, using discussion and dialogue with the intention of developing deep and honest relationships with children, families, and other educators.

intergenerational trauma. The transmission of historical oppression, abuse, or violation and its negative consequences across generations.

language development. The process of learning to understand and communicate using language.

multiculturalism. A belief or policy in which all cultural and racial/ ethnic groups have equal rights and opportunities. In Canada, multiculturalism is also understood as a policy of encouraging minority ethnocultural groups to maintain their customs and traditions (Cochrane et al., 2016)

nature deficit disorder. A term developed by Louv (2005) to describe the costs of our alienation from nature.

pedagogical documentation. A way of making children's thinking and learning visible using observations, texts, children's words, photos, evidence of children's work, interpretation, and analysis (Kashin, 2017).

pedagogy. The study of the theory and practice of teaching.

physical development. The process of learning to use one's body. Includes gross motor development (arms, legs, and torso) and fine motor development (hands, fingers, wrists, feet, and toes).

prejudice. A preconceived opinion not based on fact.

privilege. The advantages, mostly unearned and unacknowledged, that one group of people has over others.

provocation. An attractive display or activity intended to test children's curiosity, interest, and involvement in a topic before further integrating it into planning.

racism. A form of prejudice in which a person believes, consciously or unconsciously, that their race is superior to others.

scaffolding. A process of providing intentional supports during the learning process in order to lead students to a higher level of skill or understanding.

sexual orientation. A term that describes the sexes or genders to which a person is romantically or sexually attracted.

social development. The process of learning to interact effectively with others.

sociocultural theory. A theoretical framework that assumes that humans develop within the context of the culture in which they live.

stereotype. A belief (often untrue) that all people of a particular group have certain characteristics.

systemic racism. Policies and practices in the larger society that serve to give an unfair advantage to some sectors of the population based on race.

unconscious bias. Refers to stereotypes or preconceptions that people unconsciously attribute to a person or group of people. These affect the way that they understand or interact with that person or group.

whānau. A Māori word meaning extended family, often connected by physical, emotional, and spiritual bonds.

wise practice. A form of early childhood practice that works to combine the best of cultural practice with the best of early childhood practice

Bibliography

Abawi, Z., & Berman, R. (2019). Politicizing early childhood education and care in Ontario: Race identity and belonging. *Journal of Curriculum, Teaching, Learning and Leadership in Education, 4*(2), 4–13. https://digital commons.unomaha.edu/ctlle/vol4/iss2/2/

Academy of Pediatric Physiotherapy. (2018). *Fact sheet.* https://pediatricapta. org/includes/fact-sheets/pdfs/18%20Motor%20Dev%20Variations%20 Across%20Cultures%20FS.pdf

American Psychological Association. (2016, March 9). *Talking to kids about discrimination.* https://www.apa.org/topics/kids-discrimination

Association of Early Childhood Educators of Nova Scotia (AECENS). (n.d.). *Code of ethics: Guidelines for responsible behaviour in child care practice.* https://aecens.ca/wp-content/uploads/2019/04/Code-of-ethics-AECENS. pdf

August, C., & Shanahan, T. (2010). Response to a review and update on developing literacy in second-language learners: Report of the National Literacy Panel on Language Minority Children and Youth. *Journal of Literacy Research, 42*(3), 341–48. https://doi.org/10.1080/1086296X.2010. 503745

Babakr, Z., Mohamedamin, P., & Kakamad, K. (2019). Piaget's cognitive developmental theory: Critical review. *Education Quarterly Reviews, 2*(3), 517–14. https://doi.org/10.31014/aior.1993.02.03.84

Baker, C. (2006). *Foundations of bilingual education and bilingualism.* Multilingual Matters.

Balmes, T. (Director). (2010). *Babies* [Film]. StudioCanal.

Barac, R., & Bialystok, E. (2011). Cognitive development of bilingual children. *Language Teaching, 44*(1), 36–54. https://doi.org/10.1017/ S0261444810000339

Bar-Haim, Y., Ziv, T., Lamy, D., & Hodes, R.M. (2006). Nature and nurture in own-race face processing. *Psychological Science, 17*(2), 159–63. https://doi. org/10.1111/j.1467-9280.2006.01679.x

Barrett, M.S., Welch, G.F., Howard, D.M., & Nix, J. (2019). Singing and invented song-making in infants' and young children's early learning and development: From shared to independent song-making. In G.F. Welch, D.M. Howard, & J. Nix (Eds.), *The Oxford handbook of singing* (pp. 471–87). Oxford University Press.

Baumgart, C.Q., & Billick, S. (2018). Positive cognitive effects of bilingualism and multilingualism on cerebral function: A review. *Psychiatric Quarterly, 89*(2), 273–83. https://doi.org/10.1007/s11126-017-9532-9

Beck, J. (2017). Making the connection between culture and mathematics. *Northwestern School of Education and Social Policy.* https://www.sesp. northwestern.edu/news-center/inquiry/2009-spring/making-the-connection.html

Beloglovsky, M. & Spahn, D. (2021, January 27). *Provoking inquiry with loose parts* [Webinar]. Early Childhood Investigations. www.earlychildhood webinars.com/webinar-resources/

Belshaw, J.D. (2015). Canadian history: Pre-confederation. http://opentextbc. ca/preconfederation/

Bentley, S.M. (2009, December). *Friedrich Schiller's play: A theory of human nature in the context of the eighteenth-century study of life* (Paper 101). [Master's thesis, University of Louisville]. ThinkIR: The University of Louisville's Institutional Repository. https://ir.library.louisville.edu/etd/101/

Berto, R. (2014). The role of nature in coping with psycho-physiological stress: A literature review on restorativeness. *Behavioral Sciences, 4*(4), 394–409. https://doi.org/10.3390/bs4040394

Bialystok, E. (2001). *Bilingualism in development: Language, literacy and cognition.* Cambridge University Press.

Bialystok, E. (2006). The impact of bilingualism on language and literacy development. In T.K. Bhatia & W.E. Ritchie (Eds.), *The handbook of bilingualism* (pp. 577–601). Blackwell Publishing.

Boston University. (n.d.). *Parenting children with special needs.* BU Faculty and Staff Assistance. https://www.bu.edu/fsao/resources/parenting-children-with-special-needs/#:~:text=The%20usual%20challenges%20 of%20parenting%20are%20compounded%20for,Researching%2C%20 locating%20and%20accessing%20effective%20treatments%20and%20 resources

Bronfenbrenner, U. (1994). Ecological models of human development. *Readings on the Development of Children, 2*(1), 37–43.

Canadian Child Care Federation. (2020). *Our code of ethics.* https://cccf-fcsge. ca/about-canadian-child-care-federation/values/code-ethics/

Canadian Child Care Federation. (2021). *ECE guide by province or territory.* https://cccf-fcsge.ca/ece-resources/professional-development/journey-early-childhood-education/provincial-data-child-care-certification/

Canadian Heritage LGBTQ2 Secretariat. (2020, August 19). *LGBTQ2 terminology—Glossary and common acronyms.* Government of Canada. https://www.canada.ca/en/canadian-heritage/campaigns/free-to-be-me/lgbtq2-glossary.html

Canadian Children's Book Centre. (n.d.). *How to choose a book.* https://bookcentre.ca/resources/how-to-choose-a-book#:~:text=Look%20for%20these:%201%20Plenty%20of%20creative%20ideas,and%20crafts%20for%20next%20time.%20More%20ite

Canadian Human Right Commission. (2020, June 2). *Statement—Anti-black racism in Canada: Time to face the truth.* https://www.chrc-ccdp.gc.ca/eng/content/statement-anti-black-racism-canada-time-face-truth

Cannella, G.S. (2008). *Deconstructing early childhood education: Social justice and revolution.* Peter Lang.

Carr, M., & Lee, W. (2019). *Learning stories in practice.* SAGE.

Centre on the Developing Child. (2007). *In brief: The science of early childhood development.* Harvard University. https://developingchild.harvard.edu/resources/inbrief-science-of-ecd/

Centre on the Developing Child. (2011, September 29). *Toxic stress derails healthy development* [Video]. Harvard University. https://developingchild.harvard.edu/resources/toxic-stress-derails-healthy-development/

Center on the Developing Child. (2021). *Executive function and self-regulation.* Harvard University. https://developingchild.harvard.edu/science/key-concepts/executive-function/

Centre on the Social and Emotional Foundations for Early Learning (CSEFEL). (2008). *Helping children make transitions between activities* (What Works Brief Training Kit #4). http://csefel.vanderbilt.edu/kits/wwbtk4.pdf

Chard, S. (1992). *Projects and the curriculum: Seeing the possibilities* (The Project Approach Vol. 1). TheProjectApproach.org.

Chard, S. (1994). *Features of the project approach: A framework for learning* (The Project Approach Vol. 2). TheProjectApproach.org.

Chawla L., Keena, K., Pevec, I., & Stanley, E. (2014). Green schoolyards as havens from stress and resources for resilience in childhood and adolescence. *Health and Place, 28,* 1–13. https://doi.org/10.1016/j.healthplace.2014.03.001

Cherry, K. (2020, March 31). *Support and criticism of Piaget's stage theory.* Verywell Mind. https://www.verywellmind.com/piagets-stages-of-cognitive-development-2795457

Child Care Human Resources Sector Council. (CCHRSC). (2010). *Occupational standards for early childhood educators*. http://www.ccsc-cssge.ca/sites/default/files/uploads/ECE-Post-Secondary-docs/OSECE_2010_EN.pdf

Chin, N.B., & Wigglesworth, G. (2007). *Bilingualism: An advanced resource book*. Routledge.

Clements, D. & Sarama, J. (2011). Early childhood mathematics intervention. *Science, 333*(6045), 968–70. https://doi.org/10.1126/science.1204537

Cochrane, C., Blidook, K. & Dyck, R. (2016). *Canadian politics: Critical approaches* (8th ed.). Nelson Canada.

College of Early Childhood Educators (CECE). (2017, July 1). *Code of ethics and standards of practice*. https://www.college-ece.ca/en/Public/professionalstandards

Collins, C. (2018). What is white privilege, really? *Teaching Tolerance, 60*(Fall). https://www.tolerance.org/magazine/fall-2018/what-is-white-privilege-really

Craven, M.J. (2012, January 4). Cultural influences on Piagetian task performance. *MartinJamesCraven*. https://martinjamescraven.wordpress.com/2012/01/04/cultural-influences-on-piagetian-task-performance/

Crown–Indigenous Relations and Northern Affairs. (2010, September 15). *Highlights from the Report of the Royal Commission on Aboriginal Peoples: People to people, nation to nation*. Government of Canada. https://www.rcaanc-cirnac.gc.ca/eng/1100100014597/1572547985018

Dahlberg, G., Moss, P., & Pence, A. (2007). *Beyond quality in early childhood education and care: Languages of evaluation*. Routledge.

Daly, L., & Beloglovsky, M. (2015). *Loose parts: Inspiring play in young children*. Redleaf Press.

D'Ambrosio, U. (1985). Ethnomathematics and its place in the history and pedagogy of mathematics. *For the Learning of Mathematics, 5*(1), 44–48.

Daniels v. Canada (Indian Affairs and Northern Development), 12 Supreme Court of Canada (2016). 1 SCC 99. Retrieved from the Supreme Court of Canada Judgments website: https://scc-csc.lexum.com/scc-csc/scc-csc/en/item/15858/index.do

Daschuk, J. (2019). *Clearing the plains: Disease, politics of starvation, and the loss of Aboriginal life*. University of Regina Press. (Original work published 2013).

Dehaene, S. (1997). *The number sense*. Oxford University Press.

De Houwer, A. (2015). Harmonious bilingual development: Young families' well-being in language contact situations. *International Journal of Bilingualism, 19*(2), 169–84. https://doi.org/10.1177/1367006913489202

Delisle, R. (2019, August 2). This is what it's like to parent when you're struggling to make ends meet. *Chatelaine*. https://www.chatelaine.com/living/parenting-in-poverty/

Derman-Sparks, L. & Edwards, J. (2009). *Anti-bias education for young children and ourselves.* NAEYC.

Derman-Sparks, L., & Edwards, J.O. (2015, July 8). *Teaching young children about race: A guide for parents and teachers.* Teaching for Change. https://www.teachingforchange.org/teaching-about-race

Di Giorgio, E., Méary, D., Pascalis, O., & Simion, F. (2013). The face perception system becomes species-specific at 3 months: An eye-tracking study. *International Journal of Behavioral Development, 37*(2), 95–99. https://doi.org/10.1177/0165025412465362

Dunham, Y., Baron, A. & Banaji, M. (2008). The development of implicit intergroup cognition. *Trends in Cognitive Science, 12*(7), 248–53. https://doi.org/10.1016/j.tics.2008.04.006

Dweck, C. (2006). *Mindset: The new psychology of success.* Ballantyne.

Early Childhood Development Association of PEI. (2021). *Code of ethics.* https://www.ecdaofpei.ca/about/ethics.php

Early Childhood Educators of BC (ECEBC). (2008). *Code of ethics.* http://www.ecebc.ca/resources/pdf/ecebc_codeofethics_web.pdf

Educational Leadership Project Ltd. (2019a, February 19). *Part one: Learning stories—A philosophical approach* [Video]. YouTube. https://youtu.be/jpor4bXCf44

Educational Leadership Project Ltd. (2019b, March 3). *Part two: Learning stories—The key components* [Video]. YouTube. https://youtu.be/GU2ZIlfsR7s

Educational Leadership Project Ltd. (2019c, March 11). *Part three: Learning stories—Culture in the classroom* [Video]. YouTube. https://youtu.be/LrdP9EztPGA

Edwards, C., Gandini, L., & Forman, G. (Eds.). (2012). *The hundred languages of children: The Reggio Emilia experience in transformation* (3rd ed.). Praeger.

Eisenchlas, S.A., Schalley, A.C., & Guillermin, D. (2013). The importance of literacy in the home language: The view from Australia. *SAGE Open, 2013*(January). https://doi.org/10.1177/2158244013507270

Employment and Social Development Canada. (2018, September 17). *Indigenous early learning and child care framework.* Government of Canada. https://www.canada.ca/en/employment-social-development/programs/indigenous-early-learning/2018-framework.html

Eshet, D. (2015). *Stolen lives: The Indigenous Peoples of Canada and the Indian residential schools.* Facing History and Ourselves. https://www.facinghistory.org/stolen-lives-indigenous-peoples-canada-and-indian-residential-schools

Feagin, J.R. (2006). *Systemic racism: A theory of oppression.* Routledge.

Fine, S. (2015, May 28). Chief justice says Canada attempted "cultural genocide" on Aboriginals. *The Globe and Mail.* https://www.theglobeand mail.com/news/national/chief-justice-says-canada-attempted-cultural-genocide-on-aboriginals/article24688854/

First Nations Pedagogy Online. (2009) *Storytelling.* https://firstnation spedagogy.ca/storytelling.html#:~:text=First%20Nations%2C%20Inuit% 2C%20and%20Metis%20cultures%20have%20long,rituals%2C%20 history%2C%20practices%2C%

Flohr, J.W., & Perselling, D. (2011). Applying brain research to children's musical experiences. In S. Burton & C.C. Taggart (Eds.), *Learning from young children: Research in early childhood music.* R&L Education.

Fraser, S. (2012). *Authentic childhood.* Nelson Education.

Friesen, J., & Bascaramurty, D. (2011, December 16). Canadian schools struggle with what to do about Christmas. *The Globe and Mail.* https:// www.theglobeandmail.com/life/holiday-guide/canadian-schools-struggle-with-what-to-do-about-christmas/article1357339/

Gandini, L. (2012). Connecting through caring and learning spaces. In C. Edwards, L. Gandini, & G. Foreman (Eds.), *The hundred languages of children: The Reggio Emilia experience in transformation* (3rd ed.; pp. 317–42). Praeger.

Genesee, F., & Lindholm-Leary, K. (2012). The education of English language learners. In K. Harris, S. Graham, & T. Urdan (Eds.), *APA handbook of educational psychology.* APA Books.

Georgis, R., Brosinsky, L., Mejia, T., Kirova, A., Gokiert, R., & Knowledge Exchange Advisory. (2017). *RAISED between cultures: A knowledge and reflection guidebook for intercultural practice in the early years.* Edmonton: Community-University Partnership, University of Alberta.

Gifford, R. & Chen, A. (2016, March 31). *Children and nature. What we know and what we do not.* The Lawson Foundation. https://lawson.ca/wp-content/uploads/2018/04/Children-and-Nature-What-We-Know-and-What-We-Do-Not.pdf

Goldenberg, C. (2008). Teaching English language learners: What the research does—and does not—say. *American Educator, 32*(2), 8–43.

Goodfellow, J. (2001, September). Wise practice: The need to move beyond best practice in early childhood settings. *Australian Journal of Early Childhood, 26*(3), 1–5.

Gordon, T. (1970). *P.E.T.: Parent effectiveness training.* Peter H. Wyden.

Government of Alberta. (2021). *What is child abuse, neglect and sexual exploitation?* https://www.alberta.ca/what-is-child-abuse-neglect-and-sexual-exploitation.aspx

Government of Ontario. (2009). *Ontario's equity and inclusive education strategy.* http://www.edu.gov.on.ca/eng/policyfunding/equity.pdf

Gray, J., & the International Society for the Prevention of Child Abuse and Neglect (ISPCAN). (2012). *World perspectives on child abuse* (10th ed.; Dubowitz H., Ed.). ISPCAN.

Gray Smith, M. (2018, April 28). *Respectfully weaving Indigenous perspectives throughout curriculum* [Conference presentation]. Canadian Association for Young Children annual general meeting, NorQuest College, Edmonton, Alberta.

Greenman, J. (1993). Just wondering: Building wonder into the environment. *Exchange, 1993*(January/February), 32–36. https://www.childcareexchange.com/article/just-wondering-building-wonder-into-the-environment/5008932/

Griffin, S. (2004). Teaching number sense: Improving achievement in math and science. *Educational Leadership, 61*(5), 39–42.

Griffin, S., Case, R., & Siegler, R. (1994). Rightstart: Providing the central conceptual prerequisite for first formal learning of arithmetic to students at risk for school failure. In K. McGilly (Ed.), *Classroom lesson: Integrating cognitive theory and classroom practice* (pp. 24–49). MIT Press.

Hackett, C., Feeny, D., & Tompa, P. (2016). Canada's residential school system: Measuring the intergenerational impact of familial attendance on health and mental health outcomes. *Journal of Epidemiology and Community Health, 70*(11), 1096–105. https://doi.org/10.1136/jech-2016-207380

Halberstadt, A.G., Cooke, A.N., Garner, P.W., Hughes, S.A., Oertwig, D., & Neupert, S.D. (2020, July 2). Racialized emotion recognition accuracy and anger bias of children's faces. *Emotion,* (advance online publication). https://doi.org/10.1037/emo0000756

Hanson, E. (2009). *Oral Traditions.* http://indigenousfoundations.arts.ubc.ca/oral_traditions/

Head Start. (2020, October 8). Understanding and eliminating expulsion in early childhood programs. *U.S. Department of Health & Human Services.* https://eclkc.ohs.acf.hhs.gov/publication/understanding-eliminating-expulsion-early-childhood-programs

The health benefits of strong relationships. (2019, August 6). *Harvard Health.* https://www.health.harvard.edu/newsletter_article/the-health-benefits-of-strong-relationships

Heerwagen, J., & Orians, G. (2002). The ecological world of children. In P.H. Kahn & S.R. Kellert (Eds.), *Children and nature: Psychological, sociocultural and evolutionary investigations* (pp. 29–64). MIT Press.

Heran, J., & Matheson, M.L. (2016). Culturally responsive practice at the Intercultural Child and Family Centre. *Interaction, 30*(2). https://cccf-fcsge.ca/ece-resources/browse/interaction-magazine-archive/

Hewes, J. (n.d.). *Let the children play: Nature's answer to early learning*. Centre of Excellence for Early Childhood Development. http://www.child-encyclopedia.com/sites/default/files/docs/suggestions/let-the-children-play_jane-hewes.pdf

Hook, J., Davis, D., Owen, J., Worthington, E., & Utsey, S. (2013). Cultural humility: Measuring openness to culturally diverse clients. *Journal of Counseling Psychology, 60*(3), 353–66. https://doi.org/10.1037/a0032595

Hordyk, S.R., Dulude, M., & Shens, M. (2015). When nature nurtures children: Nature as a containing and holding space. *Children's Geographics, 13*(5), 571–88. https://doi.org/10.1080/14733285.2014.923814

How art promotes learning [Newsletter]. (2007, January 18). Exchange Every Day. https://childcareexchange.com/eed/issue/1640/

Howell, J., & Reinhard, K. (2015). *Rituals and traditions: Fostering a sense of community in preschool*. National Association for Young Children.

Huang, Ching-Yu. (2018, July 19). How culture influences children's development. *The Conversation*. https://theconversation.com/how-culture-influences-childrens-development-99791

Hutchinson, N., & Specht, J. (2020). *Inclusion of learners with exceptionalities in Canadian schools* (6th ed.). Pearson.

Hughes, F.P. (2009). *Children, play, and development*. SAGE.

Isik-Ercan, Z. (2017). Culturally appropriate positive guidance with young children. *Young Children, 72*(1). https://www.naeyc.org/resources/pubs/yc/mar2017/culturally-appropriate-positive-guidance#:~:text=%20Culturally%20Appropriate%20Positive%20Guidance%20with%20Young%20Childre

Jaboneta, N. (2018). *You can't celebrate that! Navigating the deep waters of social justice teaching* (A. Pelo & M. Carter, Eds.). Exchange Press

Jesuit Social Services. (n.d.). *Strong bonds fact sheet: Workers: Refugees—trauma, grief and loss*. http://www.strongbonds.jss.org.au/workers/cultures/refugees.pdf

Kaiser, B. (2020, March 25). *The link between early trauma and young children's behaviour* [Webinar presentation]. Early Childhood Investigations; ContinuEd. https://www.earlychildhoodwebinars.com/webinars/understanding-the-impact-of-trauma-on-behavior-by-barbara-kaiser/

Kappler, M. (2020, June 1) Racism in Canada is ever present but we have a long history of denial. *Huffington Post*. https://www.huffingtonpost.ca/entry/racism-canada-anti-black_ca_5ecd6c6cc5b670f88ad48d5c

Kashin, D. (2017, August 23). *Documentation: A tool for family engagement and curriculum development* [Webinar presentation]. Early Childhood Investigations; HiMama. https://www.earlychildhoodwebinars.com/webinars/documentation-tool-family-engagement-curriculum-development-diane-kashin/

Katz, L. (1996). Child development knowledge and teacher preparation: Confronting assumptions. *Early Childhood Research Quarterly 11*(2), 135–46.

Kelly, D., Quinn, P., Lee, K., Gibson, A., Smith, M., Ge, L., & Pascalis, O. (2005). Three-month-olds, but not newborns, prefer own-race faces. *Developmental science, 8*(6), F31–F36. https://doi.org/10.1111/j.1467-7687.2005.0434a.x

Kemble, T. (2019, October). *Indigenous early learning and care in the city of Edmonton: Articulating the experiences, perspectives and needs of Indigenous parents/caregivers.* Edmonton Council for Early Learning and Care.

Kirova, A. (2001). Loneliness in immigrant children: Implications for classroom practice. *Childhood Education, 77*(5), 260–68. https://doi.org/10.1080/00094056.2001.10521648

Kirova, A. (2003). Accessing children's experiences of loneliness through conversation. *Field Methods, 15*(1), 3–24. https://doi.org/10.1177/1525822X02239572

Kirova, A. (2016). Phenomenology of inclusion, belonging, and language. In *Encyclopedia of educational philosophy and theory* (M.A. Peters, Ed.). Springer Singapore. https://doi.org/10.1007/978-981-287-532-7_97-1

Korn-Bursztyn, C. (Ed.). (2012). *Young children and the arts: Nurturing imagination and creativity.* Information Age Publishing.

Lewis, P.J. (2019). Spirituality of play. In S. Jagger (Ed.), *Early years education and care in Canada* (pp. 13–26). Canadian Scholars.

Liljedahl, P., & Liu, M. (2013). Numeracy. *Vector 2*(Summer), 34–39. http://www.peterliljedahl.com/wp-content/uploads/NR-Numeracy.pdf

Lin, X. (2018, March 9) Parents' play beliefs and engagement in young children's play at home. *European Early Education Research Journal, 26*(2), 161–76.

Lindstrom, G., Choate, P., Bastien, L., Weasel Traveller, A., Breaker, S., Breaker, C., Good Striker, W., & Good Striker, E. (2016). Nistawatsimin: *Exploring First Nations parenting: A literature review and expert consultation with Blackfoot Elders.* Mount Royal University. https://cwrp.ca/publications/nistawatsimin-exploring-first-nations-parenting-literature-review-and-expert

Lourenco, O. (2012). Piaget and Vygotsky: Many resemblances, and a crucial difference. *New Ideas in Psychology, 30*(3), 281–95. https://doi.org/10.1016/j.newideapsych.2011.12.006

Louv, R. (2005). *Last child in the woods: Saving our children from nature-deficit disorder.* Algonquin Books.

MacIntosh, P. (1988). *White privilege: Unpacking the invisible knapsack.* SEED; Wellesley Centers for Women. https://nationalseedproject.org/images/documents/Knapsack_plus_Notes-Peggy_McIntosh.pdf

Madwan, S. (2018). Inuit High Arctic relocations in Canada. In *Canadian Encyclopedia*. https://www.thecanadianencyclopedia.ca/en/article/inuit-high-arctic-relocations

Makovichuk, L., Hewes, J., Lirette, P., & Thomas, N. (2014). *Flight: Alberta's Early Learning and Care Framework*. https://flightframework.ca/downloads/Flight%20Framework%20Document%20F.pdf

Malaguzzi, L. (1994). Your image of the child: Where teaching begins. *Exchange, 3*(94). https://www.reggioalliance.org/downloads/malaguzzi:ccie:1994.pdf

Manitoba Child Care Association. (2019). *Code of ethics*. http://mccahouse.org/wp-content/uploads/2019/12/Code-of-Ethics-Principles.pdf

Massing, Carole, & Shortreed, L. (2014). *Teaching and learning with immigrant and refugee child care educators*. Alberta Ministry of Human Services.

Massing, Christine. (2015). *An ethnographic study of immigrant and refugee women's knowledge construction in an early childhood teacher education program* [Doctoral dissertation, University of Alberta]. ERA: Education and Research Archive. https://doi.org/10.7939/R3445HM33

Massing, Christine. (2018). African, Muslim refugee student teachers' perceptions of care practices in infant and toddler field placements. *International Journal of Early Years Education, 26*(2), 186–200. https://doi.org/10.1080/09669760.2018.1458603

Mathews, K., & Jordan, I. (2019). *Our children, our workplace: Why we must talk about race and racism in early childhood education*. Exchange Press.

Matusov, E., & Hayes, R. (2000). Sociocultural critique of Piaget and Vygotsky. *New Ideas in Psychology, 18*(2000), 215–39.

Mayo Clinic Staff. (2019, April 5). Stress relief from laughter? It's no joke. *Mayo Clinic*. https://www.mayoclinic.org/healthy-lifestyle/stress-management/in-depth/stress-relief/art-20044456

McCarthy, C. (2017, June 13). Resilience: A skill your child really needs to learn (and what you can do to help). *Harvard Health*. https://www.health.harvard.edu/blog/resilience-a-skill-your-child-really-needs-to-learn-and-what-you-can-do-to-help-2017061311899

McCarthy, C. (2019, September 14). How racism harms children. *Harvard Health*. https://www.health.harvard.edu/blog/how-racism-harms-children-2019091417788

McCue, H. (2018). Education of Indigenous Peoples in Canada. In B. Graves (Ed.), *The Canadian Encyclopedia*. https://www.thecanadianencyclopedia.ca/en/article/aboriginal-people-education

Monkman, L. (2019, May 17). Genocide against Indigenous Peoples recognized by Canadian Museum for Human Rights. *CBC News*. https://www.cbc.ca/news/indigenous/cmhr-colonialism-genocide-indigenous-peoples-1.5141078

Montgomery, H. (2019, March 1). Different cultures, different childhoods. *OpenLearn*. https://www.open.edu/openlearn/history-the-arts/history/different-cultures-different-childhoods

Morency, J.D., Malenfont, E.C., & MacIsaac, S. (2017). *Immigration and diversity: Population projections for Canada and its regions, 2011 to 2036.* Statistics Canada. https://www150.statcan.gc.ca/n1/pub/91-551-x/91-551-x2017001-eng.htm

Morra, S., Bisagno, E., Caviola, S., & Mammarella, I. (2019, July 27). Working memory capacity and the development of quantitative central conceptual structures. *Cognition and Instruction, 37*(4), 483–511. https://doi.org/10.1080/07370008.2019.1636797

Morrison, H. (Ed.). (2012). *The global history of childhood reader.* Routledge.

Mozaffar, R. (2018). *Creativity for children: Assessing children's creativity in play and design recommendations for educational outdoor environments to enhance children's creativity* [Doctoral dissertation, University of Edinburgh] ERA: Edinburgh Research Archive. http://hdl.handle.net/1842/31113

Murnaghan, A.M., & Shillington, L.J. (Eds.). (2016). *Children, nature, cities.* Routledge.

National Inquiry into Missing and Murdered Indigenous Women and Girls. (2019). *Reclaiming power and place: The final report of the inquiry into missing and murdered Indigenous women and girls.* https://www.mmiwg-ffada.ca/final-report/

National Numeracy. (2021). *What is numeracy? It's the ability to use maths in everyday life.* https://www.nationalnumeracy.org.uk/what-numeracy#:~:text=What%20is%20numeracy%3F%20%20When%20do%20we,budget%2C%20underst%20...%20%203%20more%20rows%20

National Scientific Council on the Developing Child. (2004). *Young children develop in an environment of relationships* [Working paper no. 1]. https://46y5eh11fhgw3ve3ytpwxt9r-wpengine.netdna-ssl.com/wp-content/uploads/2004/04/Young-Children-Develop-in-an-Environment-of-Relationships.pdf

National Scientific Council on the Developing Child. (2014). *Excessive stress disrupts the architecture of the developing brain* [Working paper no. 3]. Centre on the Developing Child; Harvard University. https://developingchild.harvard.edu/wp-content/uploads/2005/05/Stress_Disrupts_Architecture_Developing_Brain-1.pdf. Original work published 2005.

National Scientific Council on the Developing Child. (2020). *Connecting the brain to the rest of the body: Early childhood development and lifelong health are deeply intertwined* [Working paper no. 15]. Centre on the Developing Child; Harvard University. https://developingchild.harvard.edu/resources/connecting-the-brain-to-the-rest-of-the-body-early-childhood-development-and-lifelong-health-are-deeply-intertwined/

Nicholson, S. (1971). How NOT to cheat children: The theory of loose parts. *Landscape Architecture, 62, 30–34.*

Parry, M. (2006). G. Stanley Hall: Psychologist and early gerontologist. *American Journal of Public Health, 96*(7), 1161. https://doi.org/10.2105/AJPH.2006.090647

Piaget, J. (1923). *The language and thought of the child.* Harper Brace.

Piaget, J., & Inhelder, B. (1973). *Memory and intelligence.* Basic Books.

Piaget, J. (1995). *Sociological studies* (L. Smith, Trans.). Routledge. (Original work published in 1977).

Pickens, I.B., & Tschopp, N. (2017). *Trauma-informed classrooms.* National Council of Juvenile and Family Court Judges. https://www.ncjfcj.org/wp-content/uploads/2017/10/NCJFCJ_SJP_Trauma_Informed_Classrooms_Final.pdf

Poole, N., Talbot, C., & Nathoos, T. (2017). *Healing families, helping systems: A trauma-informed practice guide for working with children, youth and families.* BC Ministry of Children and Family Development. https://www2.gov.bc.ca/assets/gov/health/child-teen-mental-health/trauma-informed_practice_guide.pdf

Price, C.L., & Steed, E.A. (2016). Culturally responsive strategies to support young children with challenging behavior. *Young Children, 71*(5). https://www.naeyc.org/resources/pubs/yc/nov2016/culturally-responsive-strategies#:~:text=In%20this%20article%20we%20describe%20five%20culturally%20responsive,empathy%2C%20and%20use%20group%20times%20to%20discuss%20conflict

Prochner, L., Cleghorn, A., Kirova, A., & Massing, C. (2016). *Teacher education in diverse settings: Making space for intersecting worldviews.* Sense Publishers.

Qikiqtani Truth Commission. (2014). *Thematic reports and special studies 1950–1975.* Qikiqtani Inuit Association.

Rajan, R. (2014). Supporting conflict resolution through structured dramatic play. *Exchange 2014*(May/June). https://www.childcareexchange.com/catalog/product/supporting-conflict-resolution-through-structured-dramatic-play/5021768/

Rees, A., Becker, B., Bryant, C., & Frazier, A.D. (2016). Shaping our space: Children's embodiment and engaging nature. In A.M. Murnaghan & L.J. Shillington (Eds.), *Children, nature, cities* (pp. 171–95). Routledge.

Reynolds, E. (2008). *Guiding young children* (4th ed.). McGraw Hill.

Rice, K., & Gallant, D.J. (2020, April 17). Indigenous languages in Canada. In B. Graves (Ed.), *The Canadian Encyclopedia.* https://www.thecanadianencyclopedia.ca/en/article/aboriginal-people-languages

Rice, K., Gallant, D.J. & Filice, M. (2020, April 17). Indigenous language revital-ization in Canada. In B. Graves (Ed.), *The Canadian Encyclopedia*. https://www.thecanadianencyclopedia.ca/en/article/indigenous-language-revitalization-in-canada

Rinaldi, C. (2005). Documenting and assessment: What is the relation-ship? (1995–8). In C. Rinaldi, *In dialogue with Reggio Emilia* (pp. 45–56). Routledge.

Roffey, S. (2017). Learning healthy relationships. In C. Proctor (Ed.), *Positive Psychology Interventions in Practice* (pp. 163–181). Springer.

Rogoff, B. (1990). *Apprenticeship in thinking: Cognitive development in social context*. Oxford University Press.

Rogoff, B. (2003). *The cultural nature of human development*. Oxford University Press.

Roopnarine J.L., & Davidson K.L. (2015). Parent–child play across cultures: Advancing play research, *American Journal of Play, 7*(2), 228–52.

Rubin, K.H., Fein, G.G., & Vandenberg, B. (1983). Play. In P.H. Mussen (Ed.), *Handbook of child psychology: Socialization, personality, and social develop-ment* (Vol. 4; pp. 693–775). Wiley.

Rubin, K.H., & Menzer, M. (2010). Culture and social development. In R.E. Temblay, M. Boivin, & R.D. Peters (Eds.), *Encyclopedia on early childhood development*. http://www.child-encyclopedia.com/culture/according-experts/culture-and-social-development

Rudy, L.J. (2020, April 18). Intelligence tests for children with autism. *Verywell Health*. https://www.verywellhealth.com/best-intelligence-test-for-an-autistic-child-260573

Sangrigoli, S., & De Schonen, S. (2004). Recognition of own-race and other-race faces by three-month old infants. *Journal of Child Psychology and Psychiatry, 45*(7), 1218–27. https://doi.org/10.1111/j.1469-7610.2004.00319.x

Schalley, A.C., Eisenchlas, S.A., & Gagarina, N. (2016). Conference report: HOLM 2016—The International Conference on Social and Affective Fac-tors in Home Language Maintenance and Development. *Journal of Home Language Research, 2*(2017), 1–5. http://hdl.handle.net/10092/13529

Schottenstein, Y. (n.d.). *How the language you speak affects your worldview.* Omniglot. https://omniglot.com/language/articles/languageworldviews.htm

Schreifer, P. (2016, April 18). *What's the difference between multicultural, intercultural, and cross-cultural communication?* Spring Institute. https://springinstitute.org/whats-difference-multicultural-intercultural-cross-cultural-communication/

Seitz, H. (2008). *The power of documentation in the early childhood classroom.* National Association for the Education of Young Children. https://www. naeyc.org/sites/default/files/globally-shared/downloads/PDFs/resources/ pubs/seitz.pdf

Smith, J.Y. (1980, September 17). Jean Piaget dies, was a founder of modern child psychology. *The Washington Post.* https://www.washingtonpost. com/archive/local/1980/09/17/jean-piaget-dies-was-a-founder-of- modern-child-psychology/fc04e08d-791f-4516-9015-596db2020a9f/

Smith, P. (2010). *Children and play.* Wiley Online. https://onlinelibrary.wiley. com/doi/book/10.1002/9781444311006

Sobel, D. (1996). *Beyond ecophobia: Reclaiming the heart of nature education.* The Orion Society.

Souto-Manning, M., Falk, B., López, D., Barros Cruz, L., Bradt, N., Cardwell, N., McGowan, N., Perez, A., Rabadi-Raol, A., & Rollins, E. (2019, May 22). A transdisciplinary approach to equitable teaching in early childhood education. *Review of Research in Education, 43*(1), 249–76. https://doi. org/10.3102/0091732X18821122

Stacey, S. (2009). *Emergent curriculum in early childhood settings: From theory to practice.* Redleaf Press.

Stagg-Peterson, S., Huston, L., & Loon, R. (2019). Professional lives and initial teacher education experiences of Indigenous early childhood educators, child care workers and teachers in Northern Ontario. *Brock Education, 28*(2), 17–22. https://doi.org/10.26522/BROCKED.V2812.683.

Statistics Canada. (2016, February 19). *Two-thirds of the population declare Christian as their religion.* https://www150.statcan.gc.ca/n1/pub/91- 003-x/2014001/section03/33-eng.htm

Statistics Canada. (2017a, November 26). *Statistics on official languages in Canada.* https://www.canada.ca/en/canadian-heritage/services/ official-languages-bilingualism/publications/statistics.html

Statistics Canada. (2017b, August 2). Census in brief: Same-sex couples in Canada in 2016. https://www12.statcan.gc.ca/census-recensement/2016/ as-sa/98-200-x/2016007/98-200-x2016007-eng.cfm

Statistics Canada. (2020, February 24). *Canadian income survey 2018.* https:// www150.statcan.gc.ca/n1/daily-quotidien/200224/dq200224a-eng. htm?HPA=1

Stearns, P.N. (2017). *Childhood in world history* (3rd ed.). Routledge.

Stonechild, B. (2006). Aboriginal people of Saskatchewan. In B. Stonechild (Aboriginal Ed.), *The Encyclopedia of Saskatchewan.* https://esask.uregina. ca/entry/aboriginal_peoplesof_saskatchewan.jsp

Strigley, K. (2016). Oral history: The stories our grandmothers tell us and more. In J.D. Belshaw (Ed.), *Canadian History: Post-Confederation* (Pt. 12.11). https://opentextbc.ca/postconfederation/chapter/12-11-oral-history-the-stories-our-grandmothers-tell-us-and-more/

Sutherland, N. (2014, September 19). History of childhood. In B. Graves (Ed.), *The Canadian Encyclopedia*. https://www.thecanadianencyclopedia.ca/en/article/history-of-childhood

Tabery, J. (2014, April 29). *Nature vs nurture*. Eugenics Archive. http://eugenicsarchive.ca/database/documents/535eed0d7095aa0000000241#!

Tagataga Inc. (2008, April 30). *Early childhood education and care: Present successes – Promising directions. A discussion paper for the National Inuit Education Summit, October 2007*. Inuit Tapiriit Kanatami. https://www.itk.ca/wp-content/uploads/2016/07/Inuit-Early-Childhood-Education-and-Care_0.pdf

Taylor, C.S. (2014, February 22). If we can't say "merry Christmas" in Canada, multiculturalism failed. *Huffington Post*. https://www.huffingtonpost.ca/christopher-stuart-taylor/saying-merry-christmas_b_4490555.html

TEDx Talks. (2015, June 4). *It starts at home: Letting children collaborate | Dr. Barbara Rogoff | TEDxSantaCruz* [Video]. YouTube. https://www.youtube.com/watch?v=Bu03KUNI1Zk

Teillet, J. (2019). *The Northwest is our mother: The story of Louis Riel's people, the Metis Nation*. Patrick Crean Editions.

Trent, M., Dooley, D.G., & Douge, J. (2019, July 29). The impact of racism on child and adolescent health. *Pediatrics, 144*(2), e20191765. https://doi.org/10.1542/peds.2019-1765

Truth and Reconciliation Commission (TRC). (2015). *Canada's residential schools: The history, part 1: Origins to 1939*. TRC; McGill-Queen's University Press. http://www.trc.ca/assets/pdf/Volume_1_History_Part_1_English_Web.pdf

University of Alberta. (2018, March 7). *RAISED between cultures model*. University of Alberta Community University Partnership. https://www.ualberta.ca/community-university-partnership/cup-news/2018/march/raised-video.html

University of Alberta. (2008a). *Cross-cultural handbook: Early childhood developmental screening and approaches to research and practice*. https://www.ualberta.ca/community-university-partnership/media-library/community-university-partnership/resources/publications/crosscultural handbook.pdf

University of Alberta. (2008b). *Early childhood screening in immigrant and refugee families*. University of Alberta Community University Partnership. https://www.ualberta.ca/community-university-partnership/research/early-childhood-development/cross-cultural-lessons.html

Victoria State Government. (2021, February 10). *Assessment for learning: Younger children's development.* https://www.education.vic.gov.au/childhood/professionals/learning/Pages/Assessment-for-learning-.aspx

Vizina, Y. (2008). *Métis culture.* Our Legacy. http://scaa.sk.ca/ourlegacy/exhibit_metisculture

Vygotsky, L.S. (1978). *Mind in society: The development of higher mental processes* (M. Cole, V. John-Steiner, S. Scribner, & E. Souberman, Eds.). Harvard University Press.

Vygotsky, L.S. (1986). *Thought and language* (A. Kozulin, Trans.). The MIT Press. (Original work published 1934).

Vygotsky, L.S. (1987). *Thinking and speech* (N. Minick, Trans.). Plenum Press. (Original work published 1934).

Ward, M., Azzopardi, C., & Morantz, G. (Eds.). (2018, April). *A mindful approach: Assessing child maltreatment in a multicultural setting.* Caring for Kids New to Canada; Canadian Pediatric Society. https://www.kidsnewtocanada.ca/screening/maltreatment

Wein, C.A., & Kirby-Smith, S. (1998). Untiming the curriculum: A case study of removing clocks from the program. *Young Children, 53*(5), 8–13.

Wenger, E. (1998). *Communities of practice: Learning, meaning, and identity.* Cambridge University Press.

Wenger-Traynor, E., & Wegner-Traynor, B. (2015). *Introduction to communities of practice.* https://wenger-trayner.com/introduction-to-communities-of-practice/

Wereszcynska, K. (2018). Importance of and need for intercultural education according to students, future teachers. *Polish Journal of Educational Studies, 18*(LXXI), 212–20.

Whiskeyjack, L., & Napier, K. (2020). Reconnecting to the spirit of the language. *Briarpatch, 49*(5), 27–29.

White, R. (2006). Young children's relationship with nature: Its importance to children's development & the Earth's future. *Taproot, 16*(2). http://www.outdooredcoalition.org/taproot.htm

White, R.E. (2012). *The power of play: A research summary on play and learning.* Minnesota Children's Museum. https://www.childrensmuseums.org/images/MCMResearchSummary.pdf

Woodrow, C. (1999). Revisiting images of the child in early childhood education: Reflections and considerations. *Australian Journal of Early Childhood, 24*(4), 7–12. https://doi.org/10.1177/183693919902400403

Woods, M. (2020, May 6). What does "systemic racism" mean? 20 terms to help you understand allyship. *Huffington Post.* https://www.huffingtonpost.ca/entry/what-does-systemic-racism-mean_ca_5ed97c17c5b69d703f3867c9

World Health Organization. (2013, May 7). *Social determinants of health: Key concepts.* www.who.int/social_determinants/thecommission/finalreport/key_concepts/en/

Wright, S.C., & Taylor, D.M. (1995). Identity and the language of the classroom: Investigating the impact of heritage versus second-language instruction on personal and collective self-esteem. *Journal of Educational Psychology, 87*(2), 241–52. https://doi.org/10.1037/0022-0663.87.2.241

Yeager, K.A., & Bauer-Wu, S. (2013). Cultural humility: Essential foundation for clinical researchers. *Applied Nursing Research, 26*(4), 251–56. https://doi.org/10.1016/j.apnr.2013.06.008

Young, S. (2018). *Critical new perspectives in early childhood music: Young children engaging and learning through music.* Routledge.

About the Authors

Carole Massing began her career as an elementary school teacher and developed a deep interest in early learning and child care when her own children were small. Since then, she has worked in various preschool settings and has taught in early childhood education at MacEwan University, the University of Alberta, and NorQuest College. She has also consulted on, researched, and developed curriculum in early learning and child care, interculturalism, and human service administration. Currently teaching in the Bachelor of Applied Human Service Administration program at MacEwan University, Carole recently co-authored *The Educational Assistant's Guide to Supporting Inclusion in a Diverse Society* (Brush Education, 2020). She earned her PhD in elementary education at the University of Alberta.

Mary Lynne Matheson taught in the Early Learning & Child Care program at MacEwan University for over 25 years. She also taught in the Bridging Program for Immigrant Child Care Workers. She became a pedagogical mentor as part of *Flight*, Alberta's Early Learning and Care Framework, working with the Intercultural Child and Family Centre (ICFC). She later became Education Coordinator at the ICFC, supporting educators' understanding and integration of framework concepts into their practice. She has acted in the capacity of ECEC Faculty Liaison at NorQuest College, helping to open the 1000 Women Child Care Centre (operated by ICFC) in 2017. Her work at these centres and with Carole, spanning many years, has awakened her interest in and respect for cultural differences. Mary Lynne has an MSc in Family Ecology and Practice from the University of Alberta.